InsidersChoice
to
MCP/MCSE Exam 70-291
Windows Server 2003 Certification: Implementing, Managing, and Maintaining a Microsoft Windows Server 2003 Network Infrastructure

Online practice exam provided by
BeachFront Quizzer, Inc.

Authors:
Deborah Timmons, MCT, MCSE
Patrick Timmons, MCT, MCSE+I
with the
TRP Author Certification Success Team

Published by
TotalRecall Publications, Inc.
1103 Middlecreek
Friendswood, TX 77546
281-992-3131

NOTE: THIS BOOK IS GUARANTEED
See details at www.TotalRecallPress.com

TotalRecall Publications, Inc.

This Book is sponsored by Beachfront Quizzer, Inc.

Printed in United States of America
Printed and bound by Data Duplicators of Houston, Texas
Printed and bound by Lightning Source, Inc. in the USA and UK
Printed and bound by BookSurge, Inc in the USA and around the world

Paper Back
ISBN 1-59095-042-9
UPC 6-43977-04291-0

eBook:
ISBN 1-59095-708-3
UPC 6-43977-64291-2

Worldwide eBook publication and distribution by:

The sponsoring editor is Bruce Moran and the production supervisor is Corby R. Tate.
Authors: Deborah Timmons, MCSE, Patrick Timmons, MCSE

This book, as always, is dedicated to our children,
Katie, Jamie, Alex and Lauren.
We love you.

To my mother, Dorothy Caroline (Schick) McEachern,
I will miss you every day of my life. Until we meet again.

Deborah

InsidersChoice™
to
MCP/MCSE Exam 70-291
Windows Server™ 2003 Certification: Implementing, Managing, and Maintaining a Microsoft Windows™ Server 2003 Network Infrastructure

Deborah Timmons, MCT, MCSE

Technical Editor:
Patrick Timmons, B.Sc., MCSE+I

About the Author

Deborah Timmons is a Microsoft Certified Trainer and Microsoft Certified Systems Engineer. She came into the Microsoft technical field after six years in the adaptive technology field, providing technology and training for persons with disabilities. She is the President and co-owner of Integrator Systems Inc.

Patrick Timmons is a Microsoft Certified Systems Engineer + Internet. He has been working in the IT industry for approximately 15 years, specializing in network engineering, and has recently completed his Bachelor of Science, Major in Computer Science. He is currently the CEO of Integrator Systems Inc., a company based in Nepean, Ontario, Canada.

Patrick and Deborah have four children—Lauren, Alexander, James and Katherine who take up a lot of their rare spare time.

Integrator Systems Inc. designs and implements network solutions based on Microsoft and 3Com technology, produces custom applications based on customer needs, provides local and remote network troubleshooting and support, and provides courseware, training and consultants to various horizontal and vertical markets. Integrator Systems is a Microsoft Certified Partner and 3Com Focus Partner.

The TRP Author Certification Success Team

Jada Brock-Soldavini

Jada Brock-Soldavini lives in suburban Atlanta and works for the State of Georgia as a Network Services Administrator. She has co-authored or contributed to other numerous works pertaining to Microsoft Windows technologies. She has an A.S. degree in Computer Information Systems and has been in the Information Technology industry for seven years. She is also married to Michael and the mother of three children Alyssa, Daniel and Christian. In her spare time she enjoys cooking, writing and reading anything that pertains to Network and Security technology.

Alan Grayson

Alan Grayson has a Masters Degree in Systems Management, is a Microsoft Certified Trainer, a Microsoft Certified Systems Engineer and Microsoft Database Administrator and also holds a dozen other certifications.

Patrick Simpson

Patrick Simpson is a Microsoft MCSE, MCSE +I, MCT and a Novell Master CNE and Master CNI. He has been a Microsoft Certified Trainer for five years and working in the IT industry for approximately 9 years, specializing in network consulting and technical education. Patrick has written numerous certification study aids for both Microsoft Windows 2000 exams and for Novell certification exams.

Pat is married, has three children and is currently working for a technical consulting/education company in Green Bay, WI.

David Smith

David [Darkcat] Smith is Microsoft Certified Trainer (MCT) and Microsoft Certified Systems Engineer (MCSE). He has been working in the IT industry for approximately 15+ year, specializing in directory services design and administration. He also enjoys planning and implementing large-scale rollouts.

Tom McCarty

Tom McCarty is currently an independent trainer, network engineer and consultant. He has worked in the computers and networking environment for 20 years as an administrator, end user support and instructor. Tom has the following certifications; MCSE on Windows NT 4.0, MCP+I, MCDBA, MCT on Windows 2000 and MCSA on Windows Server 2003. Along the way he has gained experience in Exchange 5.5 to 2000 upgrades, SMS 2.0 and NT to Active Directory migrations. In addition to Microsoft certification, Ton holds CompTIA A+, Network+ and IT Project+ certifications. I always enjoy seeing the light come on in someone's face when they finally nail down something new.

About the Book

Part of the TotalRecall InsidersChoice Certification System Series, this Certification System is designed to enhance you knowledge and performance. This will enable you to pass the 70-291 exam as easy as a walk on the beach.

The 70-291 Certification Exam focuses on network infrastructure management for Windows Server 2003. This InsidersChoice Certification System covers topics such as implementing, managing and maintaining IP Addressing, Name Resolution, Network Security, Routing, Remote Access, Maintaining and Troubleshooting a network infrastructure.

Work your way through each Chapter to increase your knowledge on Windows Server 2003 Network Infrastructure by working at your own pace. Each chapter in this book includes a pre- and post-assessment quiz to measure comprehension of each topic. Written to mimic the real exam, you also get complete answers and explanations, plus a detailed scoring summary showing test results at the end of each practice exam. The flexibility of the Beachfront Quizzer test engine is the best engine in the business for self-study and practicing for the real exam. The database features over 325 practice questions for the 70-291 exam with 4 major featured styles: Adaptive testing, Simulated Exams, Flash Cards and the very poplar Study Session option.

Each exam is different, because we randomize the questions and randomize the answers. In the Study Session you can focus on specific objectives or chapters, and get detailed explanations for right and wrong answers—including links to the book chapter for further study.

This book explains the concepts in a clear and easy-to-understand manner to help you not only pass the exam, but to apply the knowledge later in a real-world situation. Chapter summaries help wrap up each topic. The large glossary at the end of the book provides a review of essential exam-related terms and concepts that will prove invaluable just before taking the exam. Helpful tips and time management techniques will alleviate pre-exam jitters and put you in control.

Introduction

I've realized something as I've stared at this blank page. It can be harder to write an introduction to a book than it is to write the book itself. What can I say that is new and different and exciting?

We've all seen the commercials on television for Windows server 2003. Wonderful shadings, bodies soaring through the air and the familiar Madonna tune. The first time I installed Windows server 2003, my initial reaction was "Wow! That's colorful!" 2003 provided a shiny, new, slick user interface that removed some of the common irritants with previous incarnations of Windows—hundreds of server shortcuts cluttering up the screen, twenty copies of Internet Explorer open on the taskbar.

But having worked in the technical field for a number of years, slick and shiny wasn't going to make me want to run out and start upgrading all my systems. I needed a better reason. What's new with Windows server 2003? What makes it different? Better?

As with any new technology, it took a little while to find the answers. Those answers are the ones I've tried to provide to you in this book. I've done my best to show you all the new features of Windows XP Professional, noted the differences between Professional and Home Edition and brought you the "guts" of Windows server 2003—the similarities and differences between it and the previous versions of Windows.

Hopefully, you finish the book with a good grasp of what Windows server 2003 Professional really is. You should end up with the information you need to make the decision—to upgrade or not to upgrade. After all, that really is the question!

Deborah Timmons

President, Integrator Systems Inc.

A quick overview of the book chapters

Table of Contents

Exam Information and Resources

Exam News

The Exam 70-291 was made available August 14, 2003.

http://www.microsoft.com/traincert/exams/70-291.asp

The course provides a general introductory overview of this task.

You will need to supplement the course with additional work.

Audience Profile

The Microsoft Certified Systems Administrator (MCSA) on Windows Server 2003 credential is intended for IT professionals who work in the typically complex computing environment of medium to large companies. An MCSA candidate should have 6 to 12 months of experience administering client and network operating systems in environments that have the following characteristics:

- 250 to 5,000 or more users
- Three or more physical locations
- Three or more domain controllers
- Network services and resources such as messaging, database, file and print, proxy server, firewall, Internet, intranet, remote access and client computer management
- Connectivity requirements such as connecting branch offices and individual users in remote locations to the corporate network and connecting corporate networks to the Internet.

Credit Toward Certification

When you pass the Implementing, Managing, and Maintaining a Microsoft® Windows® Server 2003 Network Infrastructure exam, you achieve Microsoft Certified Professional (MCP) status. You also earn credit toward the following certifications:

- **Core** credit toward Microsoft Certified Systems Administrator (MCSA) on Microsoft Windows Server 2003 certification.
- **Core** credit toward Microsoft Certified Systems Engineer (MCSE) on Microsoft Windows Server 2003 certification.

Recommended Preparation Tools and Resources

We make a wealth of preparation tools and resources are available to you, including courses, books, practice tests and Microsoft Web sites. When you are ready to prepare for this exam, here's where you could start.

Recommended: Instructor-led Courses for This Exam

- Course 2276: Implementing a Microsoft Windows Server 2003 Network Infrastructure: Network Hosts.
- Course 2277: Implementing, Managing, and Maintaining a Microsoft Windows Server 2003 Network Infrastructure: Network Services.

Microsoft Online Resources

- TechNet: Designed for IT professionals, this site includes how-tos, best practices, downloads, technical chats and much more.
- MSDN: The Microsoft Developer Network (MSDN) is a reference for developers, featuring code samples, technical articles, newsgroups, chats and more.
- Training & Certification Newsgroups: A newsgroup exists for every Microsoft certification. By participating in the ongoing dialog, you take advantage of a unique opportunity to exchange ideas with and ask questions of others, including more than 750 Microsoft Most Valuable Professionals (MVPs) worldwide.

TotalRecall Self-Paced Training Products

Practice Tests

- **BeachFront Quizzer, Inc: www.bfq.com**

Web Based Training

- **www.wbtwise.com**

Books and eBooks Training Products

- **www.totalrecallpress.com**

Managing & Maintaining IP Addressing

The objective of this chapter is to provide the reader with an understanding of the following:

Implementing, Managing, and Maintaining IP Addressing

- Manage DHCP.
- Manage DHCP clients and leases.
- Manage DHCP Relay Agent.
- Manage DHCP databases.
- Manage DHCP scope options.
- Manage reservations and reserved clients.

Troubleshoot TCP/IP addressing.

- Diagnose and resolve issues related to Automatic Private IP Addressing (APIPA).
- Diagnose and resolve issues related to incorrect TCP/IP configuration.

Troubleshoot DHCP.

- Diagnose and resolve issues related to DHCP authorization.
- Verify DHCP reservation configuration.
- Examine the system event log and DHCP server audit log files to find related events.
- Diagnose and resolve issues related to configuration of DHCP server and scope options.
- Verify that the DHCP Relay Agent is working correctly.
- Verify database integrity.

Chapter 1: Managing IP Addressing

Introduction:

Windows Server 2003 has some new features not available in previous network operating systems. This chapter will cover the Transmission Control Protocol/Internet Protocol more commonly referred to as TCP/IP. TCP.IP can be defined as a routable network protocol that allows computers with the same TCP/IP protocol installed to connect and share resources on a network. This chapter will also cover the Dynamic Host Configuration Protocol also known as DHCP. DHCP is used to simplify the use of IP addresses on networked resources. DHCP works by allocating unique IP addresses to all hosts on a network. When planning a TCP/IP and DHCP network within your Windows Server 2003 environment it is important that you carefully plan out your TCP/IP and DHCP structure. Some fundamental questions and answers you need to know before you begin are:

- Are there separate network segments within your network?
- Will the network be connected to the Internet via a router?
- Will you organization be using Network Address Translation or NAT behind a firewall or Proxy server?
- Will all systems use TCP/IP or will the systems run other protocols?
- Will you be using DHCP to supply client machines with IP addresses?

Once you have this information in hand you are ready to implement your IP Addressing scheme on your Windows Server 2003 network.

Getting Ready Questions

1. Jim travels between his home and his office with his laptop that has Windows 2003 that he uses for training purposes. At home he uses DHCP to connect to his ISP, while at the office he uses a fixed IP address. What would make switching between settings quicker?

2. Twenty people fly in to company headquarters for a meeting with their laptops. After they leave a couple of company computers cannot connect to the network. Investigation reveals that their IP addresses start with 169.254. What should the administrator do?

3. From the command line how can you look up your computer name?

4. From a GUI, how can you see your IP address even if it has been obtained from a DHCP server?

5. Where would you configure a DHCP Relay Agent?

Getting Ready Answers

1. Alternate TCP/IP configuration.

2. Delete the DHCP leases for the laptops that have left in DHCP Administrator Program.

3. The following commands will show your computer name: hostname, ipconfig/all, ping -a 127.0.0.1, and nbtstat –n.

4. Double-click on your Local Area Connection and then click on the Support Tab to see your TCP/IP configuration.

5. To configure a DHCP Relay Agent you would configure a new routing protocol in the Routing and Remote Access utility.

New Features for TCP/IP and DHCP on Windows Server 2003 Networks.

Before you dive into the implementation of TCP/IP addresses and DHCP, let's take a look at some new features of these protocols available only on Windows Server 2003. Table 1.1 below lists some of these features for TCP/IP.

Feature	Description
Automatic Private IP Addressing (APIPA)	Allows a computer to use an alternate, manually configured IP address configuration. This is helpful if the DHCP server is not functioning or if a computer is used on more than one network.
IP Version 6 (IPv6)	IPv6 is quite lengthy to describe. Some of the features are: larger address space, stateless and stateful address configuration, built-in security and new header format. These are just a few of the list of IPv6 features. For more information please see the Microsoft Web site at http://www.microsoft.com or RFC 2460, which describe the protocol in detail.
IGMP version 3	This protocol allows hosts the ability to receive multicast traffic from specified sources or from all but a specific set of sources.
Alternate configuration	This feature allows the client machine to use an alternate IP address if the DHCP server is unavailable to allocate an IP address for any reason. If this is unavailable then TCP/IP will use APIPA instead.

Table 1—1: New TCP/IP features available only with Windows Server 2003.

To obtain additional information on TCP/IP features available in Windows Server 2003 just go to the Microsoft Web site at http://www.microsoft.com. Table 1.2 below lists new features only available on servers running Windows Server 2003 and DHCP.

For more information, see Technical Resources:

DHCP client alternate configuration and

Use DHCP client alternate configuration.

Feature	Description
DNS integration with DHCP.	If a DNS server on Windows 200 or Windows 2003 supports dynamic updates, then DHCP can use DNS dynamic update protocol to update their host name-to-address mapping information. This information is stored in the zone settings on the DNS Server.
Dynamic support for BOOTP clients.	BOOTP allows the DHCCP server to configure IP address information for clients without the implementation of a fixed address.
When Active Directory is used unauthorized DHCP servers can easily be detected.	When a domain member DHCP server running Windows 2000 or Windows Server 2003 attempts to start on the network, Active Directory is queried and the IP address of the server is compared to the list of authorized DHCP servers. If a match is found, the server computer is authorized as a DHCP server. If a match is not found, the following occurs: The server is identified as an unauthorized server. The server is not authorized in Active Directory. No IP addresses are leased to DHCP clients.
Alternate configuration.	This feature allows the client machine to use an alternate IP address if the DHCP server is unavailable to allocate an IP address for any reason. If this is unavailable then TCP/IP will use APIPA instead.
DHCP client alternate configuration.	This enables Network Administrators the ability to move clients between two or more networks. One configuration has a DHCP configuration and the other has a static IP address. The Network Interface Card or NIC does not need to be reconfigured.

Table 1—2: New DHCP features available only with Windows Server 2003.

Now that we have looked at some new features of TCP/IP and DHCP available in Windows Server 2003, we will cover how to configure TCP/IP addressing in a Windows Server 2003.

1.1 TCP/IP Addressing on a Server Computer

As stated earlier in this chapter you need to decide whether or not you are using Private or Public IP addressing schemes within your network. There are five different types of IP Classes that are used for address ranges. Three of these addresses are used for TCP/IP assignment and they are A, B and C. The other two address classes D and E are not used for IP address assignment. Table 1.3 below shows these addresses and their Network Identification, Host and Number of hosts supported.

The number of possible networks and hosts per network available for each class is below and uses the letters A, B, C and D to designate the four octet values in any given IP address shown in Table 1.3.

xxx.xxx.xxx.xxx

A B C D

Class	First Octet Value Number	Network Identification	Host Identification	Number of Networks	Hosts Available per Network
A	1–126	A	B, C and D	126	16,777,214
B	128–191	*A and B*	C and D	16,384	65,534
C	192–223	B, C and D	D	2,097,152	254
D	224–239	Reserved. Only used for multicast addressing	N/A	N/A	N/A
E	240–254	Reserved. Only used for trial uses	N/A	N/A	N/A

Table 1—3: The Address Classes.

These IP addresses are assigned by the Internet Assigned Numbers Authority (IANA). For better security IANA suggest that Network Administrators use private non-routable addresses behind a Firewall. This is accomplished by using Network Address Translation (NAT). It can also be accomplished by using a proxy server. Table 1.4 below shows the private IP addresses used for NAT.

Private Network ID	**Subnet Mask**	**Range of IP Addresses**
10.0.0.0	255.0.0.0	10.0.0.1 – 10.255.255.254
172.16.0.0	255.240.0.0	172.16.0.1 – 172.31.255.254
192.168.0.0	255.255.0.0	192.168.0.1 – 192.168.255.254

Table 1—4: IP Address Assignments

If you work in a corporation and need to obtain IP addresses, your Corporate ISP should be able to provide these for you. If for some reason an IP address cannot be obtained you can request that a number be assigned to your corporation by directly contacting the American Registry for Internet Numbers (ARIN). Table 1.5 below also shows some basic DHCP terminology that you need to be familiar with when configuring your DHCP Server.

Term	**Definition**
Scope	Used to define a single physical subnet within your network by using a range of IP addresses. DHCP uses these scopes to distribute IP addresses to client machines that are configured to use DHCP.
Super Scope	Used to support more than one subnet within the same physical subnet.
Exclusion Range	This option is used to exclude or leave out a certain IP address range from the scope so that it is not assigned to a network resource.
Address Pool	This is where DHCP obtains available IP addresses to assign to clients on the network. You set the address pool and all addresses in the pool minus the Excluded IP addresses will be assigned to client machines..
Lease	Used to determine the amount of time a client should have a particular IP address.
Reservation	This is used to create permanent IP address leases for hardware on the network. An example of this would be using a reservation for Servers or Network Printers on the network.
Option Types	Used to assign options such as WINS Servers, DNS servers and default gateway addresses. But you can use the DHCP console to define and add custom option types if needed.
Options Class	Used to manage clients based on their class-specified type. There are two types of option classes; user class and vendor class.

Table 1—5: Basic DHCP Terminology.

1.2 Manage DHCP

Make certain you have DHCP installed before you begin this next section. DHCP Server can be installed by clicking on **Start | Control Panel | Add/Remove Programs | Add/Remove Windows Components | Networking Services | Dynamic Host Configuration Protocol.** This is shown in Figure 1.1.

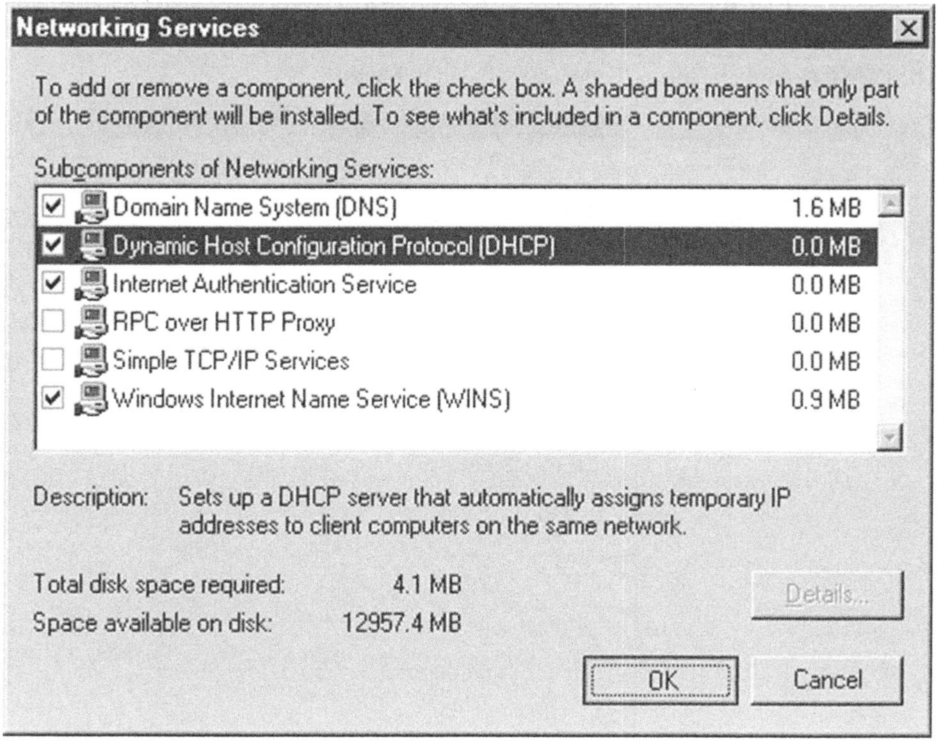

Figure 1-1: Installing the DHCP Server.

Click **OK** to begin the installation of DHCP. Once DHCP has been installed it can be accessed by clicking on **Start | Administrative Tools | DHCP**. An important item to know is that two local administrative groups are created when DHCP is installed. The two groups are the DHCP Administrators Group, which is more secure than the DHCP Users Group. The DHCP Users Group only gives read-only access to the DHCP Server. No data in the DHCP scopes can be modified when a member of this local user group is accessing the DHCP Console. The second group, DHCP Administrators Group has full access to the DCHP Server and all settings pertaining to DHCP only not to the Domain. The DHCP Console screen will appear as shown in Figure 1.2.

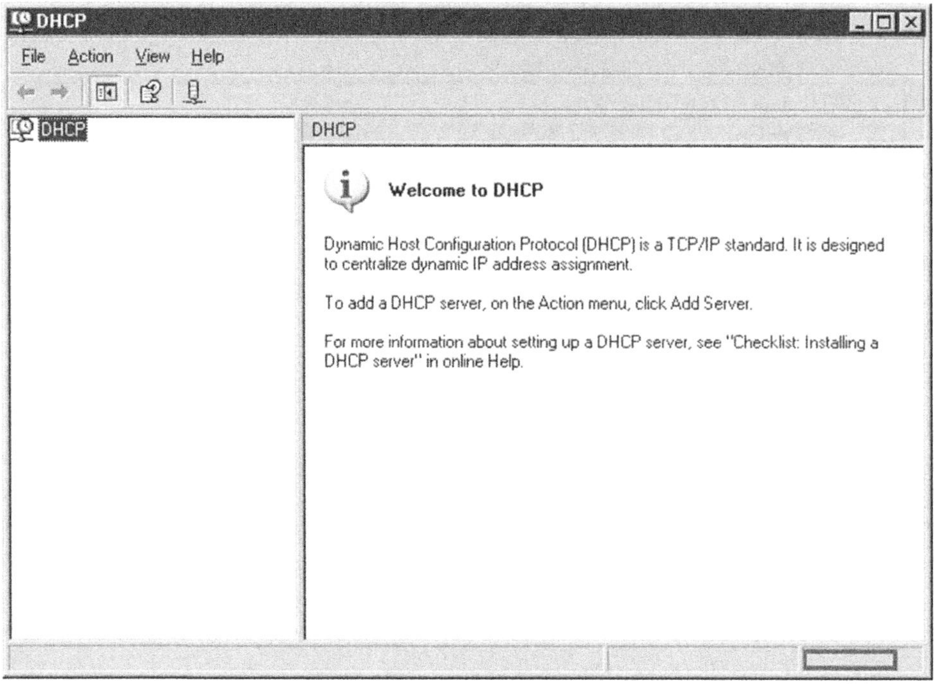

Figure 1-2: The DHCP Console in Windows Server 2003.

To begin using DHCP you need to add a server. To do this right-click the **DHCP** icon shown in Figure 1.2 above and the following options will appear as shown in Figure 1.3.

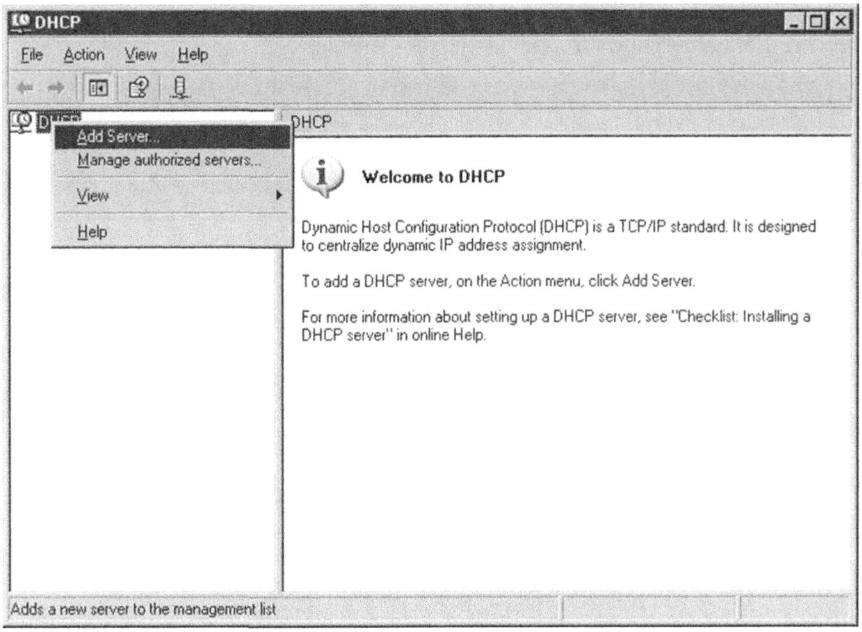

Figure 1-3: Adding a DHCP Server in Windows Server 2003.

Select the Add Server option and a new dialog box will appear, as shown in Figure 1.4, that allows you to select the Server that you wish to add to DHCP.

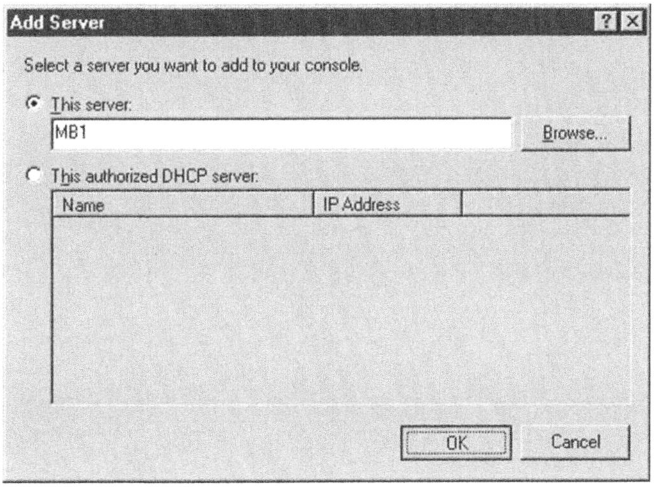

Figure 1-4: Choosing the DHCP Server.

As you can see from the option above if you are not sure of the server you can browse to the specific server. You can also use the **This authorized DHCP server** option to add another configured DHCP from within the Forest. Once the server has been selected click **OK.** Figure 1.5: below shows the DHCP Server Console.

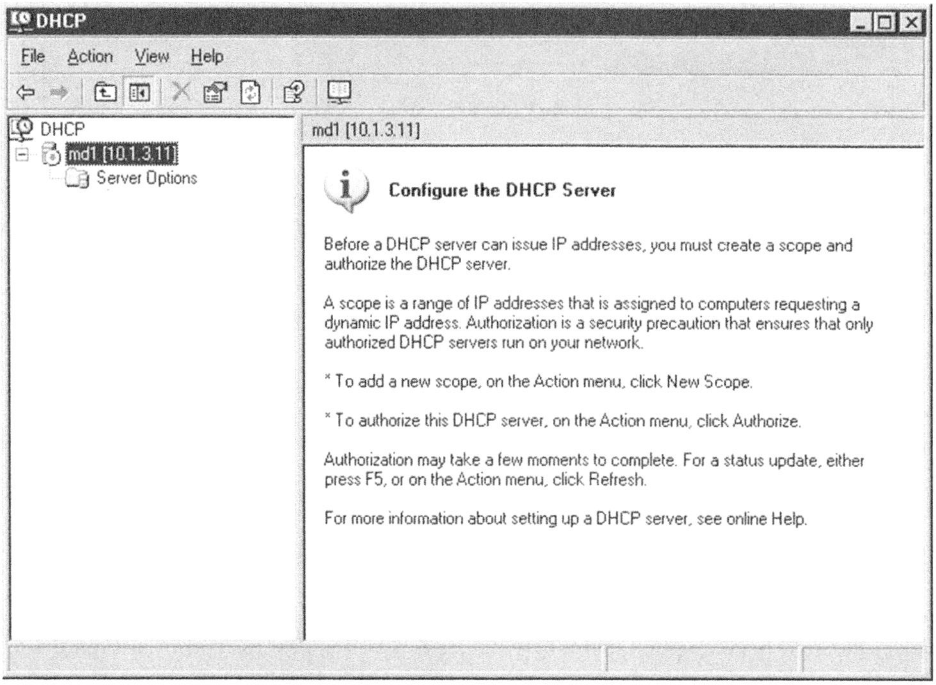

Figure 1-5: The DHCP Server Console.

Once the console is opened you can begin to configure DHCP options. Right-click the DHCP Server and a variety of options will appear as shown in Figure 1.6.

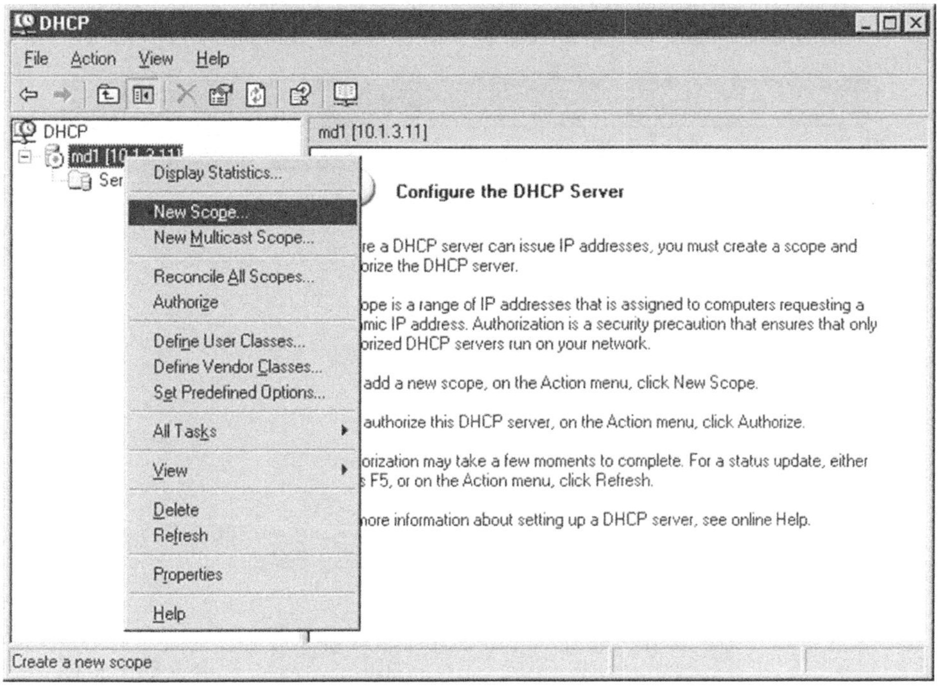

Figure 1-6: DHCP Configuration Options.

The options listed are:

- Display Statistics – Used to display DHCP Server statistical information such as start time, up time, discovers, offers, requests, etc. Because of the number of statistics available this option can be viewed below in Figure 1.7.

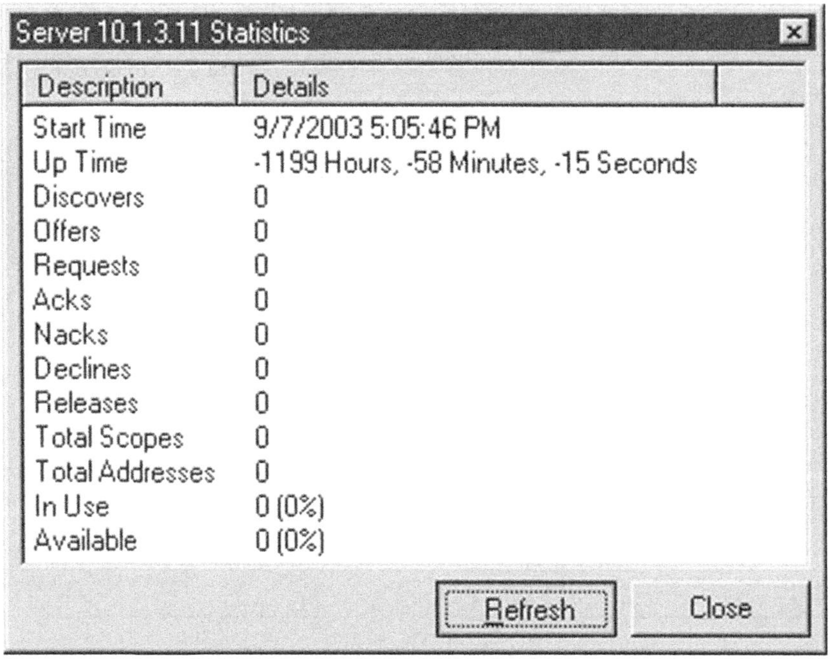

Figure 1-7: Viewing the Statistics of a DHCP Server.

- New Scope – Used to create a new scope.
- New Multicast Scope – Used to create new Multicast Scopes.
- Reconcile All Scopes – Used to resolve all Scopes in the DHCP Server.
- Authorize – Must be used to authorize the DHCP Server. If the DHCP Server is not authorized then it will not function.
- Define User Classes – Used for assigning options to clients identified as sharing a common need for similar DHCP configurations such as lease time, different router address and other WINS or DNS Server settings.
- Define Vendor Classes – Clients can be configured to use this option to identify themselves by the type of vendor they belong.
- Set Predefined Options – Used to set predefined options such as: Option Classes for Windows, Windows 2000 and Windows 98 machines, and adding a class.
- All Tasks – Used to start, stop, pause, resume and restart the DHCP server.
- View – Used to customize the MMC Console for the DHCP Server.
- Delete – Used to delete the DHCP Server.

- Refresh – Used to refresh the screen for the DHCP Console.
- Properties – Used to view the Properties of the DHCP Server such as Automatic Updating, Enabling DHCP Audit logging and the BOOTP table folder. Also gives Administrators the ability to use DNS for dynamic updates and Conflict Detection options.
- Help – Used to access the Microsoft Help files.

1.2.1 Backing Up and Restoring the DHCP Database

The DHCP console will allow Administrators the ability to back-up and restore the DHCP Server Database. To access these options use the **Action** option from the **DHCP Console**.

1.2.1.1 How to Migrate a DHCP Database from NT 4.0 to Windows Server 2003.

Microsoft Knowledge Base Article 325473 (previously Q325473) explains how to easily migrate your DHCP server database from a Windows NT 4.0 Server to a Windows Server 2003. Before you begin this process you will need the Windows 2000 Resource Kit Supplement 1 utility DHCP Export Import utility **Dhcpexim.exe** which can be downloaded via the Microsoft Download site at

http://www.microsoft.com/windows2000/techinfo/reskit/tools/new/dhcpexim-o.asp

and also make certain you have your Microsoft Server 2003 CD-ROM or DVD-ROM available.

Use the instructions below to complete this task:

- On the Windows NT 4.0 Server log in as Administrator and **Stop** the DHCP Server service.
- Open a command prompt and type the following command: **net stop microsoft dhcp server** and press the **Enter** key. A message will appear that The DHCP Server service is stopping.
- Type **Exit** at the command prompt to exit and return to Windows NT 4.0.
- Use the JetPack Utility to compact the DHCP server by using the following command at prompt: **cd %systemroot%\system32\dhcp**, then press the **Enter** key.
- Type **jetpack dhcp.mdb temp.mdb,** press **Enter**.
- Once the database has been compacted press **Enter**.
- Export the DHCP database by using the (Dhcpexim.exe utility from the Windows 2000 Server Resource Kit Supplement 1.)
- To export the database:
- **Install** the Dhcpexim.exe utility and then **Start** the Dhcpexim.exe utility.

- Choose the **Export configuration of the local service to a file** from the Welcome to DHCP Export Import tool screen. Click **OK** after this has been chosen.
- Type a **name** for the exported file in the File Name box and then select **Save** to save the file.
- Choose the **scope or scopes** that need to be exported and select the **Disable the selected scopes on local machine before export** check box, and then click **Export**.
- Click **OK**.
- On the Windows NT 4.0 Server **disable** the **DHCP Server service** by clicking on **Start | Settings** | select **Control Panel** | double-click Services | select **Microsoft DHCP Server** | choose **Startup** | select **Disabled** and then click **OK** | choose **Yes** to confirm the stopping of the service.
- Click **Close** to close the Services dialog screen.
- On the Windows Server 2003, install DHCP Service by clicking on **Start**, select **Control Panel**, choose **Add/Remove Programs**, then **Add/Remove Windows Components**, select **Networking Services**, then choose **Details** and finally the **Dynamic Host Configuration Protocol** on the Windows Server 2003 machine. Then click **OK**.
- Select **Next** to install the selected components. At this point you may want to have your Windows Server 2003 CD-ROM or DVD-ROM drive.
- Click **Finish**.

The next step is to import the DHCP Database.

- **Copy** the DHCP file from Windows NT 4.0 the exported database to the hard drive of the DHCP Server.
- Open a command prompt on the Windows Server 2003 machine and type **netsh dhcp server** import **c:\dhcpdatabase.txt all** (the full path and file name of the exported Windows NT 4.0 file) and press **Enter**.
- Exit the command prompt after this step has successfully completed.
- Make sure you are logged onto the Windows Server 2003 machine as a member of the **Enterprise Administrators Group**. The next step is to Authorize the DHCP Server by clicking on **Start**, choose **All Programs**, select **Administrative Tools** and then click **DHCP.**
- Select the **DHCP Server** and **Expand** it. Make sure the server has been authorized. The arrow over the server should be green. If it is red then it needs to be **Authorized**. To authorize right-click the DHCP server and select **Authorize**.
- The arrow should change from red to green once this has been completed. You may also need to click the refresh button.

This is all you need to do to move your DHCP Server database from Windows NT 4.0 to Microsoft Server Windows 2003.

1.2.2 Manage DHCP Clients and Leases

Managing DHCP clients and leases can be done in various ways. You can use the DHCP Console or you can use command line utilities. Once you have installed DHCP Server you need to open the DHCP Console by Clicking on **Start**, then select **Administrative Tools** and **DHCP.** Then authorize the Server by right-clicking on the server and choosing the **Authorize** option as shown in Figure 1.8 below.

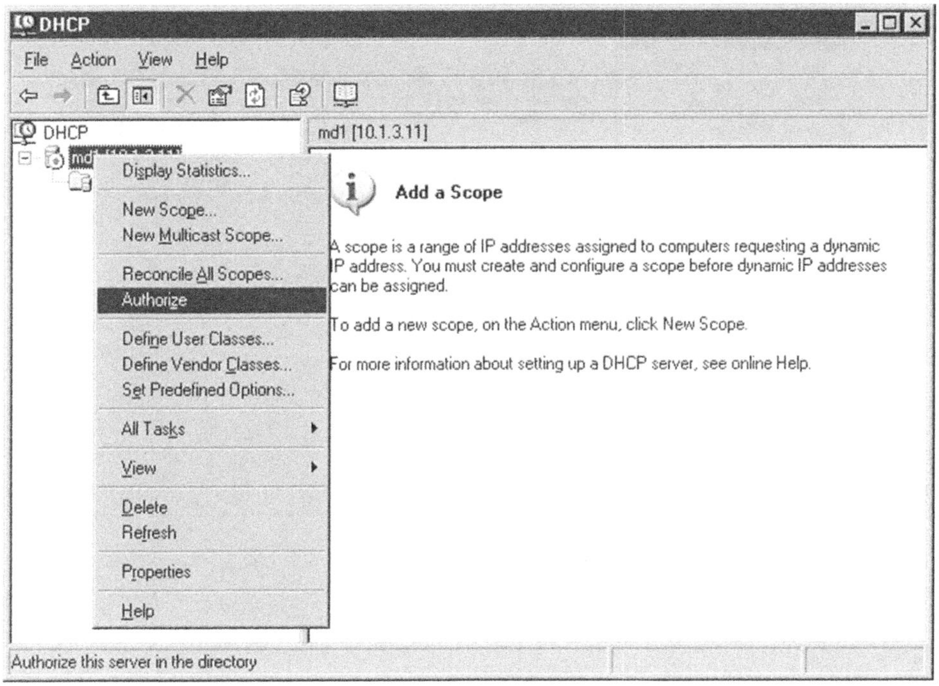

Figure 1-8: Authorizing the DHCP Server.

For this example we will add a New Scope for the DHCP Server. Right-click on the **DHCP Server** and select the **Scope** option as shown in Figure 1.9.

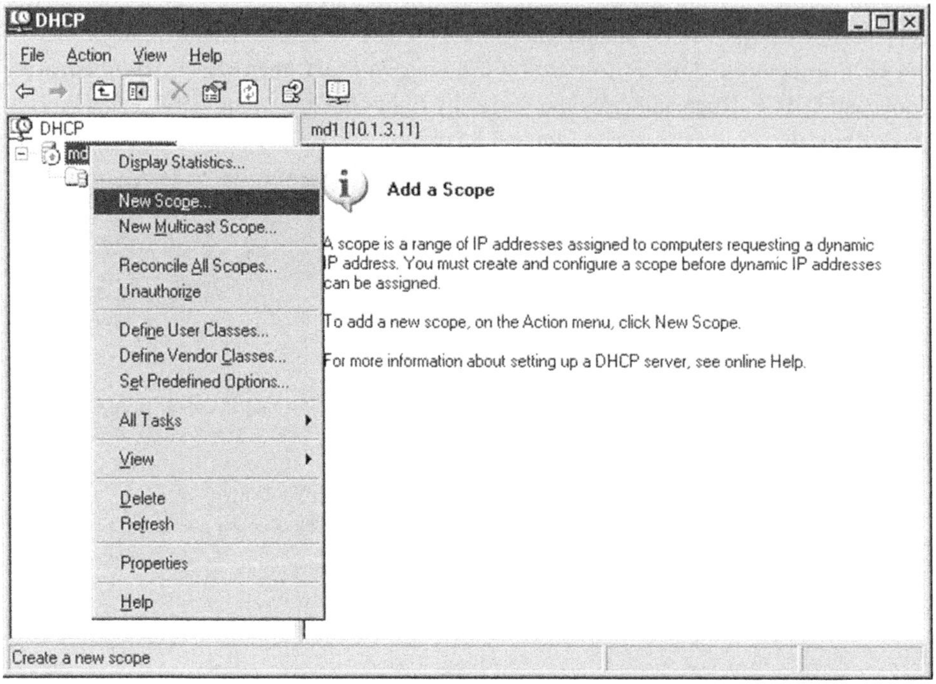

Figure 1-9: Adding a New Scope to the DHCP Server.

The New Scope Wizard will begin as shown in Figure 1.10 below.

Figure 1-10: The New Scope Wizard.

Click on the **Next** button and enter the **New Scope Name** and **Description** as shown in Figure 1.11 below.

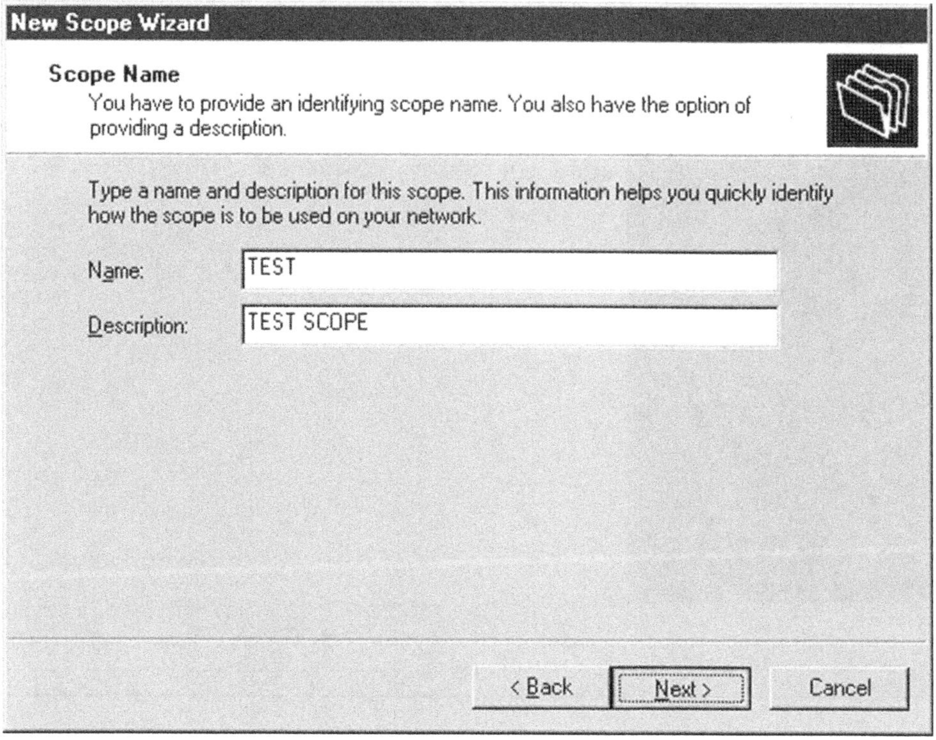

Figure 1-11: Entering a Name and Description for the New Scope.

Click on the Next Button and enter a **Starting IP Address Range, Ending IP Address Range and Subnet Length** for use in the scope as shown in Figure 1.12.

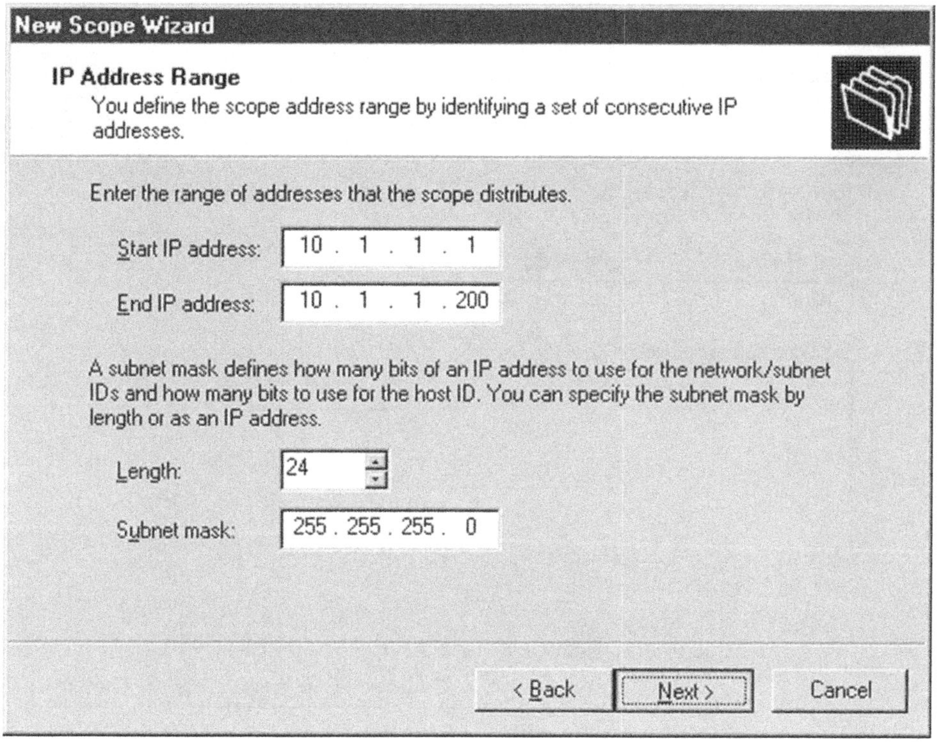

Figure 1-12: Entering the Starting, Ending IP Address ranges for the Scope and the Subnet mask information.

Click **Next** and then you will need to add the IP Address range exclusions as shown in Figure 1.13.

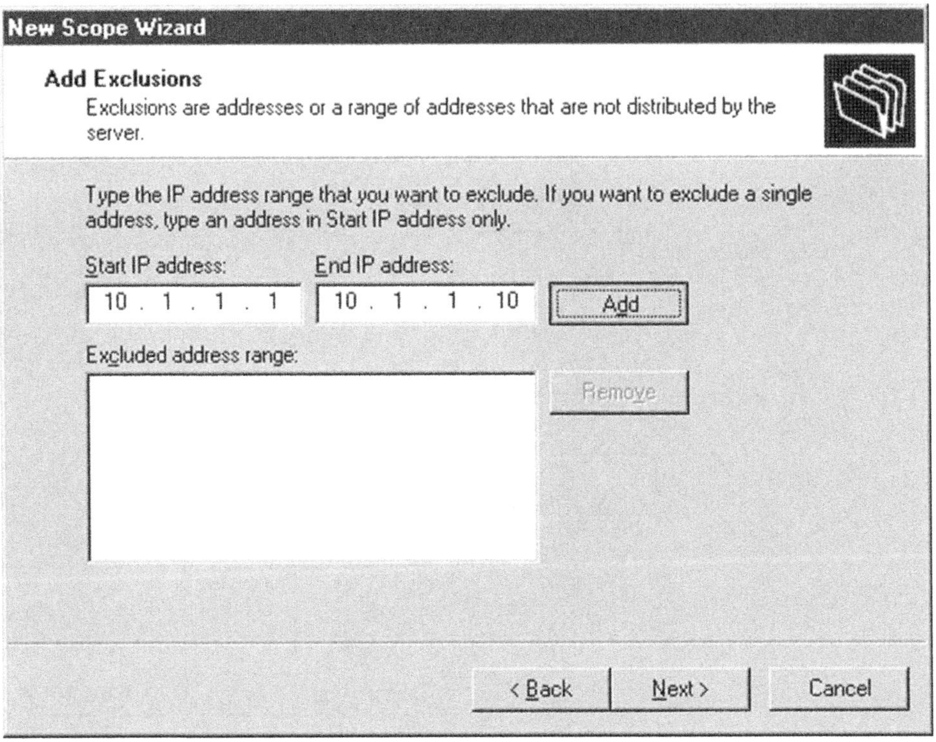

Figure 1-13: New Scope Wizard—Range Exclusions.

Enter the IP Address range that you do not wish the DHCP Server to Allocate and click on the **Add** button. If you just wish to exclude one address and not a range of addresses enter the single IP address in the Start IP Address option. Once this has been completed select the **Next** button. Figure 1.14 shows the Lease Duration Screen, which is the next option you need to configure.

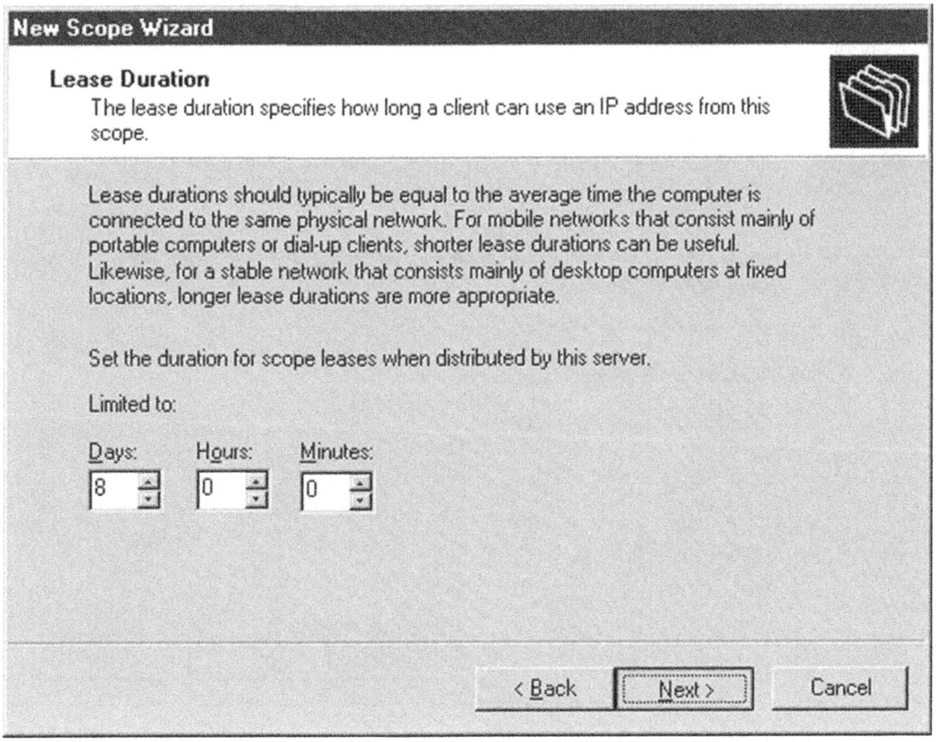

Figure 1-14: Entering in Lease Duration for the Scope.

The default lease duration is 8 hours. You can configure this to whatever you wish to use for lease durations. The rule of thumb is shorter lease duration for mobile computers and longer lease durations for stable client machines. Figure 1.15 gives you the ability to configure Advanced DHCP options.

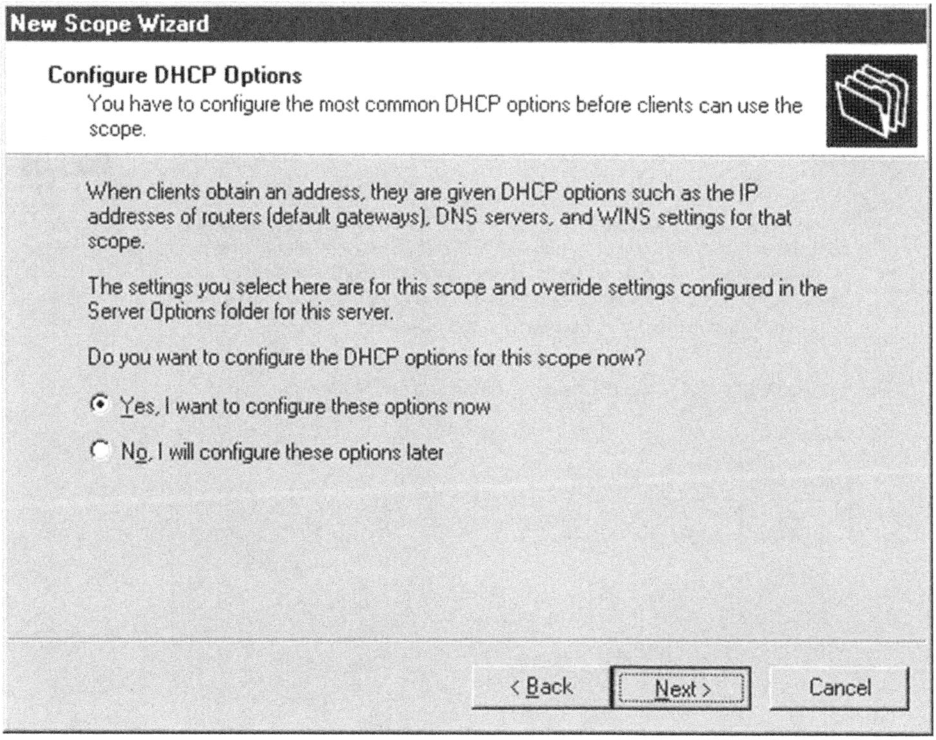

Figure 1-15: New Scope Wizard—Configure DHCP Options.

Choose **Next** to continue to configure the Advanced DHCP options. The first option will be to configure the Default Router Gateway as shown below in Figure 1.16.

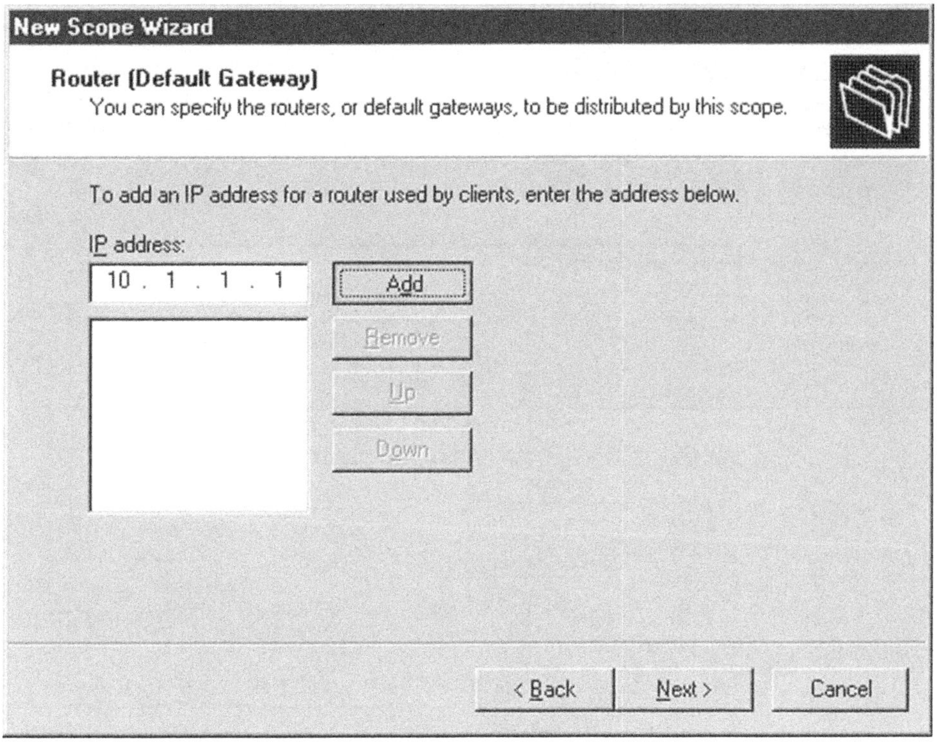

Figure 1-16: Entering an IP Address for the router to be used by the DHCP clients within this scope.

Once the IP Address has been entered click the **Add** button and then the **Next** button. The next option is to enter the DNS Server information as shown in Figure 1.17.

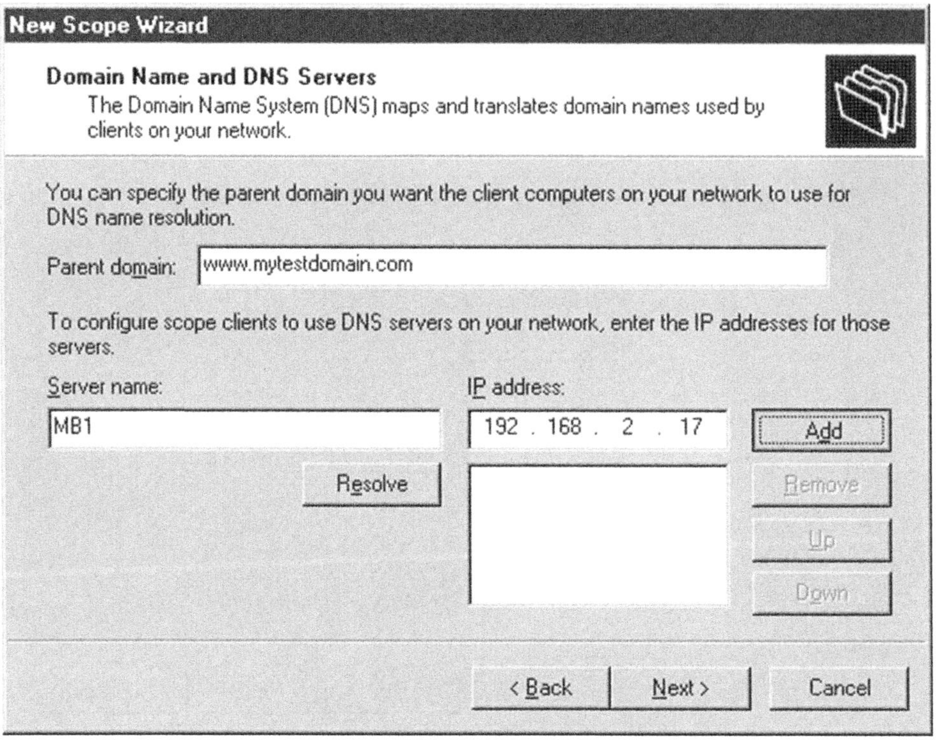

Figure 1-17: Entering the DNS Server information for the DHCP Scope.

You need to enter the **Parent Domain** information, the **DNS Server Name** and the **IP Address** of the **DNS Server.** Once this information has been entered click the **Add** button then select **Next**. The next step is to add the WINS Server information to the scope. This is shown in Figure 1.18.

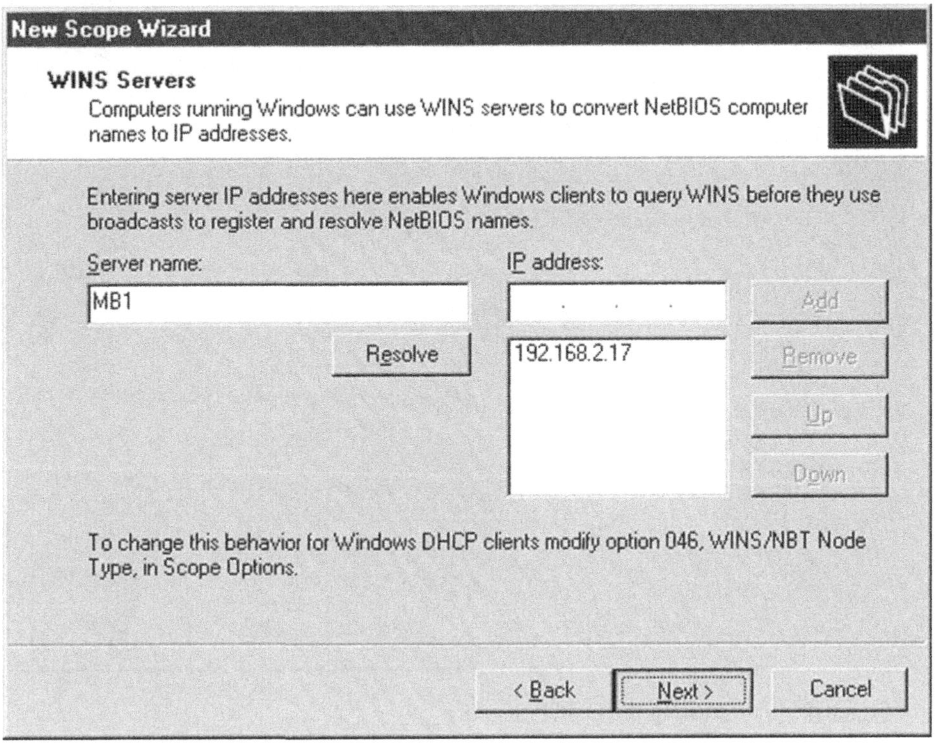

Figure 1-18: Entering the WINS Server information for the DHCP Scope.

Click **Next** once this has been entered. Figure 1.19 shows the final step, which is to activate the DHCP Scope.

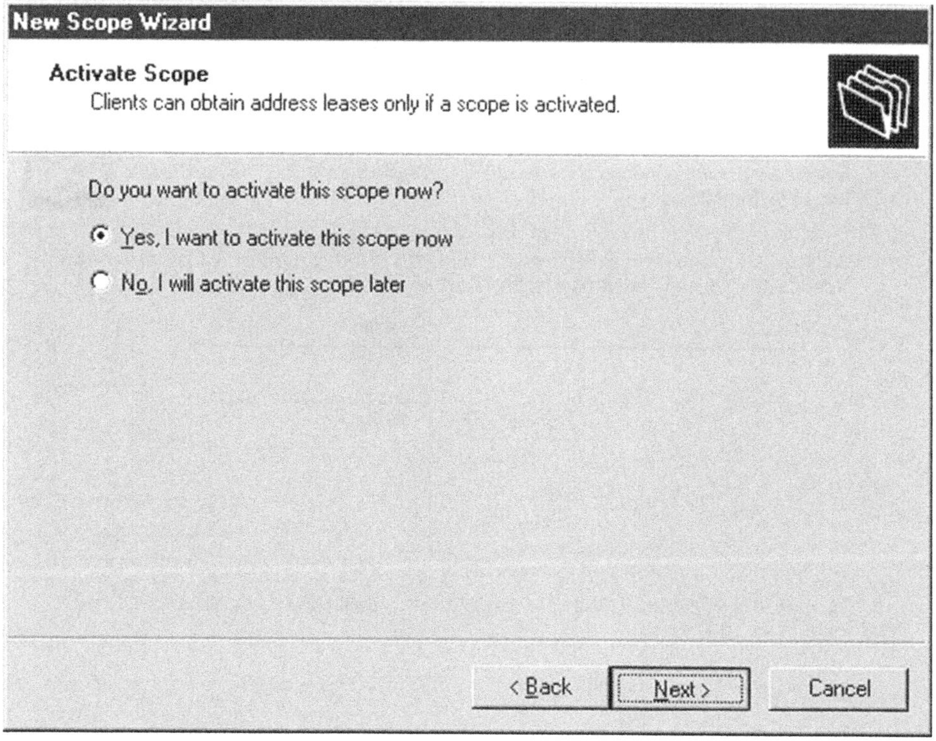

Figure 1-19: Activating the DHCP Scope.

Click the **Yes, I want to activate this scope now** option to activate the scope and then **Next**. If you decide not to activate the scope you can select **No, I will activate this scope later** and the scope properties will be saved under the DHCP Server, but not active. Once you have activated the DHCP scope you need to click on **Finish** as shown in Figure 1.20.

Figure 1-20: Finishing the Authorization of the DHCP Server Scope.

A New Scope has been added to the DHCP Server and can now be viewed from the DHCP Console as seen in Figure 1.21.

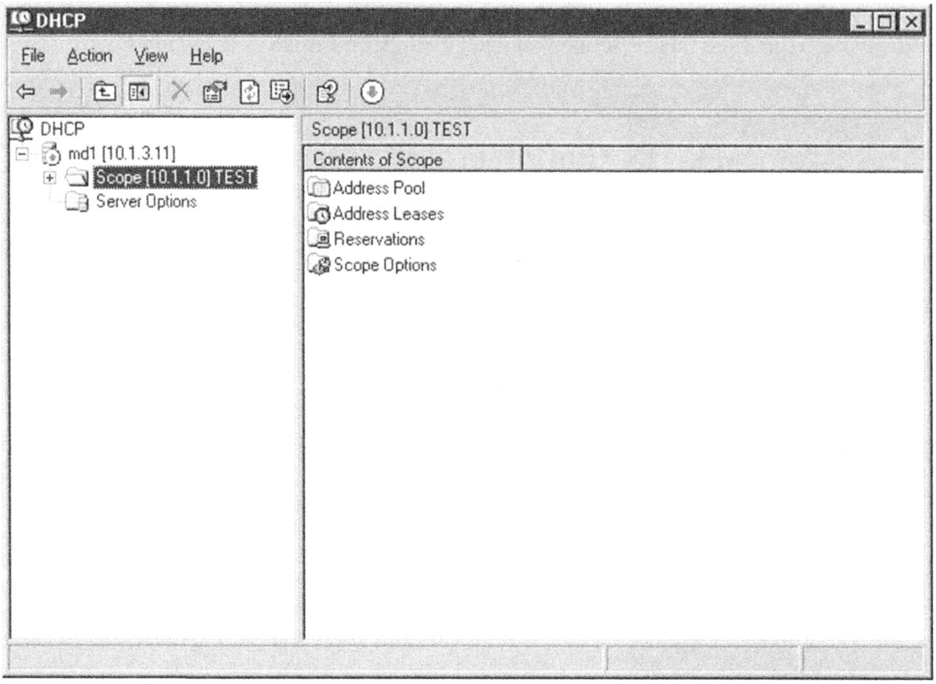

Figure 1-21: The Newly Created Scope in the DHCP Console.

If you need to deactivate this scope you can right-click on the scope and choose the **Deactivate** option. The scope for the Microsoft Windows Server 2003 DHCP service has now been created.

1.2.2.1 SuperScopes

Superscopes are used by DHCP to support DHCP networked clients that belong to a single Ethernet network segment, but have multiple logical IP addresses used within the segment. This is also referred to as multinets. Superscopes may also be used to provide support when using the multinet configuration for the DHCP server. The DHCP server can perform the task of providing multiple leases from more than one scope on a physical network to all client machines. Superscopes can also be used to manage separate IP networks using more than one DHCP server.

1.2.2.2 Multicast Scopes

The Multicast Address Dynamic Client Allocation Protocol or MADCAP is used by multicast for the distribution of IP Addresses.

1.2.3 Manage DHCP Relay Agent

The ability to relay DHCP messages between DHCP servers and clients on different IP networks can be done by using the DHCP Relay Agent. The DHCP Relay Agent cannot be configured for use when the Network Address Translation (NAT) routing protocol with automatic addressing has been enabled on a DHCP Server, or on a machine that has the Internet Connection Feature enabled. To use the DHCP Relay Agent you must have Routing and Remote Access enabled. Once this has been done use these steps to enable the DHCP Relay Agent.

Click **Start**, then select **Administrative Tools**. Choose the **Routing and Remote Access** option. Once the console has opened select **General**, then **Routing and Remote Access**. Select the **Server** and chose **IP Routing**. Right-click **General** and select New **Routing Protocol**. Next, click the **DHCP Relay Agent** from the **Select Routing Protocol** box and click the **OK** button. The DHCP Relay Agent properties can be configured by right-clicking on the **DHCP Relay Agent** and choosing **Properties**. From the **General** tab enter the **IP address** of the DHCP Server and click on the **Add** button. Click **OK** when this has been completed.

1.2.4 Manage DHCP Databases

When managing the Microsoft Windows Server 2003 DHCP Server database you have a variety of ways to complete this task. The Microsoft DHCP Console is one way to manage the DHCP Server or you can use the command line utility **Netsh**. Both of these Administrative DHCP Tools can be used to completed the following DHCP tasks.

- Create, Modify and Activate and Monitor scopes, superscopes and multicast scopes
- Create reservations
- Create advanced properties for the DHCP Scope.

The DHCP console also contains enhancements that were suggested by network managers. These include enhanced server performance monitoring, more predefined DHCP option types, dynamic update support for clients running earlier versions of Windows and detection of unauthorized DHCP servers on your network.

1.2.3.1 Netsh Commands

The Netsh command is useful in networked environments to troubleshoot DHCP. Some scenarios where this utility is beneficial are:

- Slow linked networks
- Batch File use for networks with numerous DHCP Servers.

To use the Netsh command just open a command prompt and type **netsh dhcp**. This command must be used before any commands can be issued. The netsh command has a lengthy range of available switches that support DHCP. To view a complete list, type the **netsh dhcp /?** command at the prompt.

1.2.5 Manage DHCP Scope Options

Managing scope options is easily done by using the DHCP console. Open the DHCP console and expand the server to show the scope you wish to manage as shown below in Figure 1.22.

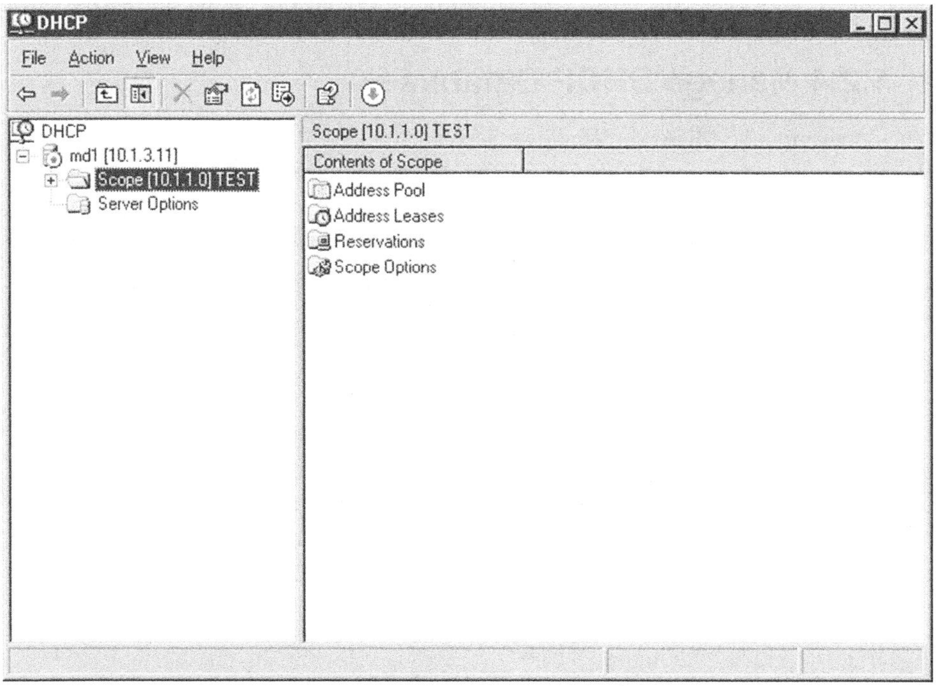

Figure 1-22: Managing the DHCP Scope from the DHCP Console.

The scope options available for management are:

- Address Pool – This contains the valid IP address pool DHCP uses to distribute IP addresses to network resources.
- Address Leases – This is the duration of the IP Address lease. Once the lease has expired a new IP address will be given to the DHCP client.
- Reservations – These addresses are not available for distribution and are reserved in the DHCP scope.
- Scope Options – These options include IP address information for the Time Server, Router addresses.

As stated earlier in this chapter, the Console is not the only way to manage the DHCP server. The Netsh command is also a way to manage the server from the prompt.

Pop Quiz 1.1

Pop Quiz 1.1 Questions

1. What is the role of Internet Assigned Numbers Authority?
2. If you are using DHCP what should you do to exclude a certain range of IP addresses from being assigned to client machines on the same network?
3. What is used to assign multicast IP Addresses within DHCP?
4. What is the octet range of a class C address?
5. What command can be used to perform batch tasks on a DHCP Server?

Pop Quiz 1.1 Answers

1. This authority is responsible for assigning companies and ISP's public IP addresses.
2. Use an address pool and set the address pool and all addresses in the pool without the Excluded IP addresses that are to be assigned to client machines.
3. The Multicast Address Dynamic Client Allocation Protocol or MADCAP is used by multicast for the distribution of IP Addresses on a Windows Server 2003.
4. 192–223 is the octet range of a Class C network of IP Addresses.
5. Batch Files for networks with numerous DHCP Servers can be done with the netsh command at the command prompt.

1.3 Troubleshoot TCP/IP Addressing

Troubleshooting TCP/IP addressing issues can be a difficult task for Network Administrators. Microsoft Windows Server 2003 has some great utilities built-in that will assist with these tasks. The steps below are taken when configuring the TCP/IP protocol is used with DHCP.

- TCP/IP configuration is successful once the DHCP server has been contacted and an IP address has been distributed to the client.
- If the DHCP server is unavailable or cannot be contacted, the client computer checks for its alternate configuration. If an alternate configuration is not available then APIPA will automatically configure TCP/IP. APIPA uses the address range 169.254.0.1 through 169.254.255.254 and a subnet mask of 255.255.0.0.

1.3.1 Diagnose and Resolve Issues Related to Automatic Private IP Addressing (APIPA)

Using APIPA within your network can be a helpful way for Network Administrators to have a backup in the event the DHCP server is unavailable and the alternate configuration on the client machine is not configured. APIPA is straightforward, so there is no configuring, but you may run into some problems. Table 1.6 below shows some common APIPA problems, resolutions and reasons for the problems.

Problem	Resolution	Reason
Client machine is receiving an IP address of 169.254.x.x instead of the IP address from the scope.	Either configure an alternate IP address for the client configuration or check the DHCP server to make certain it is available for the client machine.	The DHCP Server was not available so APIPA set the IP address for the client.
No DHCP server is available and no client alternate IP address is configured but the client is not receiving the APIPA address.	Make certain APIPA has not been disabled on the client computer.	If the DHCP Server is unavailable, no alternate IP address is configured on the client and APIPA has been disabled on the client machine then no IP address will be distributed.

Table 1.6: APIPA Problems and Resolutions.

APIPA can be disabled by using the following steps, but be careful when editing the registry and always make sure you have a current backup of the machine and a current copy of the Registry in the event of a problem. The Last Known Good Configuration will also assist you in the event of a start-up issue.

1. Click Start, type reged32.
2. Find the HKEY_LOCAL_MACHINE\SYSTEM\CurrentControlSet\Services\Tcpip\Parameters.
3. Select the Parameters folder, choose the Edit option, then New and select the DWORD value.
4. Enter the following to create a new entry: IPAutoconfigurationEnabled.
5. Right-click the new entry and then click Modify.
6. In Edit DWORD Value, under Value data, ensure that the setting is O.
7. Exit Registry Editor and reboot the computer.

APIPA should now be disabled on the client computer.

1.3.2 Diagnose and Resolve Issues Related to Incorrect TCP/IP Configuration

When troubleshooting TCP/IP configuration utilities, a host of issues could be the cause. Microsoft has tools to use to assist with the troubleshooting of TCP/IP configuration problems. Table 1.7 below contains these tools and how they can be used to troubleshoot TCP/IP.

Utility	What this Utility Does	When to Use
Ping	Sends ICMP echo request to verify connectivity. Ping has numerous switches that can be seen by typing ping /? at the command prompt.	Check network connectivity.
Netsh	This utility has a variety of functions and can be used to display TCP/IP properties at the command prompt.	Need to check network connectivity for a client computer.
Ipconfig	The ipconfig /release command can be used to release the IP Address address of a client machine. It can also be used to renew the IP address of a client by using the /renew option. The TCP/IP settings can also be viewed on a client machine by typing the ipconfig /all command at the prompt	Need to release the IP Address address of a client machine.
Netstat	Displays protocol statistics and information for TCP/IP connections. For more information.	Need to view TCP/IP statistics on a client machine.
Nbtstat	Checks the state of current NetBIOS over TCP/IP connections, updates the Lmhosts cache and determines the registered names and scope ID.	Need to check to see if NetBIOS over TCP/IP is running.
Pathping	Traces the route a packet takes to a destination and displays information on packet losses for each router in the path.	Client cannot connect to mail server. Use this command to view the route to the mail server.
Tracert	Traces the network route taken by an IP packet to the destination computer.	Client cannot connect to the Internet. Use this command to view the route to the Internet.

Table 1–7: Tools for Troubleshooting TCP/IP.

These are just a few of the utilities that can be used to diagnose TCP/IP related issues. As always before you begin to test with these utilities make certain that the CAT5 cable and Network Card on the client computer are working properly. For a more in depth look at the available utilities use the Microsoft Web Site at http://www.microsoft.com.

1.3.1 Diagnose and Resolve Issues Related to DHCP Authorization

In the event you have DHCP related authorization issues, before you begin an in depth troubleshooting session, make sure the DHCP Server and Scopes in question have been authorized.

1.3.2 Verify DHCP Reservation Configuration

To check the reservation of a DHCP client you can use the IPconfig utility. This is a simple process and all to do this follow these instructions:

- Open a command prompt.
- Type **ipconfig /all**.
- The **AutoConfiguration IP Address** should be within the range of the DHCP Server reservation that has been set.

Also, check the DHCP server and make sure the reservation has been added to the scope if you have any problems.

1.3.4 Diagnose and resolve issues related to configuration of DHCP server and scope options

In the event you are faced with issues pertaining to the DHCP server and the options set in the DHCP Scope, you can use Table 1.8 to assist you with troubleshooting. Before you begin to troubleshoot the DHCP Scope remember to always check the basics first:

- Client network card is functioning.
- CAT 5 cables are functioning properly.
- DHCP server has been Authorized.
- DHCP scope has been activated.
- Server can be reached by other client machines.

Once the above checklist has been completed you can use Table 1.8 for further troubleshooting.

Problem	Cause	Resolution
A client machine has an incorrect IP address for its adapter. The address is not from APIPA or DHCP.	Automatic IP configuration issued the address.	Make certain the DHCP server is available to distribute the IP address to the client.
Client IP address is 0.0.0.0.	DHCP server was not able to reach client machine to distribute an IP address.	Check the network cables and the Network Interface Card.
Gateway on DHCP client is incorrect.	DHCP Scope option.	Check the DHCP Server scope configuration for this setting and make certain it is correct.

Table 1–8: Common DHCP Client Issues and Resolutions.

These are some of the problems that you may have when working with the DHCP server and scopes. Double-check your scope options before you activate the scope and make sure you have entered the correct information for all information pertaining to that scope.

1.3.5 Verify that the DHCP Relay Agent is Working Correctly

When deploying the DHCP relay agent you may wish to test and make certain that it is working properly within your network. Some guidelines below can be used to verify the DHCP relay agent is functioning if it is not providing relay services for DHCP clients.

- In the event that the DHCP server IP address configured from the global properties of the DHCP relay agent are incorrect, check the DHCP relay agent properties.
- Check to see that Routing and Remote Access Server has been added to the DHCP relay agent IP routing protocol.
- If the DHCP servers are cannot be contacted go to the router that has the DHCP relay agent turned on and issue a ping command from the prompt to check for connectivity.

Chapter 1: Review Questions

1. Which of these are private network addresses?

A. 168.16.0.21

B. 12.0.0.12

C. 10.0.0.12

D. 172.16.0.13

E. 192.168.0.31

---

2. Under which of the following circumstances could your DHCP service prove a security risk?

A. When the DHCP server is configured to act as a DNS proxy server.

B. If unauthorized persons do not have physical or wireless access to your network.

C. When DHCP audit logs are ignored.

D. When the DHCP server is configured to act as a LMHOSTS proxy server.

---

3. You have two network segments but only one DHCP server. You want to broadcast DHCP traffic from the server on both segments. How can you accomplish this?

A. Ensure that your routers are RFC 1342 compliant.

B. Ensure that your routers are RFC 1542 compliant.

C. Ensure that your routers are RFC 1642 compliant.

D. Use a DHCP relay agent.

4. Which of the following are backup methods for backing up the DHCP database?
A. Synchronous
B. Asynchronous
C. Parallel
D. Backups using Windows Backup

---

5. When configuring a scope for a DHCP server, which of the following information can and should be included in the scope?
A. A range of IP addresses
B. DNS server address
C. DHCP server location
D. Router address

---

6. Which actions should you take to achieve an optimal configuration for two new DHCP servers in your brand new 2003 network?
A. Use superscopes for multiple DHCP servers on each subnet.
B. Use the 80/20 design rule.
C. Use overlapping scopes in the same subnet.
D. Use the 60/40 design rule.
E. Reservations should be created on all DHCP servers that can potentially service the reserved client.

7. If the DHCP client appears to have automatically assigned itself an IP address that is incorrect for the current network (one that start with 169.254), what could be the cause?

A. The client changed the DHCP scope.

B. The client could not find a DHCP server.

C. The client changed the DHCP lease.

D. The client is set up with a static address.

---

8. You have three print servers that need DHCP reservations. Your print servers are on the 10.30.0.0 network. 10.30.0.1 is the DHCP server's address. You want to reserve the next three addresses for the print servers. Which of the following addresses are you going to use?

A. 10.30.0.2 through 10.30.0.5

B. 10.30.0.1 through 10.30.0.4

C. 10.30.0.2 through 10.30.0.4

D. 10.30.0.1 through 10.30.0.3

9. Where are the DHCP audit logs located in 2003 Server?

A. %windir%\System32\Dhcp

B. %windir%\WINNT\System32\Dhcp

C. %windir%\WINNT32\System32\Dhcp

D. %windir%\Dhcp

---

10. Identify which of the following statements are true regarding a Class A address?

A. Class A addresses begin with a 0 when represented in binary.

B. There are 126 available networks for use with a class A address and a possible 16,777,214 hosts.

C. There are 16,384 available networks for use with a class B address and a possible 65,534 hosts.

D. The range of a Class A address is 1–127. The network ID is 8 bits in length and there are 24 host bits.

E. There are 2,097,152 available networks for use with a class C address and a possible 254 hosts.

11. Which of the following is the correct way to install Network Monitor in Server 2003?

A. Right-click the desktop and go to the Component Wizard Menu. From Subcomponents of Management and Monitoring Tools, select the Network Monitor Tools check box, click OK, and then click Next to continue the installation.

B. Go to the Program Component Wizard. From Subcomponents of Management and Monitoring Tools, select the Network Monitor Tools check box, click OK, and then click Next to continue the installation.

C. Go to the Windows Component Wizard. From Subcomponents of Management and Monitoring Tools, select the Monitoring Tools check box, click OK, and then click Next to continue the installation.

D. Go to the Windows Component Wizard. From Subcomponents of Management and Monitoring Tools, select the Network Monitor Tools check box, click OK, and then click Next to continue the installation.

---

12. You want to capture packets with Network Monitor. How can this be done?

A. Open Network Monitor. Select the Network Monitor phase. Click Start Capture on the toolbar. Then click Stop and View Capture. Don't close the capture window.

B. Open Performance. Select the network interface. Click Start Capture on the toolbar. Then click Stop and View Capture. Don't close the capture window.

C. Open Network Monitor. Select the network interface. Click Start Capture on the toolbar. Then click Stop and View Capture. Don't close the capture window.

D. Open Network Monitor. Select the network interface. Click View Capture. Don't close the capture window.

13. Identify which of the following statements are true regarding a Class C address?

A. Class C addresses begin with a 110 when represented in binary.

B. There are 2,097,152 available networks for use with a class C address and a possible 254 hosts.

C. The range of a Class C address is 128-191.

D. The range of a Class C address is 192-223. The network ID is 24 bits in length and there are 8 host bits.

E. The network ID is 8 bits in length and there are 24 host bits.

---

14. Into which class does the IP address 172.16.40.2 fall?

A. It is a Class A address.

B. It is a Class B address.

C. It is a Class C address.

D. It is a Class D address.

15. Which of the following binary octets equals 63?

A. 111111

B. 1111111

C. 11111

D. 11111111

---

16. When network connectivity is inconsistent between many routers in distant locations (i.e. Atlanta, GA, Los Angeles, CA, Houston, TX, and Philadelphia, PA), what command would you use to determine where packets are being dropped and what percentage of packets is being dropped?

A. ipconfig

B. pathping

C. tracert

D. ping

17. Which of the following statements are true?

A. No answer is correct.

B. Servers should always have a static IP address.

C. Clients can have either dynamic or static IP addresses.

D. If you statically enter an IP address on a client, you will also need to statically enter the subnet mask and the default gateway.

---

18. Should servers have dynamically assigned addresses?

A. It depends on the type of network card.

B. Yes, but only if they run DHCP and DNS.

C. Yes, they should always be dynamically assigned.

D. No, they should never be dynamically assigned.

19. Choose the Class A IP address.

A. 121.20.21.3

B. 240.221.23.45

C. 166.33.231.12

D. 255.211.34.321

---

20. Choose the Class B IP address.

A. 224.12.233.12

B. 240.221.23.45

C. 155.211.12.3

D. 119.23.12.122

Chapter 1: Review Answers

1. Which of these are private network addresses?
   A. 168.16.0.21
   B. 12.0.0.12

***C. 10.0.0.12**

***D. 172.16.0.13**

***E. 192.168.0.31**

Explanation: A private network would be a corporate network or an intranet, which would limit its access to those outside of the company. A public network would be the Internet, with open access to the global community. You can use certain IP addresses privately within your own intranet, as long as the global community does not see them. Class A is 10.0.0.0, Class B is 172.16.0.0 and Class C is 192.168.0.0.

---

2. Under which of the following circumstances could your DHCP service prove a security risk?

***A. When the DHCP server is configured to act as a DNS proxy server.**

***B. If unauthorized persons do not have physical or wireless access to your network.**

***C. When DHCP audit logs are ignored.**

D. When the DHCP server is configured to act as a LMHOSTS proxy server.

Explanation: When the DHCP server is configured to act as a DNS proxy server for DHCP clients and to perform DNS dynamic updates, it is possible for a malicious user to perform a denial-of-service attack against both the DHCP server and the DNS server by flooding the DHCP server with requests for leases. Ensure that unauthorized persons do not have physical or wireless access to your network. Use the DHCP audit logs, located by default at %windir%\System32\Dhcp, to monitor DNS dynamic updates by the DHCP server.

3. You have two network segments but only one DHCP server. You want to broadcast DHCP traffic from the server on both segments. How can you accomplish this?

A. Ensure that your routers are RFC 1342 compliant.

***B. Ensure that your routers are RFC 1542 compliant.**

C. Ensure that your routers are RFC 1642 compliant.

***D. Use a DHCP relay agent.**

Explanation: A relay agent is a small program that relays DHCP/BOOTP messages between clients and servers on different subnets. To support and use DHCP service across multiple subnets, routers connecting each subnet should comply with DHCP/BOOTP relay agent capabilities described in RFC 1542. In most cases, routers support DHCP/BOOTP relay.

---

4. Which of the following are backup methods for backing up the DHCP database?

***A. Synchronous**

***B. Asynchronous**

C. Parallel

***D. Backups using Windows Backup**

Explanation: Maintaining a backup of the DHCP database protects you from data loss if the DHCP database is lost (for example, due to hard disk failure) or becomes corrupted. The three backup methods supported by the DHCP Server service include the following: Synchronous (automatic backups, the default backup interval is 60 minutes), Asynchronous (manual backups, performed by using the Backup command on the DHCP console) and Backups using Windows Backup (ntbackup.exe) or non-Microsoft backup software.

5. When configuring a scope for a DHCP server, which of the following information can and should be included in the scope?

***A. A range of IP addresses**

***B. DNS server address**

C. DHCP server location

***D. Router address**

Explanation: A scope has a range of IP addresses from which to include or exclude addresses used for DHCP service lease offerings. A scope has a subnet mask, which determines the subnet for a given IP address. A scope has a scope name assigned when it is created. A scope has lease duration values, which are assigned to DHCP clients that receive dynamically allocated IP addresses. A scope has DHCP scope options configured for assignment to DHCP clients, such as DNS server, router IP address and WINS server address. A scope has reservations, optionally used to ensure that a DHCP client always receives the same IP address.

---

6. Which actions should you take to achieve an optimal configuration for two new DHCP servers in your brand new 2003 network?

***A. Use superscopes for multiple DHCP servers on each subnet.**

***B. Use the 80/20 design rule.**

C. Use overlapping scopes in the same subnet.
D. Use the 60/40 design rule.

***E. Reservations should be created on all DHCP servers that can potentially service the reserved client.**

Explanation: Use the 80/20 design rule for balancing scope distribution of addresses where multiple DHCP servers are deployed to service the same scope. Use superscopes for multiple DHCP servers on each subnet in a LAN environment. Deactivate scopes only when removing a scope permanently from service. Use server-side conflict detection on DHCP servers only when it is needed. Reservations should be created on all DHCP servers that can potentially service the reserved client. For server performance, note that DHCP is disk-intensive so purchase hardware with optimal disk performance characteristics. Keep audit logging enabled for use in troubleshooting. Reduce lease times for DHCP clients that use Routing and Remote Access service for remote access. Increase the duration of scope leases for large, stable, fixed networks if available address space is plentiful. Integrate DHCP with other services, such as WINS and DNS. For routed networks, either use relay agents or set appropriate timers to prevent undesired forwarding and relay of BOOTP and DHCP message traffic. Use the appropriate number of DHCP servers for the number of DHCP-enabled clients on your network. For DNS dynamic updates performed by the DHCP service, use the default client preference settings. Use the manual backup and restore methods in the DHCP server console.

7. If the DHCP client appears to have automatically assigned itself an IP address that is incorrect for the current network (one that start with 169.254), what could be the cause?

A. The client changed the DHCP scope.

***B. The client could not find a DHCP server.**

C. The client changed the DHCP lease.

D. The client is set up with a static address.

Explanation: More than likely, the client running Windows 98, Windows Millennium Edition or Windows XP. It could not find a DHCP server and has used IP autoconfiguration (APIPA) to configure its IP address.

---

8. You have three print servers that need DHCP reservations. Your print servers are on the 10.30.0.0 network. 10.30.0.1 is the DHCP server's address. You want to reserve the next three addresses for the print servers. Which of the following addresses are you going to use?

A. 10.30.0.2 through 10.30.0.5

B. 10.30.0.1 through 10.30.0.4

***C. 10.30.0.2 through 10.30.0.4**

D. 10.30.0.1 through 10.30.0.3

Explanation: You can choose to reserve some IP addresses for permanent lease assignment to specified computers or devices on your network. You should make reservations only for devices that are DHCP-enabled and that must be reserved for specific purposes on your network (such as print servers). Here we should use the 10.30.0.2 through 10.30.0.4 address range for the printers.

9. Where are the DHCP audit logs located in 2003 Server?

***A. %windir%\System32\Dhcp**

B. %windir%\WINNT\System32\Dhcp
C. %windir%\WINNT32\System32\Dhcp
D. %windir%\Dhcp

Explanation: Use the DHCP audit logs, located by default at %windir%\System32\Dhcp, to monitor DNS dynamic updates by the DHCP server. The following event IDs are used for DNS dynamic update events: 30 (DNS dynamic update request to the DNS server), 31 (DNS dynamic update failed) and 32 (DNS dynamic update successful).

---

10. Identify which of the following statements are true regarding a Class A address?

***A. Class A addresses begin with a 0 when represented in binary.**

***B. There are 126 available networks for use with a class A address and a possible 16,777,214 hosts.**

C. There are 16,384 available networks for use with a class B address and a possible 65,534 hosts.

***D. The range of a Class A address is 1-127. The network ID is 8 bits in length and there are 24 host bits.**

E. There are 2,097,152 available networks for use with a class C address and a possible 254 hosts.

Explanation: Class A addresses begin with a 0 when represented in binary. The range of a Class A address is 1-127. The network ID is 8 bits in length and there are 24 host bits. There are 126 available networks for use with a class A address and a possible 16,777,214 hosts. Class B addresses begin with a 10 when represented in binary. The range of a Class B address is 128-191. The network ID is 16 bits in length and there are 16 host bits. There are 16,384 available networks for use with a class B address and a possible 65,534 hosts. Class C addresses begin with a 110 when represented in binary. The range of a Class C address is 192-223. The network ID is 24 bits in length and there are 8 host bits. There are 2,097,152 available networks for use with a class C address and a possible 254 hosts.

11. Which of the following is the correct way to install Network Monitor in Server 2003?
A. Right-click the desktop and go to the Component Wizard Menu. From Subcomponents of Management and Monitoring Tools, select the Network Monitor Tools check box, click OK, and then click Next to continue the installation.
B. Go to the Program Component Wizard. From Subcomponents of Management and Monitoring Tools, select the Network Monitor Tools check box, click OK, and then click Next to continue the installation.
C. Go to the Windows Component Wizard. From Subcomponents of Management and Monitoring Tools, select the Monitoring Tools check box, click OK, and then click Next to continue the installation.
***D. Go to the Windows Component Wizard. From Subcomponents of Management and Monitoring Tools, select the Network Monitor Tools check box, click OK, and then click Next to continue the installation.**

Explanation: You install Network Monitor from the Windows Component Wizard. From Subcomponents of Management and Monitoring Tools, select the Network Monitor Tools check box, click OK, and then click Next to continue the installation.

---

12. You want to capture packets with Network Monitor. How can this be done?
A. Open Network Monitor. Select the Network Monitor phase. Click Start Capture on the toolbar. Then click Stop and View Capture. Don't close the capture window.
B. Open Performance. Select the network interface. Click Start Capture on the toolbar. Then click Stop and View Capture. Don't close the capture window.
***C. Open Network Monitor. Select the network interface. Click Start Capture on the toolbar. Then click Stop and View Capture. Don't close the capture window.**
D. Open Network Monitor. Select the network interface. Click View Capture. Don't close the capture window.

Explanation: To capture frames by using Network Monitor, open Network Monitor. Select the network interface that you want to use (if it has not already been selected). Start the capture process by clicking Start Capture on the toolbar. To stop the capture, on the toolbar, click Stop and View Capture. Do not close the capture window.

13. Identify which of the following statements are true regarding a Class C address?

***A. Class C addresses begin with a 110 when represented in binary.**

***B. There are 2,097,152 available networks for use with a class C address and a possible 254 hosts.**

C. The range of a Class C address is 128-191.

***D. The range of a Class C address is 192-223. The network ID is 24 bits in length and there are 8 host bits.**

E. The network ID is 8 bits in length and there are 24 host bits.

Explanation: Class A addresses begin with a 0 when represented in binary. The range of a Class A address is 1-127. The network ID is 8 bits in length and there are 24 host bits. There are 126 available networks for use with a class A address and a possible 16,777,214 hosts. Class B addresses begin with a 10 when represented in binary. The range of a Class B address is 128-191. The network ID is 16 bits in length and there are 16 host bits. There are 16,384 available networks for use with a class B address and a possible 65,534 hosts. Class C addresses begin with a 110 when represented in binary. The range of a Class C address is 192-223. The network ID is 24 bits in length and there are 8 host bits. There are 2,097,152 available networks for use with a class C address and a possible 254 hosts.

---

14. Into which class does the IP address 172.16.40.2 fall?

A. It is a Class A address.

***B. It is a Class B address.**

C. It is a Class C address.

D. It is a Class D address.

Explanation: The IP address 172.16.40.2 falls into the Class B address range.

15. Which of the following binary octets equals 63?

***A. 111111**

B. 1111111
C. 11111
D. 11111111

Explanation: The binary octet 00011111 equals 31. The binary octet 00111111 equals 63. The binary octet 01111111 equals 127. The binary octet 11111111 equals 255.

---

16. When network connectivity is inconsistent between many routers in distant locations (i.e. Atlanta, GA, Los Angeles, CA, Houston, TX, and Philadelphia, PA), what command would you use to determine where packets are being dropped and what percentage of packets is being dropped?

A. ipconfig

***B. pathping**

C. tracert
D. ping

Explanation: Pathping combines the functionality of the ping and tracert commands. Pathping also shows what percentage of packets is being dropped. Ping and Tracert don't show this information. An example of using pathping from Atlanta to test connectivity to Los Angeles, CA would be: pathping LOSANG01.

17. Which of the following statements are true?
A. No answer is correct.
***B. Servers should always have a static IP address.**
***C. Clients can have either dynamic or static IP addresses.**
***D. If you statically enter an IP address on a client, you will also need to statically enter the subnet mask and the default gateway.**

Explanation: Servers should always have a static IP address. Clients can have either dynamic or static IP addresses. If you statically enter an IP address on a client, you will also need to statically enter the subnet mask and the default gateway.

---

18. Should servers have dynamically assigned addresses?
A. It depends on the type of network card.
B. Yes, but only if they run DHCP and DNS.
C. Yes, they should always be dynamically assigned.
***D. No, they should never be dynamically assigned.**

Explanation: Servers should never use dynamically assigned addresses, because clients who try to access them (for gateway services) don't know the address. Statically assign addresses on servers and leave the DHCP services for the clients.

19. Choose the Class A IP address.

***A. 121.20.21.3**

B. 240.221.23.45
C. 166.33.231.12
D. 255.211.34.321

Explanation: Class A will have a number between 1 and 126 in the first octet. Class B will have a number between 128 and 191 in the first octet. Class C will have a number between 192 and 223 in the first octet. Class D (broadcast or multicast) will have a number between 224 and 239 in the first octet. Class E (set aside for experimentation and research) will have a number between 240 and 255 in the first octet. The 127 range is set aside for loopback.

---

20. Choose the Class B IP address.
A. 224.12.233.12
B. 240.221.23.45

***C. 155.211.12.3**

D. 119.23.12.122

Explanation: Class A will have a number between 1 and 126 in the first octet. Class B will have a number between 128 and 191 in the first octet. Class C will have a number between 192 and 223 in the first octet. Class D (broadcast or multicast) will have a number between 224 and 239 in the first octet. Class E (set aside for experimentation and research) will have a number between 240 and 255 in the first octet. The 127 range is set aside for loopback.

Implementing, Managing, and Maintaining Name Resolution

The objective of this chapter is to provide the reader with an understanding of the following:

Install and configure the DNS Server service.

- **Configure DNS server options.**
- **Configure DNS zone options.**
- **Configure DNS forwarding.**

Manage DNS.

- **Manage DNS zone settings.**
- **Manage DNS record settings.**
- **Manage DNS server options.**

Monitor DNS. Tools might include:

- **System Monitor**
- **Event Viewer**
- **Replication Monitor**
- **DNS debug logs.**

Chapter 2: Managing Name Resolution

Introduction:

The Domain Name System or DNS is the basis for name resolution on the Internet and in Windows Server 2003. A thorough understanding of DNS concepts and their implementation on Windows Server 2003 will make your planning and deployment much easier and possibly much faster. Windows Server 2003 provides several tools to make the implementation and maintenance of DNS easier for the network administrator. We'll explore these at the end of this chapter, after examining some basic configuration and management issues.

DNS stores the host name information in a database that is distributed among multiple servers, thus decreasing the load on any one server. Each server is responsible for answering queries about a subsection of the entire database. Because the entire database is distributed, the size of the database is unlimited, and performance does not suffer as the database size increases. This area is called a zone, and we will find out about different types of zones in the following sections.

DNS is responsible for providing the information to resolve a host name to an IP address. The DNS namespace is a hierarchical naming tree that allows DNS to identify and locate a specific host in the tree. DNS uses the DNS namespace to precisely identify the exact host you desire to connect with. The name of the host is traced from the top of the tree (or root) down through a top level domain (such as .com), a second level domain (such as microsoft.com), to possibly a sub-domain (sales.microsoft.com) to the host (server42.sales.microsoft.com).

Getting Ready Questions

1. To configure a DNS server as a caching only DNS server, how must this server be configured?

2. How could you check your DNS server?

3. How could you clear the DNS resolver cache for a client computer?

4. What kind of DNS record is required for a client computer to find a Windows 2003 Domain Controller?

5. A copy of a ____ zone file contains only the records needed to identify the authoritative DNS server for the zone. Typically this is used to point to a child domain to allow for faster query performance.

Getting Ready Answers

1. To configure a DNS server as a caching only DNS server, it must be configured as a forwarder.

2. You could check your DNS server using the Monitoring tab of your DNS server properties or you could use the nslookup command.

3. Ipconfig /flushdns

4. Service (SRV) record

5. Stub

The entire name is referred to as the fully qualified domain name for the host. It traces the one path through the DNS namespace tree to that specific machine.

There are three main components to the DNS system in Windows Server 2003—the DNS Name Server, the DNS client and the resource records the name servers hold in their databases. Let's look at each of these for a bit.

The **DNS Serve**r or Name Server is a computer running the DNS service on Windows Server 2003 (or some earlier version of Windows). It can also be a Unix or Linux based machine running the equivalent software for whatever flavor of Unix or Linux is on the machine. It hosts a namespace or a portion of the namespace (or domain). It is authoritative for that namespace or domain, which means that it can answer queries about its namespace from other DNS servers or client machines. It resolves the name resolution requests that DNS clients submit.

The **DNS client** is simply a machine that runs the DNS client service. Typically one thinks of the workstation machines as DNS clients, but the DNS server also needs to be configured as a client, as it uses the client software to perform the queries it needs to service client name resolution requests.

A **Resource Record** is merely an entry in the DNS database that maps a host name to a resource. There are many types of resource records, which we will discuss in a later section. These records are stored in a zone file on the DNS server.

All name resolution in DNS is based upon a query. A DNS client makes a request of the server for a name resolution in the form of a query. Basically the client is asking the server to match an alphanumeric name to an IP address of the resource, so that the resource can be accessed. Both clients and servers can initiate a query. The client would query its assigned DNS server. Depending upon the query, the DNS server may respond directly to the request, or initiate a query to another DNS server to obtain the needed information.

The way that a DNS server responds to a query depends upon if it is authoritative or non-authoritative for the namespace in that particular query. Authoritative means that the DNS server is responsible for that particular namespace. Non-authoritative simply means that the DNS server is not responsible for that namespace. If the query contains a namespace that the DNS server is authoritative for, it will check its cache and zone file for the information and return the information to the requestor, or return an authoritative no to the requestor. If the DNS server is non-authoritative for the namespace in the query, it will either forward the request to another server, or attempt to research the request for the client. What it does specifically depends on the servers' configuration, as discussed in a later section.

For example, your domain is named smallcorp.com. You need to use a resource on your intranet, like a Web page found on a machine named internalweb.smallcorp.com. You type that hostname into your Web browser, and the DNS client on your machine queries the DNS server it is assigned with a name resolution request. The DNS server checks it cache and zone file, and returns the IP address to your DNS client, which lets the rest of the TCP/IP stack do its job. Your Web browser brings up the default page assigned to the default Web site on internalweb.smallcorp.com. You get the information you need and go on with your tasks. Your DNS server has given you an authoritative answer to your query.

Now, you decide you need to make plans for your weekend camping trip. You need to get some information from Bob's Bait and Tackle Shop. They recently implemented a new Web site that gives you lots of information you need for your trip planning. You type in the Web site name, and your DNS client passes the query to your DNS server. Your DNS server is not authoritative for www.bobsbandt.com. Your DNS server is configured not to forward requests, so it makes several queries on your behalf until it finds the DNS server that is authoritative for bobsbandt.com. Your query is answered, and your DNS server returns the information to you, based upon its query to the bobsbnadt.com server. Your server is returning a non-authoritative answer to your query, because it was using the information it obtained about a name outside of its own namespace.

There are two types of queries in DNS—recursive and iterative. Both types of queries are used to resolve name resolution requests. In a recursive query, a client is requesting a complete answer from the server. The client either wants to know the correct answer, or it wants to know the fact that given the information in the query, no name resolution is possible. This puts the responsibility of an answer on the queried server. Either the client or a server that is configured to forward queries can initiate a recursive request. More on forwarding in a minute. An iterative query is a query made between DNS servers to help the DNS server making the query obtain the best answer for its client. In an iterative query the DNS server making the query will accept an authoritative answer, or a referral. The referral points the requesting DNS server to another DNS server that might have a more complete answer.

Typically the DNS server with the query to resolve will start at the top of the hierarchical tree, or root. It makes an iterative query to a top level server. This root server points to the server responsible for the first level domain, like .com or .net or .org. The DNS server for the first level points to the server the next level down responsible for that namespace, or some superset of that namespace.

This continues until your DNS server finds the name server that is authoritative for the namespace. It gets the authoritative answer for its query instead of a referral. It then returns the authoritative answer to the client requesting it.

For example—you key www.louisville.edu into your Web browser, because you are interested in the recent academic accomplishments of the business school. While you are there, you also intend to check the basketball schedule, but that's between you and your boss. (I promise I won't tell.) Your DNS client sends a recursive query to your DNS server. It checks its cache and doesn't find an entry. Because it is not authoritative for the louisville.edu namespace and it doesn't forward requests, it uses an iterative query to check with the root name servers to find out what they know about Louisville.edu. The root name server refers your DNS server to the name server responsible for .the .edu namespace. Your DNS server makes an iterative query to the .edu name server. It refers your DNS server to the name server for louisville.edu. Your DNS server makes another iterative query to the louisville.edu name server, which provides an authoritative response to the name resolution! Yeah!! Your DNS server returns this answer to the DNS client, and your requested page loads. It probably takes a lot less time than it did for you to read the last couple of paragraphs.

Two more things we need to cover quickly—forwarding and root hints. **Forwarding** is when a DNS server answers requests for the namespace it is authoritative for, but sends a recursive request to another DNS server for anything else. This "other" DNS server is configured in the server setup. Windows Server 2003 provides several types of forwarding, depending upon your needs. More later on that. The "other" server goes through the necessary steps to resolve the query, depending upon the way it is configured. **Root Hints** are special resource records kept on the server that typically point to the root name servers for the Internet. This may be configured to point just to a local DNS server. If so, that server will only resolve local host names, and return unknown host for any other records. If configured in this manner, the only names resolved are on your local intranet. This is typically done for security reasons, as only your internal domains can be resolved.

2.1 Install and Configure the DNS Server Service

Installation of the DNS Server Service is a straightforward matter. You need to log in with an account that has administrative rights on the server, or use the run as option and provide an administrator account name and password, then install the service.

The step-by-step instructions follow shortly. These steps assume you have logged into the network with an account that DOES NOT have administrative credentials. You will use the run as command to run the installation with the necessary rights. Why do you perform the operations this way? This method allows you to log in with an account that has normal user privileges. A majority of the tasks you need to perform probably do not need the additional credentials of an administrator. The run as allows you to switch to a different set of credentials for that particular task. When you exit the program you started using run as, you revert to your normal user privileges. While running the program, you have the credentials of the account you entered in the run as dialog box. This method allows just one more layer of security for your network. If someone ends a program and walks away from their computer without locking or logging out, you just have an open user account, not an administrator.

Before you install, you need to do a bit of planning and make some decisions. Some of these may be provided for you already. You must have TCP/IP configured with a static IP address. You need to select your domain name. If you are going to use this domain name on the Internet, it must be registered with Internic or another authority. Some others we'll discuss as we explore the server and zone options.

Okay, so let's get started now! Here are the installation steps.

1. Log in with a non-administrative account.
2. Click on **Start**, then click on **Control Panel** or **All Programs**.
3. Open Administrative Tools from whichever selection you chose. Right-click **Manage Your Server**, then select **Run As** (see figure 2.1).

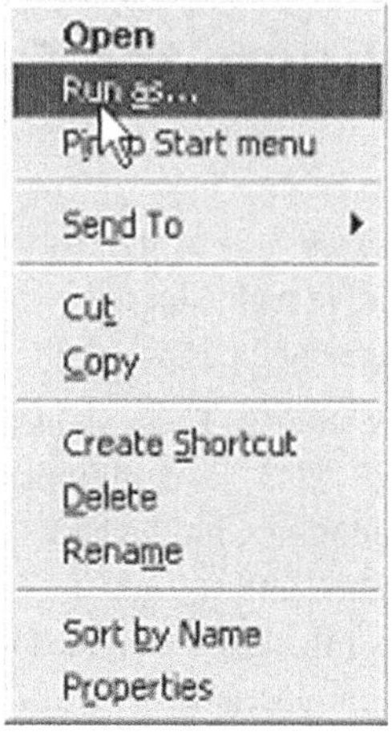

Figure 2-1: Installation Steps.

In the Run As dialog box, select **The following user** radio button, then supply a user account and password that has the appropriate permissions to complete our task. Then click on the **OK** button. Figure 2.2 shows the dialog box.

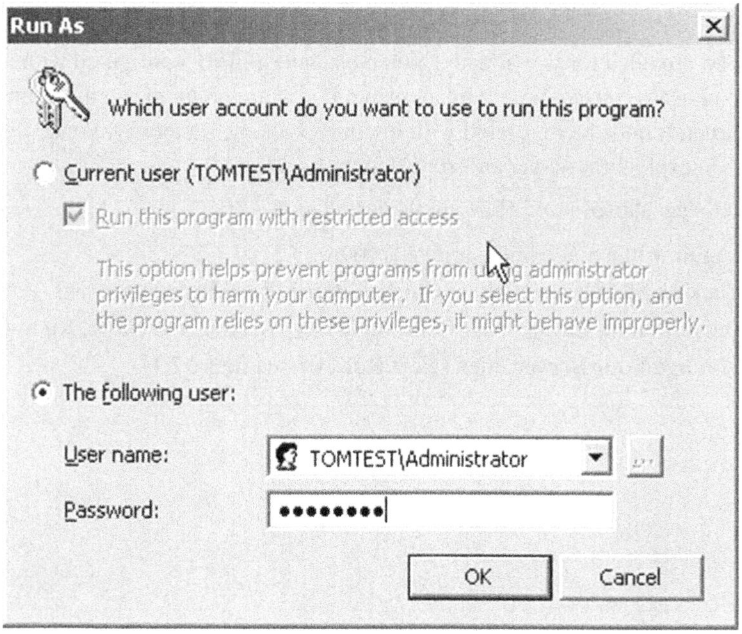

Figure 2-2: Dialog Box.

1. In the Manage Your Server Wizard, click **Add or Remove A Role**. Click **Next** on the Preliminary Steps page.
2. On the Server Role page, select **DNS Server** and again click **Next**.
3. Review the Summary of Selections page, and click **Next**. If prompted for your CD, supply it or a path to the files on your server.
4. You will be taken to the Configure A DNS Server Wizard. This concludes the basic installation. You can select **Cancel** and configure the server later, or you can continue here with the server and zone options.

2.1.1 Configure DNS Server Options

So, DNS is installed on your server. Great!! Now let's make it useful. Let's examine the various options available to you and what they mean. The DNS server property sheet appears in figure 2.3.

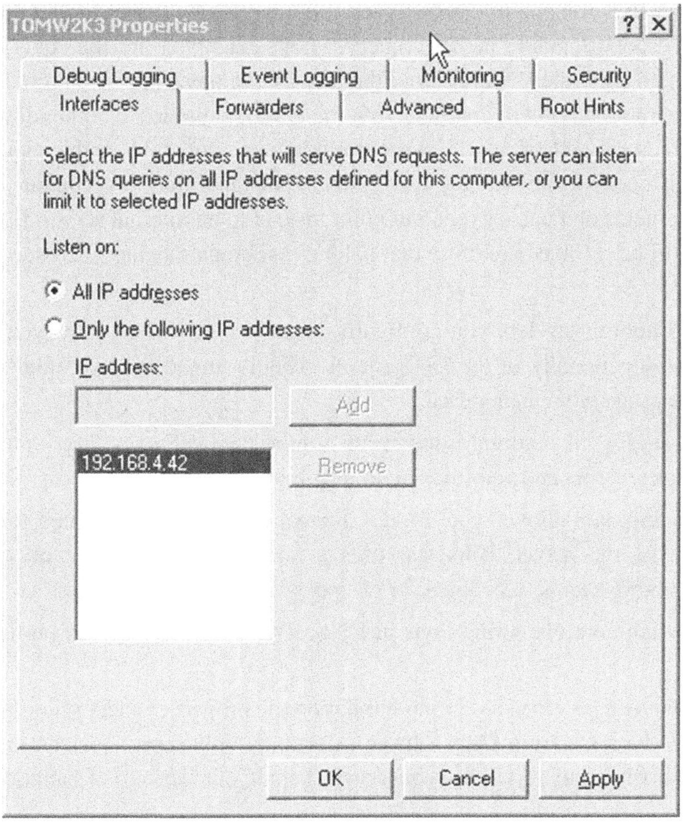

Figure 2-3: DNS Server Property Sheet

Some of the tabs on the dialog box will be discussed later in this chapter. Lets talk about the general use of each briefly. The properties sheet can be reached by launching the DNS MMC from the **Administrative Tools** menu. You can access it from **Control Panel** or the **All Programs** selection from the **Start** button.

The **Interfaces** tab allows you to define which network interfaces the server listens for DNS queries on. By default, it listens on all interfaces, but you can select to limit that by entering the IP address for the specific interface you want to answer queries.

The **Forwarders** tab to configure DNS forwarding. We discuss the different methods used to forward queries in a later section.

The **Root Hints** tab allows you to view and update the root hints for your server. You can add a new server, edit an existing one, remove one or copy the list from another server. When a query is received from a client, the DNS cache is checked. If there are no entries in cache that apply, and the DNS server does not have the IP address for authoritative DNS server for that domain, the DNS server will query a root server for the domain to the left of the root domain in the query. For example, if the query was for www.bigdomain.com, the DNS server will query for the name server for .com. When that information is returned, it will continue with the iterative queries, walking down the DNS tree until it finds the authoritative server for bigdomain.com and gets the name resolution information it needs to answer the query. The root hints may not contain information about the Internet root name servers, but point instead to an internal server. If so, the only names that will be resolved are those that belong that domain being referenced in the root hints.

The **Debug Logging** tab lets you configure the debug packet captures you can use to check various functionally in the DNS server. This is turned off by default, due to the high resource usage while being used.

The **Event Logging** tab configures the events sent to the DNS event log. You can choose all events, errors, errors and warnings or no information at all.

The **Monitoring** tab allows you to do manual or automatic testing to verify the configuration of the server. This test uses a simple or a recursive query to verify operation. The tests can be scheduled for off–peek use or run in real time.

The **Security** tab controls permissions in DNS. This controls who can perform specific tasks in DNS.

One option that is a server wide setting but not on the properties sheet is configuring your DNS server to be a **Caching Only Server**. A caching only server does not maintain any zone database files, but forwards requests on behalf of clients if it cannot answer the query from its current cache.

Thus, a caching only server is always a forwarder, or it would have nothing to cache! A caching only server is easy to configure. Configure it to forward (more on that topic shortly) and do not configure any zone files. Point clients to it and you are ready to go. Typically you would use a caching only server to cut down on replication traffic over a slow WAN link. It will still have name resolution query network traffic, but no zone transfer network traffic. Zone transfers can be somewhat resource intensive, depending on the size of the file and the method used to do the transfer.

2.1.2 Configure DNS Zone Options

Zone files are where the various resource records are stored. The resource record is data used to resolve queries. There are several types. Depending upon your server and what it does, you may need to enter several types. A zone is the portion of the DNS database that contains the resource records for a particular contiguous portion of the DNS namespace. The zone file is the file on the server hard disk that contains these records. There are several types of zone files, but the basic options are the same for most of the types. Your server is not completely configured until you add the hostname to IP address mappings into your zone file, unless your server is going to be set up to perform caching only functions that we mentioned before.

Because there are various different types of resources on a network, DNS has several types of records. Some of the more common ones are listed in Table 2.1.

Record Type	Description	Example of Use
Host or A Record	Represents a computer or other device and will resolve from a host name to IP address. Most common DNS record type.	Server1.bigdomain.com resolves to 192.168.51.12.
Pointer or PTR Record	Found only in a reverse lookup zone, this record is used to resolve from an IP address to a DNS Host name. Finds the name corresponding to an IP address. Used to match domain membership for a particular IP address by mail servers and other applications to see if what the client is telling the server is really true.	192.168.51.12 resolves to server1.bigdomain.com.

Record Type	Description	Example of Use
Start of Authority (SOA) Record	The first record in any zone file, it identifies the primary DNS name server for the zone. It also contains replication information for the zone, such as serial number, refresh interval, retry interval and expiration values (TTLs) for the zone.	Bigdomain.com resolves to NS1.bigdomain.com (and the next record is usually the A record for the name server).
Service Record (SRV)	This record type indicates the various network services a particular host provides. Here the query resolves a service name to a host name, protocol and port.	_TCP._LDAP.bigdomain.com would resolve to DC1.bigdomain.com (A domain controller. The LDAP in the query is the type of service, TCP is the protocol being used.
Nameserver (NS)	Identifies the name servers for a zone. It appears in both forward and reverse lookup zones. It helps identify where to send a query for a delegated domain (sub domain). It resolves from a domain name to a host name (like an SOA).	Bigdomain.com resolves to NS1.bigdomain.com.
Mail Exchanger (MX)	The record identifies the existence of a SMTP e-mail server. It resolves to a host name.	Bigdomain.com resolves to Exchange1.bigdomain.com.
Alias or CNAME Record	Refers one host name to another, an alias. Usually used to map a generally accepted Internet name (www or ftp for example) to the actual host providing the service.	www.bigdomain.com resolves to web1.bigdomain.com or ftp.bigdomain.com resolves to fxfer1.bigdomain.com.

Table 2—1: Types of DNS Records.

When configuring your server, you need to determine the role of the server, and then set up the zone or zones to match that role. Your server may host several zone types. The standard ones are shown in Table 2.2.

Zone Type	Description
Primary	Contains the authoritative (read/write) copy of the zone database. All changes are made here. You need one primary zone file for each zone.
Secondary	Contains a read-only copy of the zone database. Depends upon zone transfer to be updated by the primary zone file. You should configure at least one secondary zone file for fault-tolerance. You may position secondary servers on each side of a slow WAN link to improve resolution without the query traffic crossing the slow WAN links.
Stub	A copy of a zone file that contains only the records needed to identify the authoritative DNS server for the zone. Typically this is used to point to a child domain to allow for faster query performance. This allows the DNS server to resolve the query from its client with one iterative query of its own.

Table 2—2: Zone Type.

Another twist to zone configuration is the type of query it will respond to, forward or reverse. Remember that a forward lookup resolves a host name to IP address. A reverse lookup does the opposite, resolving an IP address to a host name. Each of the above types of zone files can support either a forward or reverse lookup. What do you need to have on your network? Typically client applications do forward lookups. Some server applications (typically e-mail) like to do a reverse lookup to match an IP address to a hostname that was provided by the client side of the application. If the two match, the server continues its processing. If the two don't match, the server refuses to continue.

Adding a new zone is done through the new zone wizard. From the DNS MMC snap-in, right-click on the server you want to add a new zone to. Then click on **New Zone**. Then click **Next** on the **Welcome to the New Zone Wizard** page. Your screen will look like figure 2.4.

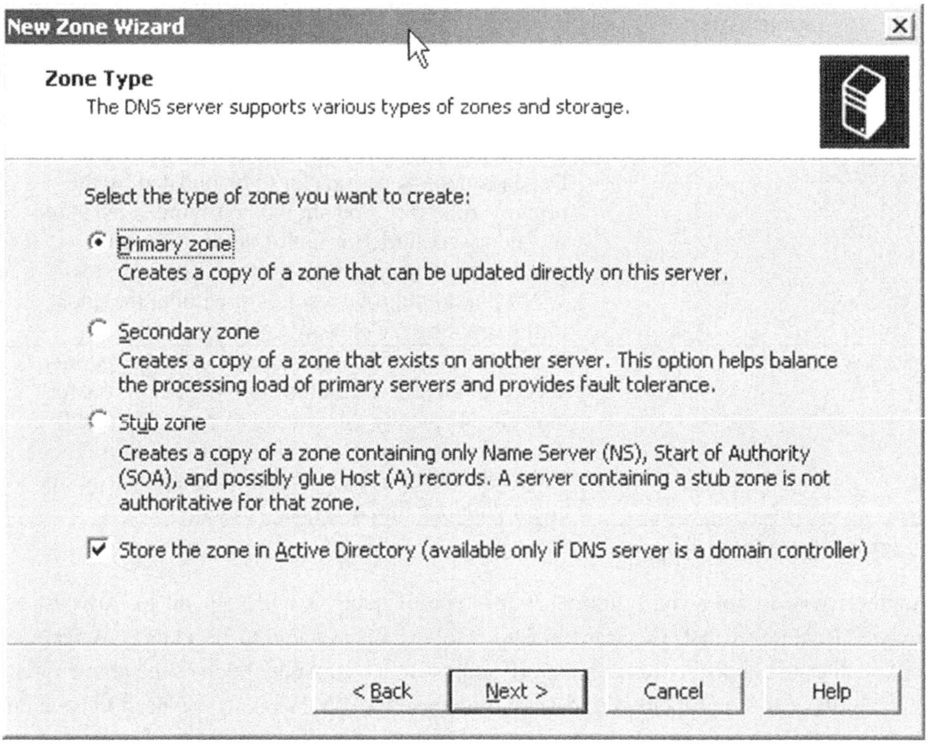

Figure 2-4: New Zone Wizard.

Here you can select a Primary Zone, Secondary Zone or Stub Zone. If you are creating the zone on a domain controller, you can store the zone in active directory (active directory integrated). We'll look at this last option more later on in the chapter.

If you are going to create a secondary or stub zone, make sure you know the IP address of the master DNS server for the zone before you start. Note that you can only do a forward lookup stub zone. The primary and secondary zone file can support both forward and reverse lookups. The steps for completing the configuration of the various types are below. All of these will pick up from the **Zone Type** page. Note that these are quite similar. Make sure you pay attention to each selection so that you achieve your desired results.

To configure a forward lookup zone on a primary zone type:

1. On the **Zone Type** page, verify that **Primary zone** is selected, and then click **Next**.
2. On the **Forward or Reverse Lookup Zone** page, verify that **Forward lookup zone** is selected, and then click **Next**.
3. On the **Zone Name** page, type the DNS name of the zone that this server will be authoritative for, and then click **Next**.
4. On the **Zone File** page, click **Next** to accept the defaults.
5. On the **Dynamic Update** page, select one of the following options, and then click **Next**. (More on dynamic updates later in the chapter.)
   - **a.** Allow only secure dynamic updates (**recommended for Active Directory**). **This option is only available for Active Directory-integrated zones.**
   - **b.** Allow both nonsecure and secure dynamic updates. **This option is not recommended, because updates can be accepted from untrusted sources.**
   - **c.** Do not allow dynamic updates. **This option requires you to update records manually.**
8. After completing the **New Zone Wizard** page, click **Finish**.
9. Close the DNS console if desired.

To configure a forward lookup stub zone:

1. On the **Zone Type** page, select **Stub zone**, and then click **Next**.
2. On the **Forward or Reverse Lookup Zone** page, select **Forward lookup zone**, and then click **Next**.
3. On the **Zone Name** page, type the DNS name of the zone that this server will be authoritative for, and then click **Next**.
4. On the **Zone File** page, click **Next** to accept the defaults.
5. On the **Master DNS Servers** page, in the **IP address** field, type the IP address of the DNS server that this DNS server will copy the zone from. Click **Add**, and then click **Next**.
6. On the **Completing the New Zone Wizard** page, click **Finish**.
7. Close the DNS console if desired.

To configure a forward lookup zone on a secondary zone type:

1. On the **Zone Type** page, select **Secondary zone**, and then click **Next**.
2. On the **Forward or Reverse Lookup Zone** page, verify that **Forward lookup zone** is selected, and then click **Next**.
3. On the **Zone Name** page, type the DNS namespace, and then click **Next**.
4. On the **Master DNS Servers** page, in the **IP address** field, type the IP address of the master DNS server, click **Add**, and then click **Next**.
5. On the **Completing the New Zone Wizard** page, click **Finish**.
6. Close the DNS console if desired.

To configure a reverse lookup zone on a primary zone type:

1. On the **Zone Type** page, verify that **Primary zone** is selected, and then click **Next**.
2. On the **Forward or Reverse Lookup Zone** page, select **Reverse lookup zone**, and then click **Next**.
3. On the **Reverse Lookup Zone Name** page, in the **Network ID field**, type the network ID portion of the IP address of the zone, and then click **Next**.
4. On the **Zone File** page, click **Next** to accept the defaults.
5. On the **Dynamic Update** page, select one of the following options, and then click **Next**.
    d. Allow only secure dynamic updates (**recommended for Active Directory**).
    e. Allow both nonsecure and secure dynamic updates.
    f. Do not allow dynamic updates.
8. On the Completing the **New Zone Wizard** page, click **Finish**.
9. Close the DNS console if desired.

To configure a reverse lookup zone on a secondary zone type:

1. On the **Zone Type** page, select **Secondary zone**, and then click **Next**.
2. On the **Forward or Reverse Lookup Zone** page, select **Reverse lookup zone**, and then click **Next**.
3. On the **Reverse Lookup Zone Name** page, in the **Network ID** field, type the network ID portion of the IP address of the zone, and then click **Next**.
4. On the **Zone File** page, click **Next** to accept the defaults.
5. On the **Master DNS Servers** page, in the **IP address** field, type the IP address of the master DNS server, click **Add**, and then click **Next**.
6. On the Completing the **New Zone Wizard** page, click **Finish**.
7. Close the DNS console.

So, now we have a zone file. But except for records associated with the name servers, it's quite empty. How do we get resource records into the database? You can elect to create, register or update DNS records in one of two ways, manually or dynamically.

Manual updating is done by opening the DNS console, selecting the server and zone to work with, and then editing or adding the record. To edit a record, select the desired record in the right panel of the MMC, right-click on it and select properties. You can change the IP address, and also elect to update the reverse lookup PTR record also associated with host. See Figure 2.5.

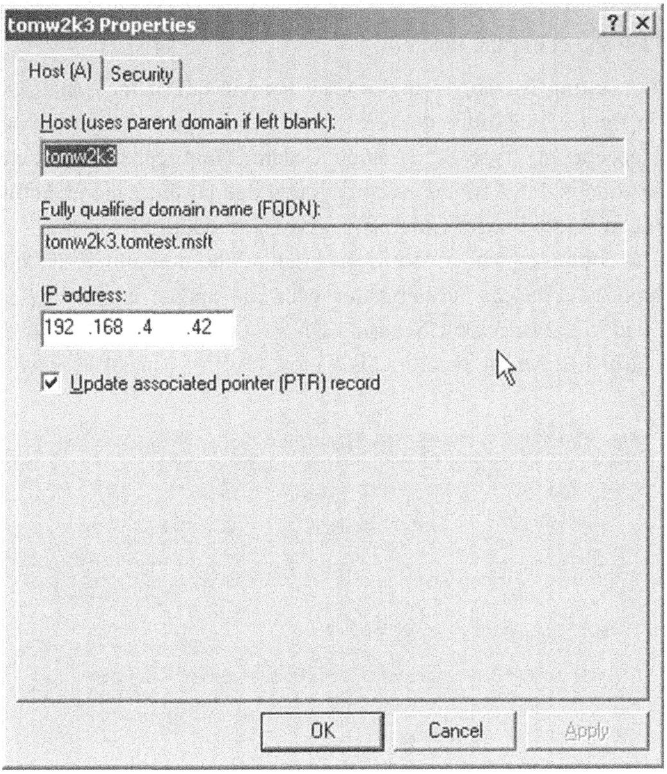

Figure 2-5: Reverse Lookup PTR Record.

The manual process is fine if you have few changes and a small number of hosts. Windows Server 2003 will also allow for dynamic updates, where a client running Windows 2000, Windows Server 2003 or Windows XP can initiate an update of its resource record(s). Dynamic updates can also be down for down level clients if they are DHCP clients and the DHCP server is Windows 2000 or Windows Server 2003 based.

For the client to dynamically update the DNS server, three settings must be configured. The DNS server must be set to allow dynamic updates. The client must be configured to update the DNS server. Also, the DHCP server must provide update services for down level clients, and the reverse lookup PTR records. The client settings are under the TCP/IP advanced properties DNS tab. The checkbox to allow the client to update the DNS server automatically must be checked.

Each interface must have this setting configured, so if there is more than one network card in the machine, be sure to get all of them. Servers with static IP addresses can also update their service resource records if the DHCP client service is running on the machine (this is running by default on Windows 2000 servers and Windows Server 2003). This is important for all of the specific network services to be entered into the proper DNS zones. Again, you must go to the advanced TCP/IP properties for each network interface and configure this.

The DNS server setting is easily found on the general tab of the zone SOA properties sheet, shown in figure 2.6. Notice the selections in the drop down box. None means the zone will not accept any type of dynamic update. Nonsecure and secure updates is available if the zone is not Active Directory-Integrated. If the zone is Active Directory-Integrated you can select Secure Only. This gives you control over who can update the DNS records. A computer who is not a member of the domain would not be able to update their records. You can further tailor who can update records by following the suggestions found in the help topic Securing DNS by using ACLs. The ability to modify the Access Control List for the record adds a great level of control over who can change the DNS records.

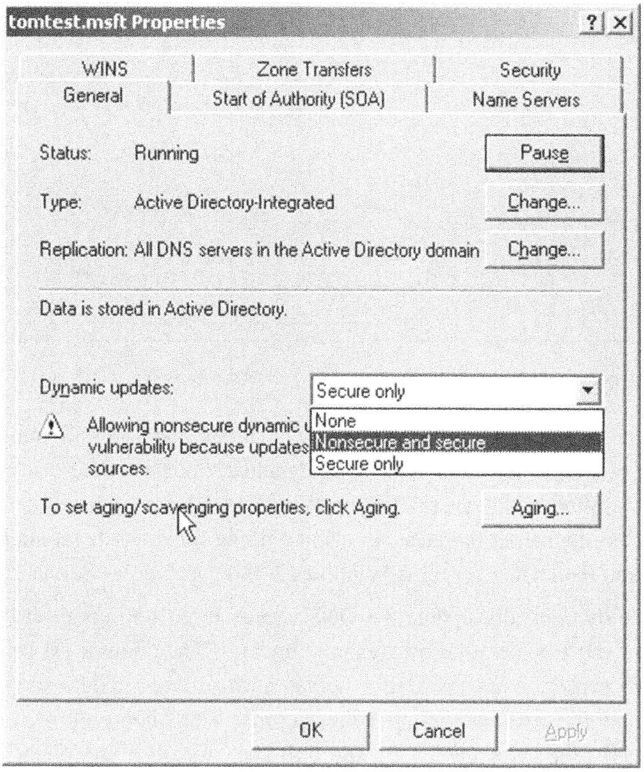

Figure 2-6: Zone SOA Properties Sheet.

Zone Transfer is the process that DNS uses to replicate zone data from the primary to secondary zone servers. There are two types of transfers, full and incremental. A full transfer will send the entire database, even though one IP address may have changed. An incremental transfer sends just the changed data. When a secondary zone server is configured, a full zone transfer is performed to populate the database on the new secondary. Zone transfers are performed to insure all zone files servers have the same zone information.

Now that you have primary and secondary zones figured out, we need to discuss the concept of a master DNS server. The master DNS server is responsible for distributing zone information to other servers using the same zone file(s). The server hosting the primary zone is always a master DNS server. The secondary zone file machines typically receive their updates from the master. These machines are also referred to as slaves. Sometimes a secondary or slave depends on another secondary server for its update information, instead of the primary. This is done in a larger organization with lots of zone transfer traffic to balance the load across several servers.

Two examples follow. We have 3 DNS servers PRIDNS, SEC1DNS and SEC2DNS. PRIDNS had the primary zone file for the namespace; SEC1DNS and SEC2DNS both have a secondary zone for the namespace. You could configure SEC1DNS and SEC2DNS as slaves to PRIDNS for zone transfers. Then SEC1DNS and SEC2DNS would each interact separately with PRIDNS for updates.

Example two has the same 3 DNS servers as before. However, this time PRIDNS is the master server for SEC1DNS. SEC1DNS then acts as the master for SEC2DNS. A benefit to this configuration is that there is less zone transfer traffic for PRIDNS. A drawback is that there is some latency (or time lag) in the transfer across the entire zone. You need to decide if this drawback is acceptable in your situation. Can you configure the transfer intervals so that SEC2DNS is not left with outdated information for long periods of time?

Where is zone transfer configured you may be wondering. Things concerning the zone are usually found in the SOA record. In the DNS console, expand the zone file you want. In the details pane on the right, locate and right-click on the SOA record. Then select properties. Figure 2.7 shows the information we're concerned with as to timings and other things. Figure 2.8 shows the zone transfer tab and how the servers would interact. Lets talk about these settings and how they are used to get data to the secondary servers.

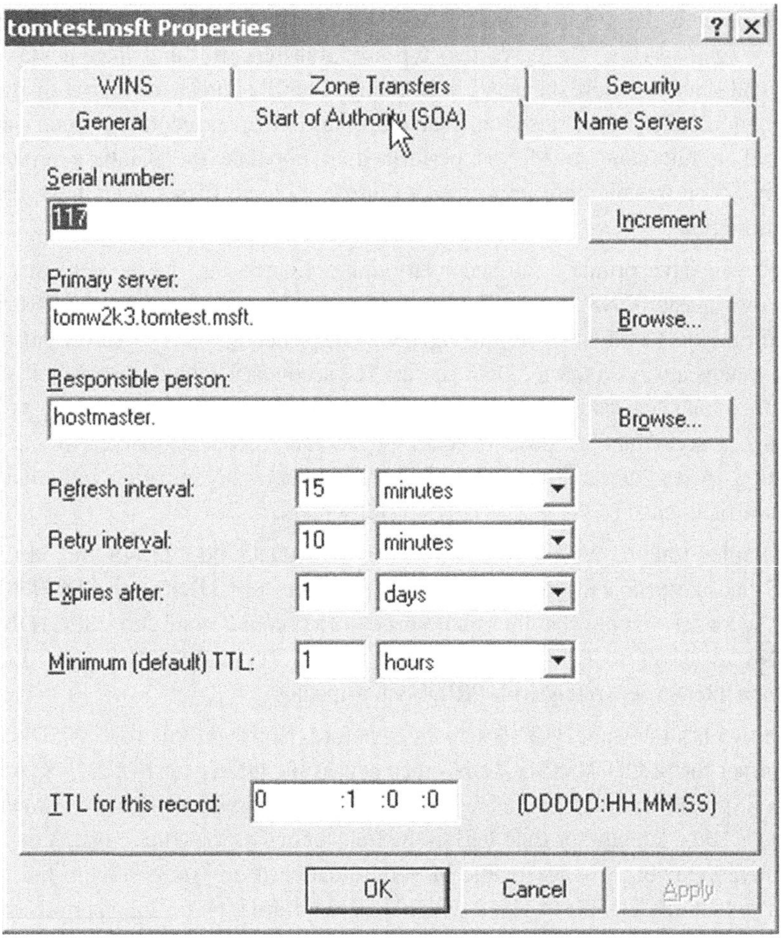

Figure 2-7: Start of Authority.

Note that on a secondary zone, you would be able to view but not change these. This screen shot is taken from a primary server. The serial number controls the version of the primary zone file. Each time a change is made to the file, the serial number is updated. It also can be manually to force a zone transfer. The primary server box identifies the host name for the primary server. The Responsible person can contain the e-mail address of the DNS admin for this zone. The refresh interval is the amount of time between attempts to determine the accuracy of the zone file at the primary server. This zone would be checked every 15 minutes. The retry interval is the amount of time the server will wait to retry the transfer if the refresh interval has expired and no successful transfer has been completed. Retry should be shorter than refresh.

The expires after will determine how long the server will answer requests with its current information without talking to its master server for a refresh of the zone. If this period expires, the secondary server will stop answering requests for the zone. The minimum default TTL value provides a default if no entry is added to an individual resource record. This is the amount of time another server or a client would keep this information in cache. The TTL for this record provides a place to enter a TTL different than the default. Note that the screenshot in Figure 2.7 contains the default time settings.

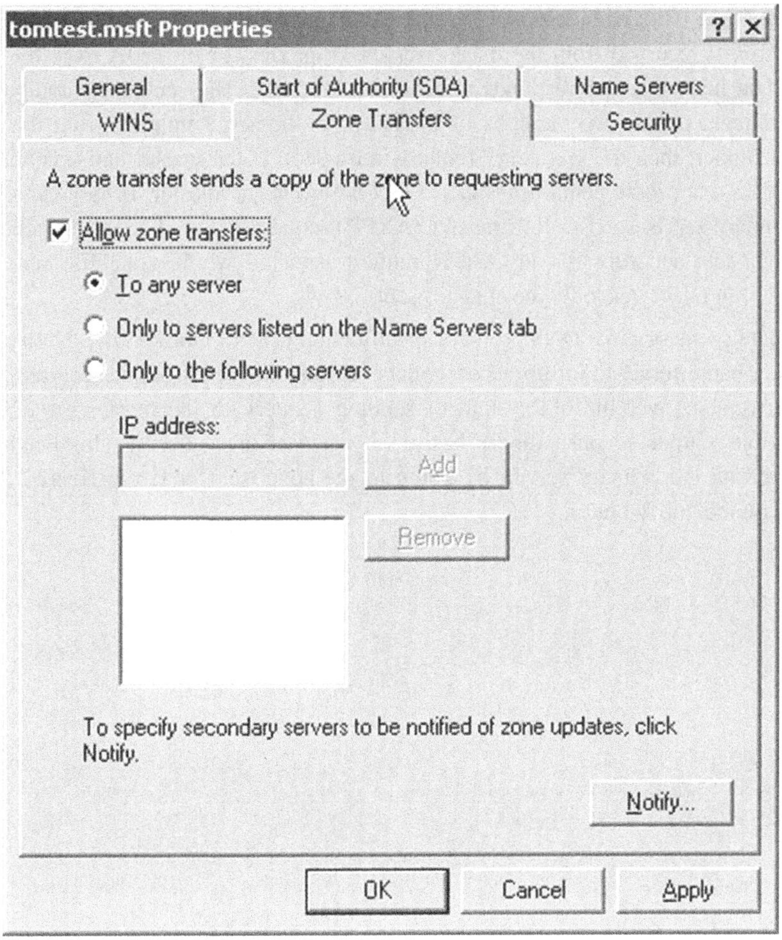

Figure 2-8: Zone Transfer.

A zone transfer can be sent to one of three choices as shown in Figure 2.8. When you click on the allow zone transfers box, the radio buttons become active. The first allows a transfer to any server requesting it. This is a bad thing. Typically zone transfers are only allowed with other name servers listed on the name server tab. This is the second choice. You can narrow that list further by clicking on the third choice of only the following servers, and add name server IP addresses to the list box.

Now that we know some of the options, how does this all work? It's really quite straightforward. The secondary server waits for the time entered in the refresh field in the SOA record it received from the master server. It queries for the SOA from the master server. The master server responds with its SOA record. The secondary compares the serial numbers in the two versions of the SOA. If the serial number from the master server is higher, then the secondary requests a transfer. If the master and secondary can both handle it, an incremental transfer (IXFR) is sent to the master. If they cannot, then the secondary server sends a full transfer (AXFR) request. When the master receives the request, it acts accordingly—an AXFR request gets the whole zone file sent to the secondary, an IXFR gets only the changes sent.

One update to the original DNS protocol specification is DNS Notify. DNS Notify allows the master name server to inform its secondary servers that a change has occurred. This is an improvement over the old system of sending a query to the master server, as the information is updated on a timely basis, i.e. when changes occur! This needs to be configured on the primary server, by going to the zone transfer tab in figure 2.8, then clicking on the notify button.

There you enter the IP addresses of the name servers you wish to notify, or select all of the servers as listed in the name server tab, as in Figure 2.9.

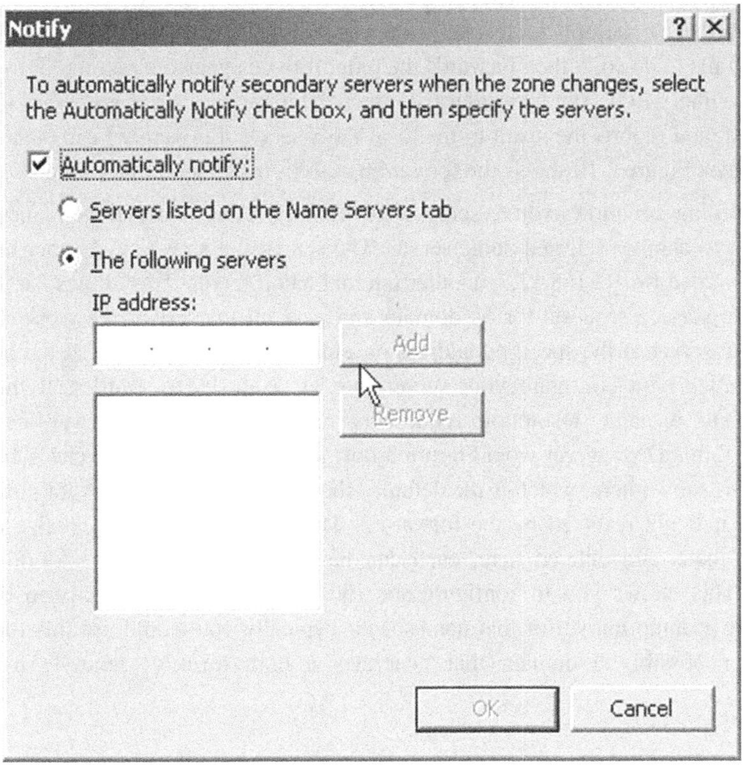

Figure 2-9: Secondary Server Notification.

When the local zone file on the primary DNS is updated, the serial number in the SOA record is changed. After this occurs, a notification message is sent to the secondary servers as configured in the notify dialog box. When the secondary receives the change notification, it will query the master for its current SOA record, and the transfer occurs as described previously.

A zone can also be configured as **Active Directory-integrated**. This can be accomplished when DNS is installed on a domain controller. The zone data is stored as an Active Directory object. It will also use Active Directory replication instead of zone transfers to transfer data. It will also use a multi-master database model, where any domain controller can process a change and replicate it to the others. There is single "primary" file that is the only copy that can be changed. This provides further fault tolerance for your namespace, as no one host is responsible for the changes.

2.1.3 Configure DNS Forwarding

We discussed the concept of forwarding briefly earlier. When a DNS server is configured as a forwarder, it attempts to reconcile the resolution request from its cache and zone files. If it fails to do so, it then forwards the request to designated name server by sending a recursive query to it. The forwarder then does the iterative queries necessary to resolve the request, and reports the result to the local DNS server. Forwarding can be configured several ways. Figure 2.10 shows the forwarding tab from the server properties.

The forwarding tab allows you to select to forward all requests not in the namespace for that server to another selected name server. The screenshot shows "All Other Domains" being forwarded to 192.168.12.2, another internal name server. This allows the tomw2k3 machine to service requests for its domain and pass all the rest of the work off to the other name server at the specified address or addresses. The check box at the bottom of the screen lets you configure your server into an exclusive forwarder. If the box is checked and a name resolution request is returned from the forwarding partner unresolved, this DNS server would return a host name not found. If the check box is not checked (as shown here, which is the default), the DNS server will attempt to resolve the request if it is not resolved by the forwarder. This is known as nonexclusive mode. If several domains are entered here, each can have its own separate set of forwarding partners. This allows you to configure specific domain requests directly to the name server that is authoritative for that namespace. Typically you would use this for a close partner, or possibly a domain that generates a high level of requests from your namespace.

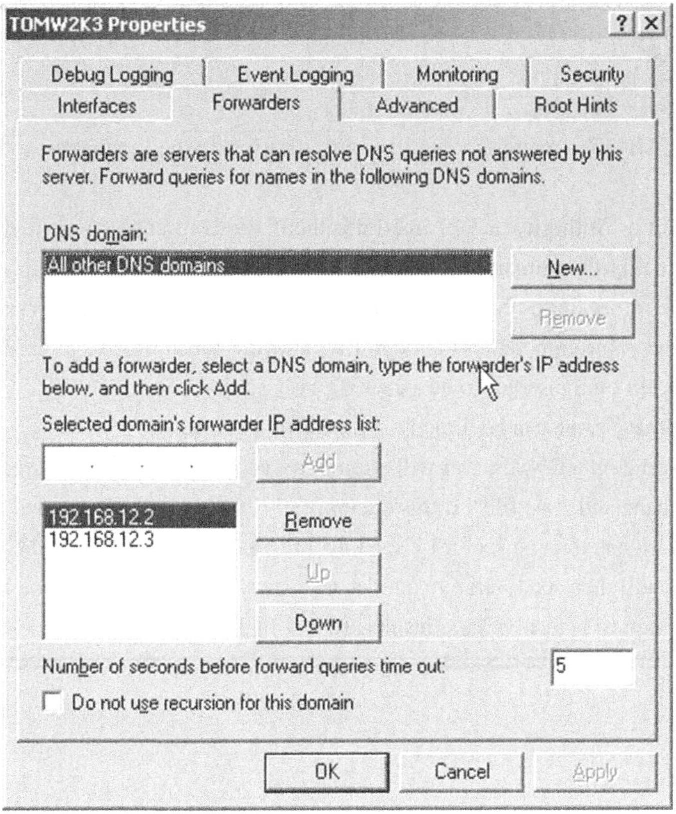

Figure 2-10: DNS Forwarder Server.

Pop Quiz 2.1

Pop Quiz 2.1 Questions

1. You need to troubleshoot a server to see if it can receive packet requests. What utility can you use for this purpose?
2. What is the Start of Authority record used for in DNS?
3. What should you do if you need a server to forward any client requests to another DNS Server?
4. Which zone updated directly on the DNS Server?
5. What is DNS Forwarding used for on a Windows Server 2003?

Pop Quiz 2.1 Answers

1. Send ICMP echo requests to verify connectivity with the Ping command at the prompt.
2. The Start of Authority or SOA record is the first record in any zone file. It is used to identify the primary DNS name server for the zone. It also contains replication information for the zone, such as serial number, refresh interval, retry interval and expiration values (Time to Live) for the zone
3. Setup DNS on the server to be a caching only server.
4. The Primary Zone can be directly updated from the server.
5. Forwarding on a DNS Server will attempt to reconcile the resolution request from its cache and zone files. If this attempt fails the request is forwarded to another designated name server by sending a recursive query to it and the forwarder will then send iterative queries necessary so the request can be resolved. Once the request is resolved the results are reported to the local DNS server

2.2 Manage DNS

If dynamic updates are used, once the DNS is configured and tested, management is fairly straightforward. There are settings for Time-To-Live (TTL) for zones and records, and aging and scavenging settings for the zone and the server. Let's define these, and look at each one at the record, zone and server levels as they apply. TTL applies to a record you receive and store in cache. It is configured on the zone SOA record, or in the properties of an individual record. Aging and scavenging are operations you perform on your database to update the information. These must be configured on both the server and the zone.

Time-To-Live (TTL) value is a setting returned with the other information in a DNS query that tells the recipient how long to hold on to the information contained in the record. The DNS server and DNS client keep the record in cache until the TTL value is reached, and then the record is discarded. This value is expressed in seconds. If the TTL is too short, the DNS client and server will generate more name resolution traffic because they have discarded the value from cache. If the TTL is too long, they may be depending on outdated information by keeping it in cache too long.

Checking the TTL is quite simple. Change the desired settings for the zone, or a specific record. Then use ipconfig at a Windows 2000, or better, client to flush the DNS cache (**ipconfig /flushdns** at a command prompt). Still at the command prompt, ping another client whose DNS setting was affected by the change you just made. Then use ipconfig to display the DNS cache and check for the proper settings. At the command prompt, type **ipconfig /displaydns** to display the client cache settings. Check to ensure your changes have taken place.

Aging and scavenging is the process that DNS uses to remove outdated, or stale, records from the database. Aging determines the DNS record should be removed; scavenging is the process that performs the removal. Typically when a computer is removed from the network and it is using dynamic update, the A record is removed from DNS. If a computer is NOT removed properly (mobile user in a hurry, motherboard decides to take an extended vacation, etc.) the A record may not get properly removed. Aging and scavenging helps take care of that issue.

When a DNS record is dynamically added to the zone database file(s), it receives a time stamp from the service, based on the current computer time. If you manually add a record, it, by default, receives a time stamp of 0. You can change that when you create the record. With dynamic update, a DNS client can try to either update or refresh the resource record in the database. An update occurs when something changes in the record, like the IP address for the host. A refresh attempt is when the client attempts to re-register it's resource record with the DNS server.

By default this occurs every 24 hours. When the client re-registers its record, it changes the time stamp. This will cause zone transfer or AD replication traffic, depending upon the settings of the zone. So what if nothing has really changed? Do we really need to start more network traffic? Probably not a great idea, wouldn't you think? So did the DNS designers.

Two settings that must be configured on both the server and the zone are the refresh interval and the no-refresh interval. The value for both is expressed in days. The no-refresh interval is the period of time that the DNS server will NOT allow a client to refresh its resource record. If I am a client and have a time stamp of 15 May and the no-refresh interval is set to 5 days on the server and zone, I will not be able to refresh my resource record on the server. This is no big deal if nothing in the record has changed. Do you need network traffic to tell you everything is still the same? Probably not in this case. If I have an update (IP address, for example), that is accepted and the record is updated.

The refresh interval is the time I allow a refresh to occur to a record before it is discarded as old. As before my DNS resource record has a time stamp of 15 May. The no-refresh and refresh intervals are both set to 5 days. DNS will allow me to refresh my record on 21 May. It will allow me to refresh my record until 25 May. If I am attempting to do this every 24 hours, I should be successful some time on the 21st. When my record is refreshed, it receives a new timestamp, and the process starts over again.

The two intervals will determine the amount of time a record can remain in the database without a refresh. If your machine is connected to the network, it is attempting regular refreshes. If it becomes disconnected improperly, the record will be removed after the sum of the two intervals. For example, if both intervals are set to 5 days each (a total of 10), the record can be removed on day 11. I have a record timestamp of 15 May. The timestamp date plus 10 days is compared to the current system date. If the current system date is greater than that sum, the record will be removed.

Scavenging can be set to run automatically, or you can initiate it manually. We'll discuss that in the server setting later in this chapter.

This process insures you have current information in the database. You may want to examine the interval settings to determine what is best for your network. The intervals may need to be adjusted for your particular needs. If your network is fairly static, in that hosts do not frequently change IP address, etc. and you are careful about moving machines, longer intervals will work fine. The more dynamic your network, the shorter the interval should be to provide DNS clients with up-to-date information.

Now let's look at the configuration involved in setting these processes in motion!

2.2.1 Manage DNS Zone Settings

The TTL setting for the zone can be found on the general tab in properties. Remember that if the zone is not Active Directory-Integrated, you must change this at the primary zone server. The following steps will configure the TTL at the zone level. If you do not add a value for an individual record, this will act as the default for the entire zone. The fields in question were shown previously in Figure 2.6. Here are the steps:

1. In the DNS console tree, right-click the applicable zone, and then click **Properties**.
2. On the **General** tab, verify that the zone type is either **Primary** or **Active Directory-integrated**.
3. Click the **Start of Authority (SOA)** tab.
4. In the **Minimum (default) TTL** section, select the interval, seconds, minutes, hours or days, and then, in the text box, type a number.
5. Click **OK** to save the adjusted interval.

Scavenging is performed at the server level, based on the server and zone settings. To set scavenging properties for the zone, follow these steps from the DNS console. Figure 2.10 shows the dialog box for the zone, which is the interface as the server.

1. In the console tree, right-click the applicable zone, and then click **Properties**.
2. On the **General** tab, click **Aging**.
3. In the **Zone Aging/Scavenging Properties** dialog box, select **Scavenge stale resource records**.
4. In the **No-refresh interval** field, select the increment, and then type a value. (For example: the increment is **days** and the value is **5**, for a No-refresh interval of 5 days.)
5. In the **Refresh** field, select the increment, and then type a value. (For example: increment is **days** and the value is **5**, for a refresh interval of 5 days.)
6. In the **Zone Aging/Scavenging Properties** dialog box, click **OK**.

To verify the settings, follow these steps from the DNS console:

1. On the **View** menu, verify that **Advanced** is selected. (If **Advanced** is not selected, click **Advanced** to select it.)
2. Right-click the applicable zone, and then click **Properties**.
3. On the **General** tab, click **Aging**.
4. In the **Zone Aging/Scavenging Properties** dialog box, view the value in the **Date and time** field to ascertain the date after which the zone is eligible to be scavenged for outdated resource records, and then click **OK**.
5. In the **Zone Properties** dialog box, click **OK**.

2.2.2 Manage DNS Record Settings

The default TTL value for the zone can be overridden for the record, if you have a specific record that requires a different TTL value. You have to turn on the advanced view to see the additional fields on the record properties. Follow these steps. The additional fields are shown in figure 2.11. Note the additional fields for both the TTL, and the scavenging settings and time stamp supplied by DNS.

1. Open the DNS console.
2. In the console tree, click **DNS**.
3. On the **View** menu, click **Advanced**.
4. In the console tree, expand the applicable zone, and then, in the details pane, right-click the applicable record, and then click **Properties**.
5. In the **Properties** dialog box for the record, in the **Time to live (TTL)** field, adjust the TTL.
6. Click **OK** to save the adjusted TTL.

To configure the time stamp on a manually entered DNS resource record, follow these steps from the DNS console.

1. On the **View** menu, verify that **Advanced** is selected. (If **Advanced** is not selected, click **Advanced** to select it.)
2. Right-click the applicable resource record, and then click **Properties**.
3. In the **Resource Record Properties** dialog box, select **Delete this record when it becomes stale**, and then click **Apply**.
4. Verify that a date and time value displays in the **Record time stamp** field. In the **Resource Record Properties** dialog box, click **OK**.

To view the time stamp on a DNS resource record, from the DNS console do the following:

1. On the **View** menu, verify that **Advanced** is selected. (If **Advanced** is not selected, click **Advanced** to select it.)
2. Right-click the applicable resource record, and then click **Properties**.
3. In the **Resource Record Properties** dialog box, view the value in the **Date and time** field to ascertain when the resource record was created in DNS.
4. In the **Resource Record Properties** dialog box, click **OK**.

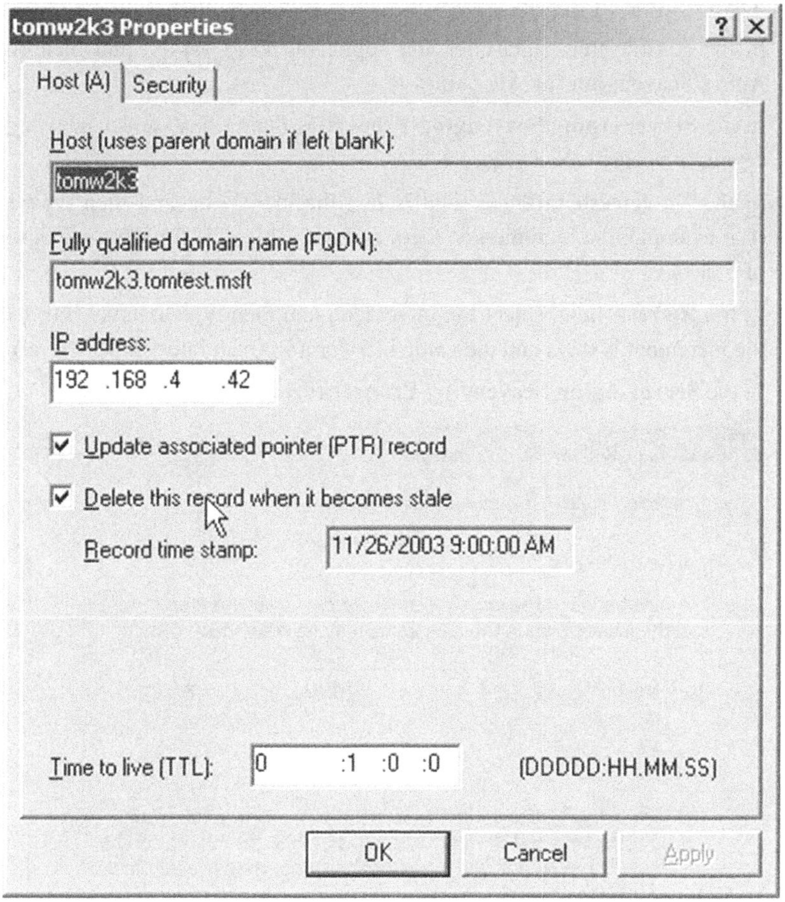

Figure 2-11: NSLookup.

NSLookup, a command line tool can be used to verify the existence of a resource record, among a multitude of other things. At a command prompt, type nslookup. Then type set q=A to set the query for A records. Then type in the name of the host you need to verify. The information should be returned for the host, and the DNS server servicing the query.

2.2.3 Manage DNS Server Options

Aging and scavenging needs to be configured at the server and the zone level. Server settings act as defaults for all new zones. You also need to check the intervals settings at the zone level. Follow these steps to set the interval fields for the server.

From the DNS console:

1. In the console tree, right-click the applicable DNS server, and then click **Set Aging/Scavenging for All Zones**.
2. In the **Server Aging/Scavenging Properties** dialog box, select **Scavenge stale resource records**. See Figure 2.12.
3. In the **No-refresh interval** field, select the increment, and then type a value. (For example: the increment is **days** and the value is **5**, for a No-refresh interval of 5 days.)
4. In the **Refresh** field, select the increment, and then type a value. (For example: the increment is **days** and the value is **5**, for a Refresh interval of 5 days.)
5. In the **Server Aging/Scavenging Properties** dialog box, click **OK**.

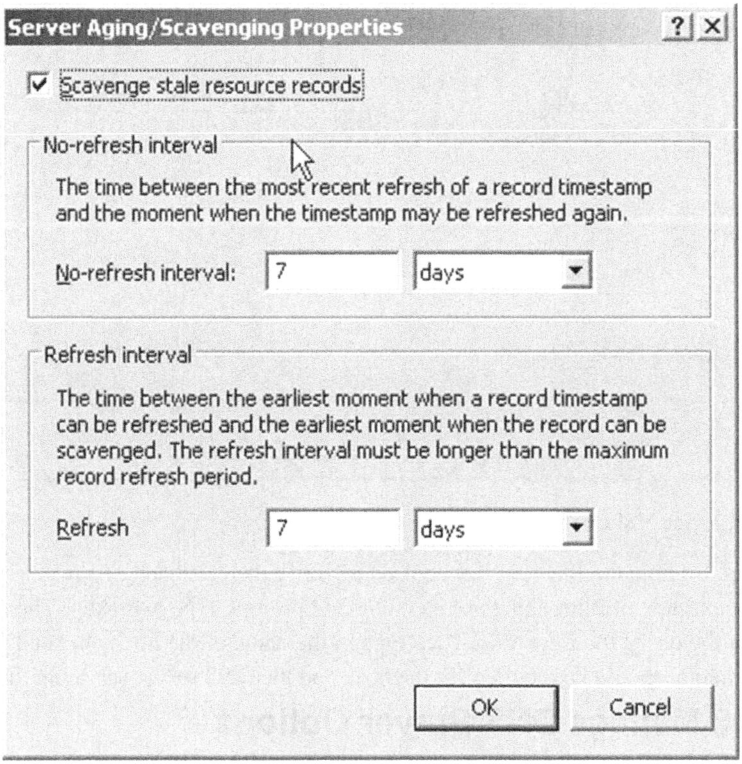

Figure 2-12: Advanced Tab from the Server Properties Sheet.

After the server and zone settings are configured, you can have the server scavenge the stale records automatically. If this is not set, the process will only occur when it is manually started. Figure 2.13 shows the Advanced tab from the server properties sheet. Again from the DNS console:

1. In the console tree, right-click the applicable DNS server, and then click **Properties**.
2. Click the **Advanced** tab.
3. Select **Enable automatic scavenging of stale records**.
4. In the **Scavenging period** field, select the increment, and then type a value.
5. In the **DNS server Properties** dialog box, click **OK**.

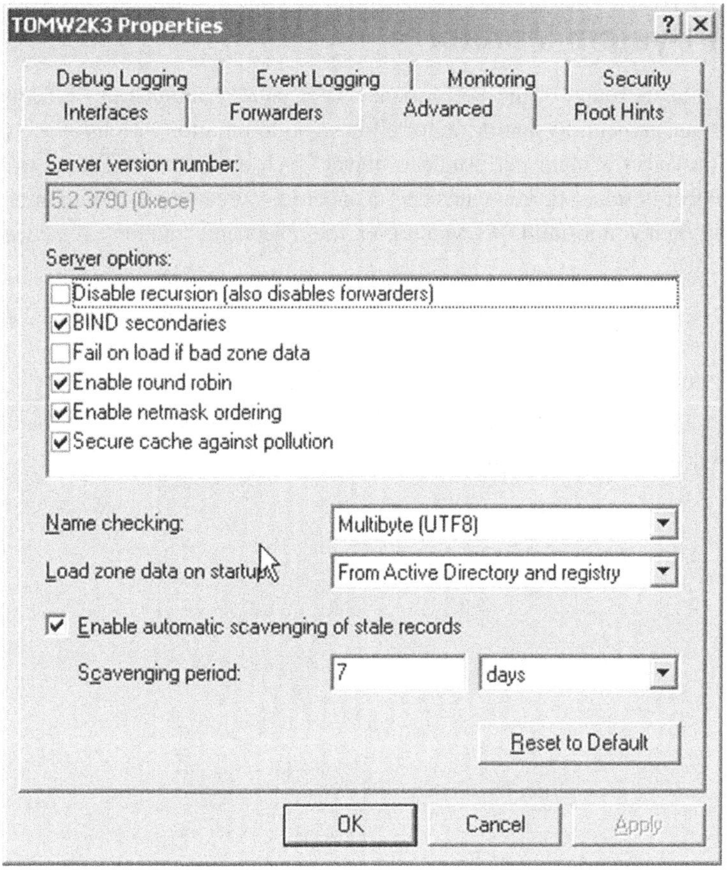

Figure 2-13: Advanced Properties.

Immediate scavenging of stale resource records can be manually set in motion. From the DNS console, take the following steps:

1. In the console tree, right-click the applicable DNS server, and then click **Scavenge Stale Resource Records**.
2. When asked to confirm that you want to scavenge all stale resource records on the server, click **OK**.

2.3 DNS Tools Might Include

Several tools exist to assist in the overall network monitoring, and thus the health of your DNS configuration. Monitoring performance is very important to the overall health of your network, and your DNS implementation. A baseline needs to be established while your network is operating normally for comparisons in the future. Then you have an idea of what is "normal" for your network before you attempt troubleshooting using the tools.

2.3.1 System Monitor

System Monitor is found in the Performance Tool under Administrative Tools, or from Computer Management. System Monitor allows you to monitor various aspects of server activity. You select a main performance object, such as Memory, Processor, or DNS. Once the object is selected, you can select a specific counter for a certain area you wish to monitor. When you install DNS on a server, the object and counters are added.

The Performance Console also allows you to create various kinds of alerts that monitor for a certain condition to occur for a particular counter, such as an unusually high level of a particular activity. The system can then do various things to warn you of a potential problem, from running a script or program to sending a network message.

You should monitor critical DNS activity, such as dynamic updates, zone transfers, queries and general server health. Some counter suggestions:

Performance Counters	What Data is Collected	What the Data Means	What to Look for After Baseline is Established
Dynamic Update Rejected	The total number of dynamic updates that the DNS server rejects.	A high number of rejections to a DNS server configured to allow secure updates could mean that unauthorized computers are attempting to update.	Any increase over the baseline may be cause for further investigation.
Recursive Queries/sec	Recursive queries/sec is the average number of recursive queries received by a DNS server in each second.	This counter provides a view of the query load on the DNS server.	If this counter goes dramatically up or down, then it should be investigated further.
AXFR Request Sent	The total number of full zone transfer requests sent by the DNS server service when operating as a secondary server for a zone.	The DNS server hosting the secondary zone is requesting incremental zone transfers. If this number is high, then there are a lot of changes happening on the primary zone.	If this counter goes dramatically above the baseline, then it could reflect a need to review the number of changes in the zone and the configuration of zone transfers.

Table 2—3: Performance Counters.

This is not meant to be an all-inclusive list. In the Windows Server 2003 Help documentation for DNS performance (search for DNS Monitoring or DNS Performance) you will find some samples collected during product testing by Microsoft. The collections of counters and their explanations are well worth the review for a comprehensive monitoring program for DNS.

2.3.2 Event Viewer

Event viewer allows you to review entries in various event logs, which can be an excellent aid in problem identification during troubleshooting. Such events range from service startup or shutdown to various errors produced during operation. The DNS Client Service writes to the System event log.

The DNS Server Service has its own Event Log containing only DNS events. This allows you to more easily focus on the DNS events. The server properties on the DNS console allow you to select the level of event logging you desire from the Event Logging tab on the properties sheet.

2.3.3 Replication Monitor

If your zone files are Active Directory-Integrated, your zone transfer traffic is a part of Active Directory replication. If you are experiencing DNS transfer issues, the tool you need to use to check replication activity is Replication Monitor. It is installed from the Windows Server 2003 Support Tools. It allows you to monitor and test replication activity between two direct AD replication partners, and to monitor the overall replication activity in your domain. The tool allows you to compare and see if all domain controllers (and thus the DNS servers) have an up-to-date copy of the AD database, and thus the DNS zone files.

2.3.4 DNS Debug Logs

DNS Debugging allows you to keep additional detailed event information, as compared to what the DNS event log or system monitor will capture. Debugging will give this additional detail at a cost. It is quite resource intensive, and should only be used on a temporary basis to troubleshoot a particular problem. It will consume mass quantities of disk space if not configured. This is configured on a server basis from the server properties debug tab.

Once enabled, logging will continue until the specified log size is met, or until the hard drive the log is saved on runs out of space. At that point (hard drive full), other things may stop as well. Logging will overwrite the older entries, but remember you are losing details that may be important. Review your settings carefully. Figure 2.14 shows the debug settings.

Quite a bit of information can be gathered to allow you to narrow down to a particular issue. It will also provide a great deal of information as to the traffic involved in a particular operation. If configured in a lab setting, you can examine the type of traffic generated by each DNS operation by preparing logging, enabling logging, performing the operation and then turning logging off.

Note you can also filter the packets logged by IP address, so you can focus on a suspected problem host and its communication with the DNS server.

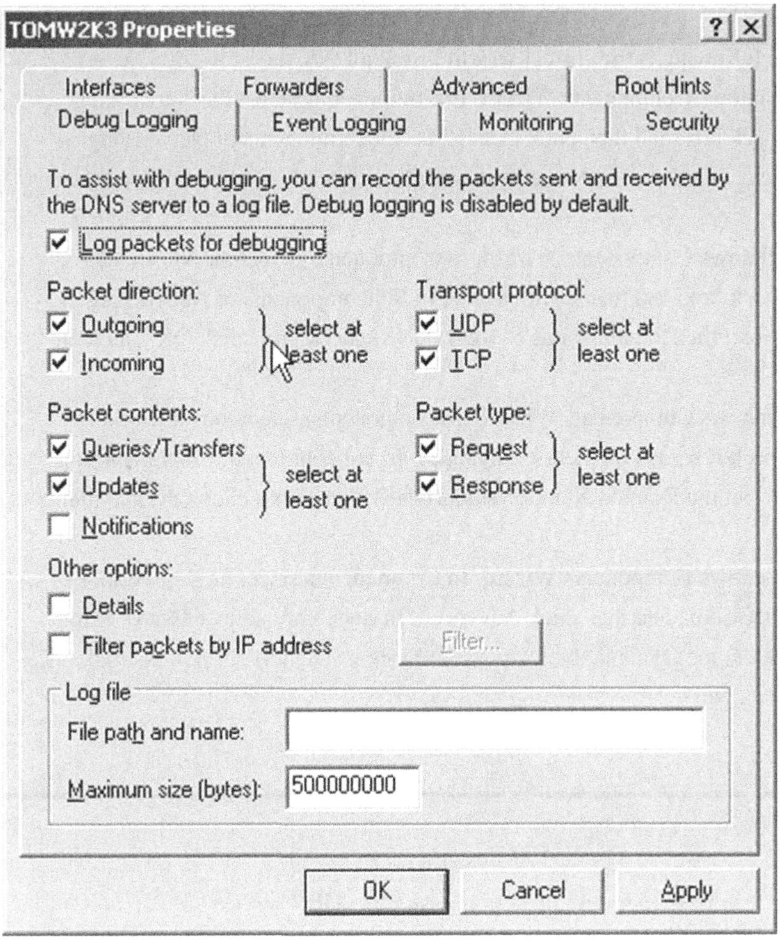

Figure 2-14: Debug Logging.

Chapter 2: Review Questions

1. Which of the following is the correct way to install a DNS server in 2003 Server?

A. Open the Windows Components Wizard. In Components, select the Networking Services check box, and then click Details. In Subcomponents of Networking Services, select the Domain Name System (DNS) check box, click OK, and then click Next.

B. Open the Windows Components Wizard. In Components, select the Multimedia Services check box, and then click Details. In Subcomponents of Networking Services, select the Domain Name System (DNS) check box, click OK, and then click Next.

C. Open the Windows Components Wizard. In Components, select the Networking Services check box, and then click Advanced. In Subcomponents of Networking Services, select the Domain Name System (DNS) check box, click OK, and then click Next.

D. Open the Windows Components Wizard. In Components, select the Networking Services check box, and then click Advanced. In Subcomponents of Networking Services, select the Dynamic Domain Name System (DDNS) check box, click OK, and then click Next.

---

2. Which of the following methods allow you to stop the DNS service?

A. To stop a DNS server, open DNS. In the console tree, click the applicable DNS server. On the Action menu, point to All Tasks and then click Stop to stop the service.

B. To stop a DNS server, open DNS. In the console tree, click Action. On the Action menu, point to All Tasks and then click Stop to stop the service.

C. To stop a DNS server, open DNS. In the console tree, click Action. On the Action menu, point to All Tasks and then click Null to stop the service.

D. To stop a DNS server, open Windows Services. In the console tree, click Action. On the Action menu, point to All Tasks and then click Stop to stop the service.

3. You suspect that bad data is causing you problems when one of your zones is loaded in DNS. How can you prevent this?

A. In the DNS console tree, click the applicable DNS server. On the Action menu, click Properties. Click the General tab. In Server options, select the Fail on load if bad zone data check box, and then click OK.

B. In the DNS console tree, click the applicable DNS server. On the Action menu, click Properties. Click the Advanced tab. In Server options, select the Stop load if bad zone data check box, and then click OK.

C. To prevent loading of a zone when bad data is found, open DNS. In the console tree, click the applicable DNS server. On the Action menu, click Properties. Click the Advanced tab. In Server options, select the Fail on load if bad zone data check box, and then click OK.

D. In the DNS console tree, click the applicable DNS server. On the Action menu, click Properties. Click the Zones tab. In Server options, select the Stop load if bad zone data check box, and then click OK.

E. In the DNS console tree, click the applicable DNS server. On the Action menu, click Properties. Click the Advanced tab. In Server options, select the Fail on load if bad zone data check box, and then click OK.

---

4. When working with UNIX BIND-based DNS servers, what type of DNS zones do we have to use?

A. Active-Directory primary zones

B. Standard secondary zones

C. Standard primary zones

D. Active-Directory Integrated zones

E. Active-Directory secondary zones

5. How can you clear out the cache on a server and a client? (Choose one for the server and one for the client.)

A. Use the ipconfig /registerdns (server).

B. Use the ipconfig /all (client).

C. Use the ipconfig /flushdns (client).

D. Use the DNS console (server).

---

6. If a Windows 2003 member server received the message, 'Network path not found,' which of the following would you use to make sure that you didn't have old DNS information on the 2003 member server?

A. Ipconfig /flushdns

B. Nbtstat -RR

C. Nslookup

D. Netdiag /l

7. Which of the following DNS servers reduce load?

A. Primary

B. Caching server

C. Secondary

D. Non-caching

---

8. If you want users in the company.com domain to access a new Web site by the URL home.portal.company.com, what would you do?

A. On a DNS server, create a new zone named portal.company.com. In portal.company.com create a CNAME record named home and specify company.com as the target host.

B. On a DNS server, create a second zone named company.com. In portal.company.com create a CNAME record named home and specify company.com as the target host.

C. On a DHCP server, create a new zone named portal.company.com. In portal.company.com create a CNAME record named home and specify company.com as the target host.

D. On a DNS server, create a new zone named portal.company.com. In portal.company.com create a CNAME record named portal.company.com and specify company.com as the target host.

9. After disabling dynamic registration, what should you remove on a domain controller with two NIC cards if Active Directory fails between it and other domain controllers in the network?

A. Remove the first NIC card's address.

B. Remove the second NIC card's address.

C. Remove host records from the DNS zone from the first NIC.

D. Remove host records from the DNS zone from the second NIC.

---

10. What type of request tells DNS to give the best response that it can?

A. Recursive

B. Qualitative

C. Iterative

D. Bombastic

11. What types of DNS zones are available in Windows 2000?

A. Secondary

B. Extended

C. Primary

D. Active Directory Integrated

---

12. What is a NetBIOS name?

A. NetBIOS is a user name.

B. NetBIOS is a machine name.

C. NetBIOS is a trust name.

D. NetBIOS is a group name.

13. Which of the following is a text file?

A. DHCP

B. WINS

C. LMHosts

D. DNS

---

14. Which of the following can be found in WINS?

A. Replication Partners

B. Parallel Registrations

C. Active Registrations

D. Dynamic Partners

15. Which of the following will display the ARP cache table specifically for the 192.168.1.1 interface?

A. arp -N 192.168.1.1

B. arp -a 192.168.1.1

C. arp -a -N 192.168.1.1

D. arp 192.168.1.1

---

16. NetBIOS names typically contain the type of computer, its location and the unique ID. They can be up to ________ in length and may not contain spaces or backslashes.

A. 10 characters

B. 8 characters

C. 15 characters

D. 20 characters

Chapter 2: Review Answers

1. Which of the following is the correct way to install a DNS server in 2003 Server?

***A. Open the Windows Components Wizard. In Components, select the Networking Services check box, and then click Details. In Subcomponents of Networking Services, select the Domain Name System (DNS) check box, click OK, and then click Next.**

B. Open the Windows Components Wizard. In Components, select the Multimedia Services check box, and then click Details. In Subcomponents of Networking Services, select the Domain Name System (DNS) check box, click OK, and then click Next.

C. Open the Windows Components Wizard. In Components, select the Networking Services check box, and then click Advanced. In Subcomponents of Networking Services, select the Domain Name System (DNS) check box, click OK, and then click Next.

D. Open the Windows Components Wizard. In Components, select the Networking Services check box, and then click Advanced. In Subcomponents of Networking Services, select the Dynamic Domain Name System (DDNS) check box, click OK, and then click Next.

Explanation: To install a DNS server, open the Windows Components Wizard. In Components, select the Networking Services check box, and then click Details. In Subcomponents of Networking Services, select the Domain Name System (DNS) check box, click OK, and then click Next. If prompted, in Copy files from, type the full path to the distribution files, and then click OK. Required files are copied to your hard disk.

---

2. Which of the following methods allow you to stop the DNS service?

***A. To stop a DNS server, open DNS. In the console tree, click the applicable DNS server. On the Action menu, point to All Tasks and then click Stop to stop the service.**

B. To stop a DNS server, open DNS. In the console tree, click Action. On the Action menu, point to All Tasks and then click Stop to stop the service.

C. To stop a DNS server, open DNS. In the console tree, click Action. On the Action menu, point to All Tasks and then click Null to stop the service.

D. To stop a DNS server, open Windows Services. In the console tree, click Action. On the Action menu, point to All Tasks and then click Stop to stop the service.

Explanation: To start or stop a DNS server, open DNS. In the console tree, click the applicable DNS server. On the Action menu, point to All Tasks and then click Start to start the service, click Stop to stop the service, or click Pause to interrupt the service. To stop and then automatically restart the service, click Restart.

3. You suspect that bad data is causing you problems when one of your zones is loaded in DNS. How can you prevent this?
   A. In the DNS console tree, click the applicable DNS server. On the Action menu, click Properties. Click the General tab. In Server options, select the Fail on load if bad zone data check box, and then click OK.
   B. In the DNS console tree, click the applicable DNS server. On the Action menu, click Properties. Click the Advanced tab. In Server options, select the Stop load if bad zone data check box, and then click OK.

***C. To prevent loading of a zone when bad data is found, open DNS. In the console tree, click the applicable DNS server. On the Action menu, click Properties. Click the Advanced tab. In Server options, select the Fail on load if bad zone data check box, and then click OK.**

   D. In the DNS console tree, click the applicable DNS server. On the Action menu, click Properties. Click the Zones tab. In Server options, select the Stop load if bad zone data check box, and then click OK.
   E. In the DNS console tree, click the applicable DNS server. On the Action menu, click Properties. Click the Advanced tab. In Server options, select the Fail on load if bad zone data check box, and then click OK.

---

4. When working with UNIX BIND-based DNS servers, what type of DNS zones do we have to use?
   A. Active-Directory primary zones

***B. Standard secondary zones**

***C. Standard primary zones**

   D. Active-Directory Integrated zones
   E. Active-Directory secondary zones

Explanation: BIND DNS servers cannot work with Active Directory zones, but BIND can work with the standard primary and secondary zones. Active Directory only uses integrated zones, since Active Directory uses multimastering.

5. How can you clear out the cache on a server and a client? (Choose one for the server and one for the client.)
   A. Use the ipconfig /registerdns (server).
   B. Use the ipconfig /all (client).

***C. Use the ipconfig /flushdns (client).**

***D. Use the DNS console (server).**

Explanation: You can use the DNS console to clear the server and execute the ipconfig /flushdns command on the client to clear out the cache (for incorrect and dated DNS information).

---

6. If a Windows 2003 member server received the message, 'Network path not found,' which of the following would you use to make sure that you didn't have old DNS information on the 2003 member server?

***A. Ipconfig /flushdns**

   B. Nbtstat -RR
   C. Nslookup
   D. Netdiag /l

Explanation: Nbtstat -RR will release and refresh the name registration at the WINS server. Ipconfig /flushdns gets rid of any cached DNS information. Ipconfig /release and /renew will allow a client to get a fresh IP address and other information, such as a subnet mask and a default gateway. Nslookup (with the host name) will give you the IP address of the host. Netdiag /l will send the lengthy results of the client network capability test to netdiag.log.

7. Which of the following DNS servers reduce load?

A. Primary

***B. Caching server**

***C. Secondary**

D. Non-caching

Explanation: Secondary and caching servers reduce the load on primary DNS servers.

---

8. If you want users in the company.com domain to access a new Web site by the URL home.portal.company.com, what would you do?

***A. On a DNS server, create a new zone named portal.company.com. In portal.company.com create a CNAME record named home and specify company.com as the target host.**

B. On a DNS server, create a second zone named company.com. In portal.company.com create a CNAME record named home and specify company.com as the target host.

C. On a DHCP server, create a new zone named portal.company.com. In portal.company.com create a CNAME record named home and specify company.com as the target host.

D. On a DNS server, create a new zone named portal.company.com. In portal.company.com create a CNAME record named portal.company.com and specify company.com as the target host.

Explanation: Since a DNS zone can only resolve host to IP addresses within the namespace of the zone, you will need to create the new zone, create the CNAME which maps the home.portal.company.com to company.com.

9. After disabling dynamic registration, what should you remove on a domain controller with two NIC cards if Active Directory fails between it and other domain controllers in the network?

A. Remove the first NIC card's address.

***B. Remove the second NIC card's address.**

C. Remove host records from the DNS zone from the first NIC.

***D. Remove host records from the DNS zone from the second NIC.**

Explanation: After disabling dynamic registration, remove the second NIC card's address as well as host records from the DNS zone from the second NIC card. If Active Directory fails between the second NIC card and other domain controllers in the network, It will force it to go to the good NIC card, which in this scenario is the first NIC card.

---

10. What type of request tells DNS to give the best response that it can?

A. Recursive

B. Qualitative

***C. Iterative**

D. Bombastic

Explanation: An Iterative request tells DNS to give the best response that it can.

11. What types of DNS zones are available in Windows 2000?

***A. Secondary**

B. Extended

***C. Primary**

***D. Active Directory Integrated**

Explanation: Primary, Secondary and Active Directory Integrated zones are all types of DNS zones available in Windows 2000.

---

12. What is a NetBIOS name?

A. NetBIOS is a user name.

***B. NetBIOS is a machine name.**

C. NetBIOS is a trust name.

D. NetBIOS is a group name.

Explanation: NetBIOS is a machine name.

13. Which of the following is a text file?
    A. DHCP
    B. WINS
***C. LMHosts**
    D. DNS

Explanation: LMHosts is a static text file used for NetBIOS name resolution.

---

14. Which of the following can be found in WINS?
***A. Replication Partners**
    B. Parallel Registrations
***C. Active Registrations**
    D. Dynamic Partners

Explanation: Active Registrations and Replication Partners are options available to us in WINS.

15. Which of the following will display the ARP cache table specifically for the 192.168.1.1 interface?
    A. arp -N 192.168.1.1
    B. arp -a 192.168.1.1
***C. arp -a -N 192.168.1.1**
    D. arp 192.168.1.1

Explanation: To display the ARP cache table specifically for the interface that is assigned the IP address 192.168.1.1, type arp -a -N 192.168.1.1.

---

16. NetBIOS names typically contain the type of computer, its location and the unique ID. They can be up to ________ in length and may not contain spaces or backslashes.
    A. 10 characters
    B. 8 characters
***C. 15 characters**
    D. 20 characters

Explanation: NetBIOS names are 16 characters long, but only 15 are used for the name and one is used as a variable.

Implementing, Managing, and Maintaining Network Security

The objective of this chapter is to provide the reader with an understanding of the following:

Implement secure network administration procedures.

- **Implement security baseline settings and audit security settings by using security templates.**
- **Implement the principle of least privilege.**

Monitor network protocol security.

Tools might include:

- **The IP Security Monitor Microsoft Management Console (MMC) snap-in**
- **Kerberos support tools.**

Troubleshoot network protocol security. Tools might include:

- **IP Security Monitor MMC snap-in**
- **Event Viewer**
- **Network Monitor.**

Chapter 3: Managing Network Security

Introduction:

To apply proper security strategies within a Windows Server 2003 network, both the Local Computer and Network need attention. At the local computer, security revolves around tasks: that is, what tasks can a locally logged-on user perform? Typically, we think in terms of adding drivers, changing settings and installing programs as candidates for scrutiny at the local level. When it comes to securing the network at large, then the issues generally revolve around initial access, and then securing shared resources appropriately. With the exception of securing shared resources, use security templates to address these issues. Securing shared resources will be addressed later with the discussions of NTFS permissions and printer permission.

Getting Ready Questions

1. What are the types of security templates that come with Windows 2003?
2. Before applying a security template, what tool should be used to see the effect of the template on the target computer?
3. Which Windows operating systems have support for SUS natively?
4. How should Windows clients be configured for SUS?
5. What tool provides advanced monitoring and troubleshooting capabilities for the Kerberos authentication protocol?

Getting Ready Answers

1. Windows 2003 comes with templates for workstations and domain controllers, which are then "grouped" as default, secure or high secure templates.

2. Before applying a security template, the target computer should run the Security Configuration and Analysis mmc to determine the changes that the template will affect.

3. The client components for SUS are contained in Windows 2000 SP 3, Windows XP SP 1, in all Windows 2003 installations and as an msi file. For Windows 2000 SP 3 or later, no additional component installation is necessary. For earlier versions of Windows, clients can download the necessary components from the Microsoft public Web site, or the update can be distributed internally with a package created from the msi file and Group Policy.

4. The recommended way to configure SUS behavior for Windows 2000 and Windows XP clients is through Group Policy. For earlier Windows operating systems, Group Policy will not be effective. For Windows NT, Microsoft recommends using the System Policy editor. For all down-level clients, registry edits can be used, even while being generally discouraged by Microsoft. The registry settings are stored in HKLM\Software\Policies\Microsoft\Windows\WindowsUpdate\AU.

5. Kerbtray allows viewing of the ticket-granting process, and is an advanced tool for network support.

3.1 Implement Secure Network Administration Procedures

Microsoft ships security templates with Windows 2003 (as they did with Windows 2000) to provide a starting point for securing servers and workstations. The graphic below, Figure 3.1, shows an MMC with the Security Templates snap-in and the templates that come with Windows 2003. Note that there are templates for workstations and domain controllers, which are then "grouped" as default, secure or high secure templates. The set of templates that come with Windows has changed from 2000 to 2003, but the underlying concepts for use remain the same.

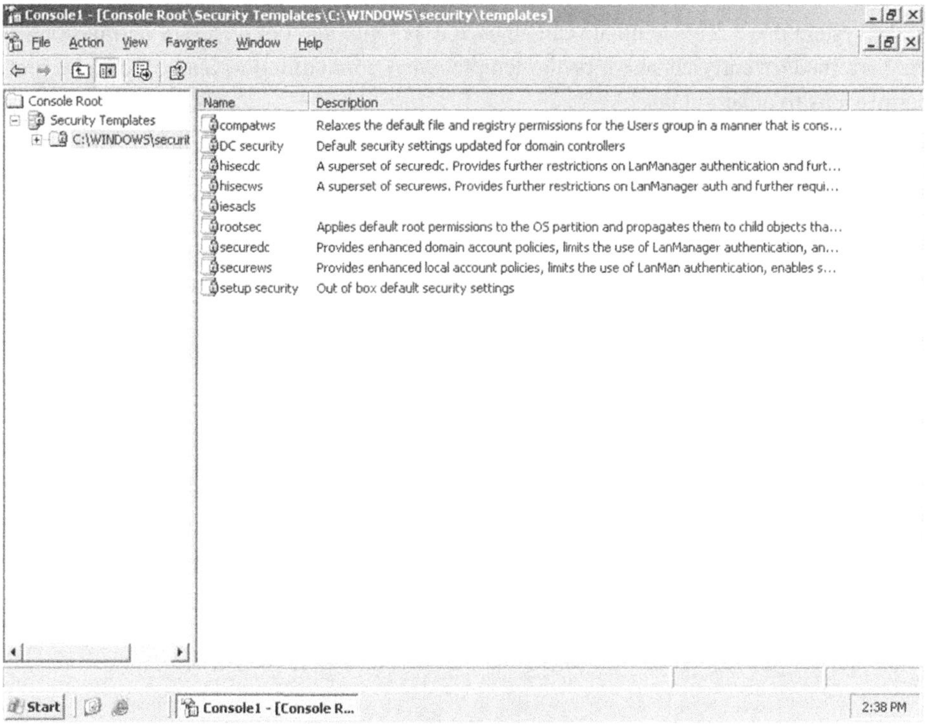

Figure 3-1: The Security Templates Snap-in to MMC.

In addition to these, Windows 2003 introduces two new templates. The setup security template is created upon installation of the operating system and can be used to restore the security settings for the computer, or can be imported into Group Policy. It represents the default security settings that are applied during installation of the operating system, including the file permissions for the root of the system drive. It can be used on servers and client computers; it cannot be applied to domain controllers. Microsoft suggests that Setup security.inf should never be applied using Group Policy. It contains a large amount of data and can seriously degrade performance if it is applied through Group Policy, because policy is periodically refreshed and a large amount of data would move through the domain. The rootsec template can be used to reset the security settings for the root volumes of the computer. By default, Rootsec.inf defines these permissions for the root of the system drive. This template can be used to reapply the root directory permissions if they are inadvertently changed, or the template can be modified to apply the same root permissions to other volumes.

Within each of the templates is a complete set of security settings, duplicating those found in the Local Security Policy, or in the Group Policy|Computer|Windows Settings|Security settings. Figure 3.2 shows the same settings within the Default Domain Policy. Again, Microsoft provides the templates as a starting point for securing both the local computer and the network. The templates are actually found in %systemroot%\system32\security as .inf files.

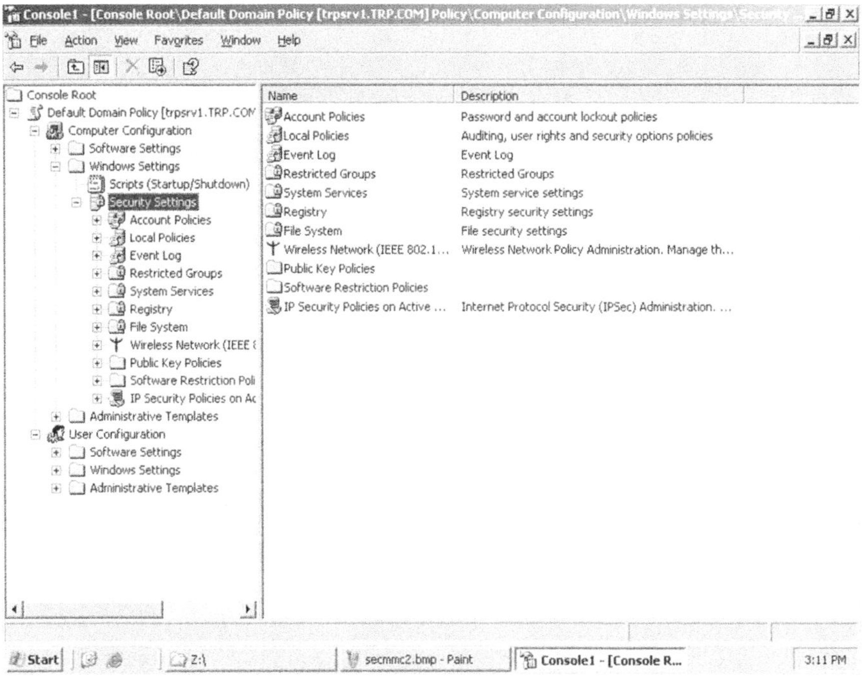

Figure 3-2: Default Domain Policy Showing Security Settings.

3.1.1 Implement Security Baseline Settings and Audit Security Settings by Using Security Templates

All Windows 2003 installations use the Setup Security template by default. You can then apply the secure and high secure templates to increase the level of security. Microsoft recommends that you copy an existing template, and then modify the copied template to create your own custom settings. Templates are applied to multiple Windows 2003 computers by importing the appropriate template into a Group Policy and then linking that Group Policy with appropriate container in Active Directory. To secure the network, create a security policy that sets the minimum password length to 10 characters, requiring password complexity, with the minimum age setting of 45 days, and allow three unsuccessful logon attempts before account lockout. The policy then is importable into the Default Domain Controller Policy, so that all Domain Controllers would then enforce those settings across the entire network. See Figure 3.3 below:

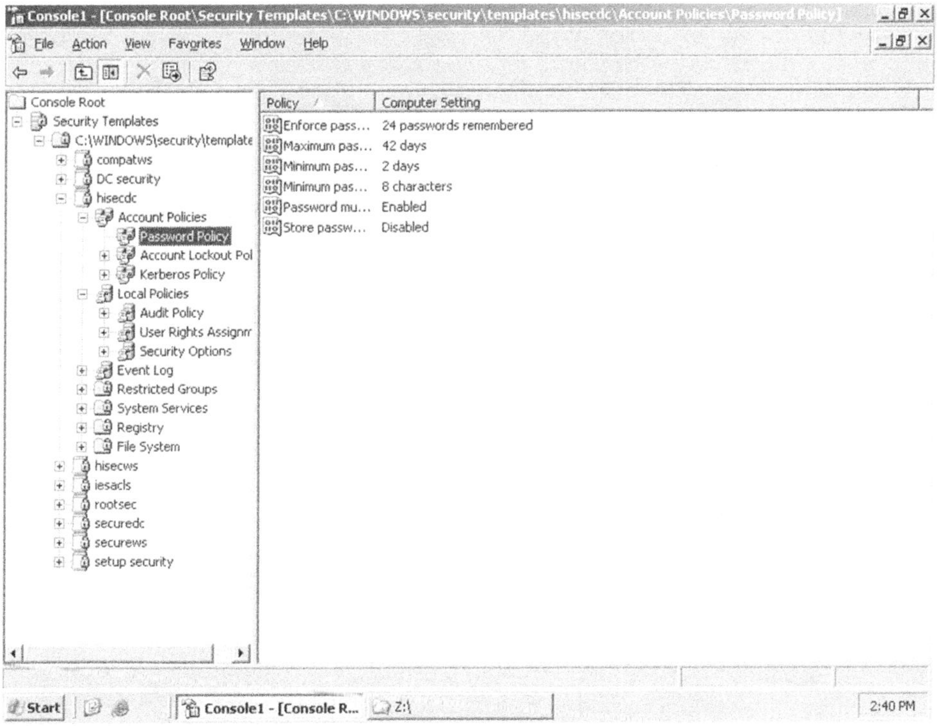

Figure 3-3: Password Policy within the Hisecdc Security Template.

Similarly, Local Policies within a security template can be set to disallow the installation of unsigned drivers, or to deny the user the ability to change the system time. As with Account Policies, these policies are importable into Group Policy, which link with a container. These containers show the objects that represent which Windows 2003 computers received the security settings configured in the security template.

Microsoft provides another snap-in for their MMC, the Security Configuration and Analysis snap-in, to allow the administrator the opportunity to analyze the affect of the policy on the local computer prior to actual implementation. To use the Security Configuration and Analysis tool, we would open an MMC on the desired computer and add the snap-in. Once added, then we would open a new database and perform an analysis. The results of the analysis would show differences in the existing configuration and the template as a red "X", as shown in Figure 3.4 below. This gives us the ability to see the impact of our template on an existing machine before we actually make the changes. Reversing the effect of security templates is not an easy matter, and requires extensive documentation and a manual setting-by-setting process of restoration.

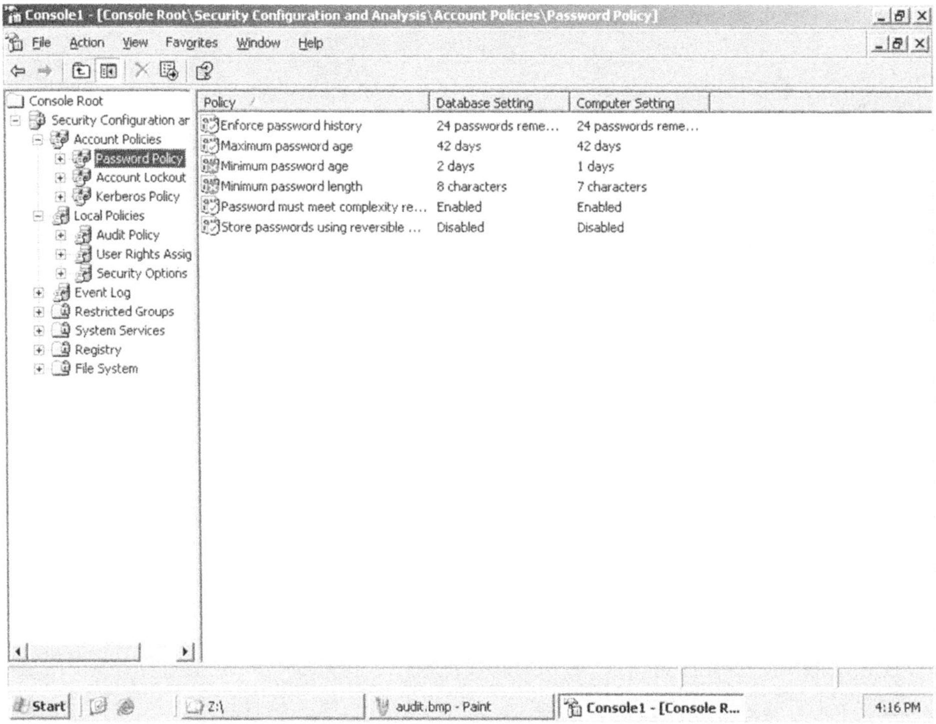

Figure 3-4: Security Configuration and Analysis.

Use this method to implement a standard audit of domain controllers. Once the configuration is finished, import the template into the default Domain Controller Policy to apply the settings to all domain controllers. Auditing is ready for use by importing the security templates. For example, earlier we only allowed three unsuccessful logon attempts prior to account lockout. An audit policy is now ready to track the failure of account logon to verify that the account lockout has occurred after the three unsuccessful attempts. All audited events are "captured" in the Security log and examined with Event Viewer. See Figure 3.5 below, which shows the Audit portion of a security template.

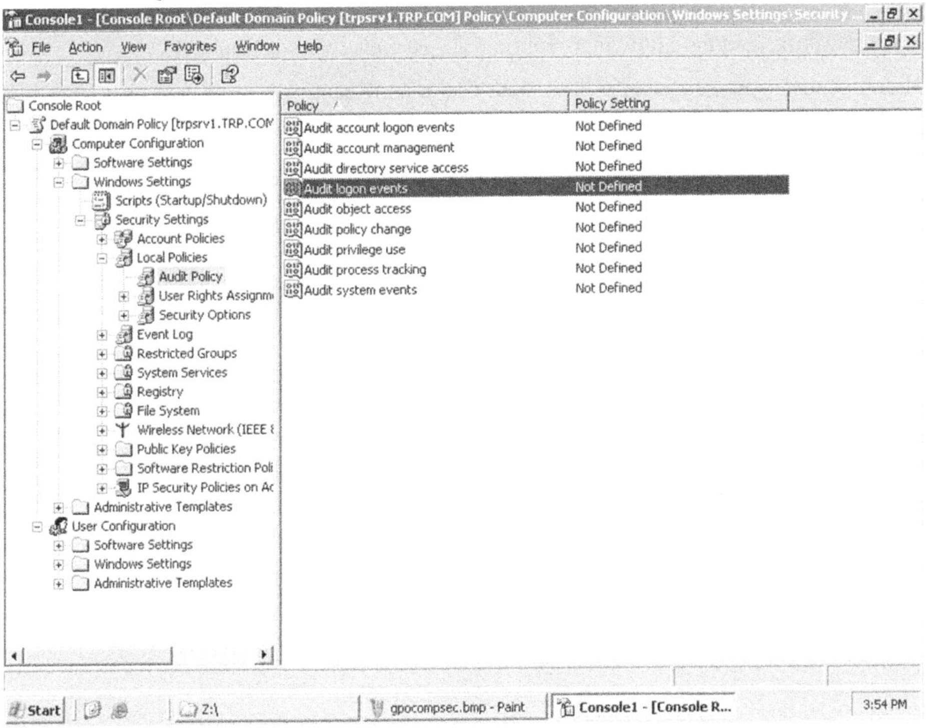

Figure 3.5 Audit Settings.

3.1.2 Implement the Principle of Least Privilege

The Microsoft Principle of Least Privilege, simply stated, suggests that we should logon using an account that only has the privileges necessary to perform general user-related tasks, such as retrieval and saving of files, printing, etc. When a user wishes to perform administrative tasks, then the user can choose the appropriate tool from Administrative Tools, right-click and choose Run As. This allows the user to run the administrative tool with administrative privileges, while only having their "normal" user rights for all other tasks. Once the tool is closed, the user's computer, if accessed when the user is away from their desk, will not allow inappropriate access to network resources.

Of course, users are supposed to lock their desktops when away from their desk, but this provides an additional level of security for your network.

Pop Quiz 3.1

Pop Quiz 3.1 Questions

1. What are the names of the two templates that were introduced with Windows Server 2003?
2. What is the Security.inf template used for on a Windows Server 2003?
3. What is the principle behind the least privilege?
4. How are security templates grouped on a Windows 2003 Domain Controller?
5. If you need to reset the security settings for the root volumes of a machine which template can be used?

Pop Quiz 3.1 Answers

1. Security.inf and Rootsec.inf.
2. The Security.inf template represents the default security settings applied during installation of the operating system, including the file permissions for the root of the system drive.
3. When logging onto a machine always use an account with the least number of elevated privileges. Use the RunAs command to use elevated privileges.
4. Templates for domain controllers (and workstations) are grouped either secure or high secure templates.
5. The rootsec template can be used to reset the security settings for the root volumes of the computer.

3.2 Install and Configure Software Update Infrastructure

To help centralize the deployment of patches and fixes, Microsoft has released Software Update Services (SUS). With SUS, an organization can have a single internal server serve as a central point for downloading and then updating all other servers and workstations. Use multiple servers to provide fault tolerance and load balancing for this service in larger implementations. Not only can this provide efficiencies in the update process, since most of the updates can be delivered across high-speed infrastructure, but it can also provide better control over who updates and what updates can and are applied throughout the network.

SUS has components that need to reside on the server, and components that need to be present at the client's. Use Internet Explorer on the server to administer SUS. To administer client behavior use the Group Policy MMC. Clients then connect to the SUS server and pull updates based upon the settings that are in effect at the server and those applied through Group Policy.

3.2.1 Install and Configure Software Update Services (SUS)

The installation of Software Update Services (SUS) is a two-step process. Use the link listed on the Web Resources page at,

http://www.microsoft.com/windows/reskits/webresources.

Click the SUS Server Component to begin the download. On the SUS Server Component download site, follow the on-screen instructions to download and install **Software Update Server**. Once the SUS server component installs, open the program by using the shortcut located in Start | Programs | Administrative Tools for administration.

Configuration of the SUS server begins with naming the server. Microsoft uses NetBIOS to find default clients. SUS is configurable to use the Microsoft DNS to find clients as well.

Since most SUS servers will reside behind a proxy server of some sort, the next step is to configure the proxy settings, which are very similar to the settings in Internet Explorer. If your network supports automatic proxy server configuration, select **automatically detect proxy server settings**. If your network does not support automatic proxy server configuration, select **Use the following proxy server to access the Internet**. To bypass the proxy server for local addresses, select the **Bypass proxy server for local addresses** check box.

If your proxy server requires a user ID and password to access the Internet, select the **Use the following user credentials to access the proxy server** check box, and then enter the proxy authentication user ID and password. Lastly, if your proxy server requires credentials but uses basic authentication, select the **Allow basic authentication when using proxy server** check box.

You will also specify from where downloads should come, directly from Microsoft or from another SUS in your intranet. It is Synchronize Content in the administrative tool. This area of the configuration also allows for scheduling of the synchronization process.

Next, specify what to approve for client machines. The packages may be marked as Approved or Not Approved, or may show a status of New, Updated or Temporarily Unavailable. A New, Not Approved or Temporarily Unavailable package will not be available for download by clients. An Approved package is available for download, and may change its status to Updated if the SUS server synchronizes with its source and changes the content prior to download.

An SUS server needs to be minimally a Pentium III 700 MHz, with 512 Mb of RAM, and must have the system partition formatted as NTFS. Additionally, the installation of the SUS components must be in an NTFS partition. A Windows 2000 server with SP2 or any Windows Server 2003 will support SUS, and you will also need IE 5.5 and IIS 5.0 or later.

3.2.2 Install and Configure Automatic Client Update Settings

The client components for SUS are contained in Windows 2000 SP 3, Windows XP SP 1, in all Windows 2003 installations and as an msi file. For Windows 2000 SP 3 or later, no additional component installation is necessary. Older client operating system machines can either download the necessary components from the Microsoft public Web site, or create a package from the msi file and Group Policy for distribution internally.

The recommended way to configure SUS behavior for Windows 2000 and Windows XP clients is through Group Policy. Group Policy settings always take precedence over local settings. In Group Policy, select Computer Configuration | Administrative Templates | Windows Components | Windows Update as shown in Figure 3.6.

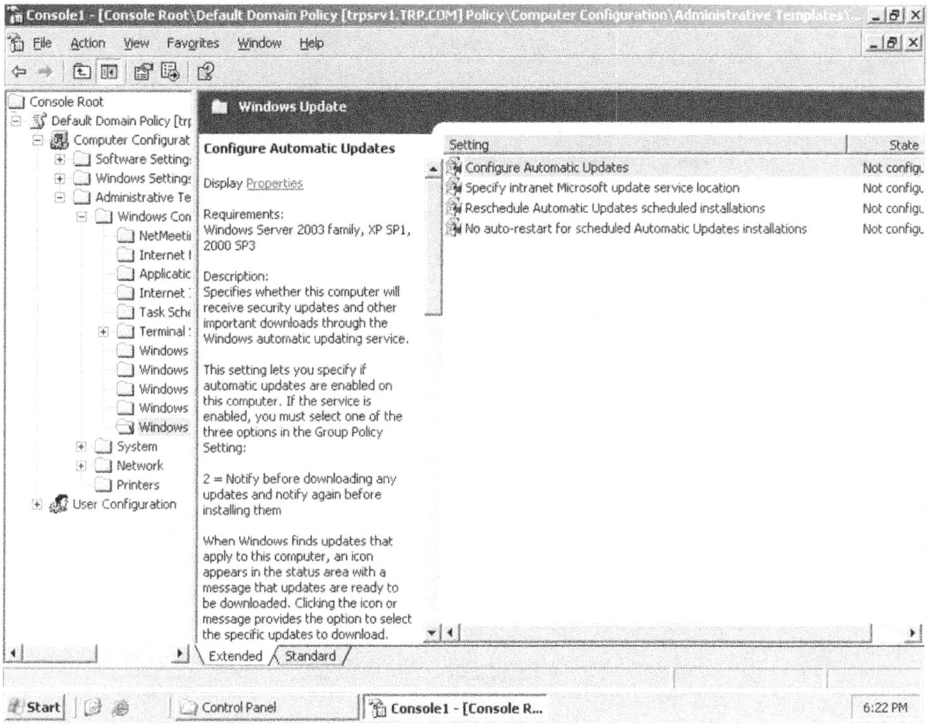

Figure 3-6: Configuring Windows Update in Group Policy.

Double-clicking on Configure Automatic Updates will open the initial configuration dialog, as shown in the next figure.

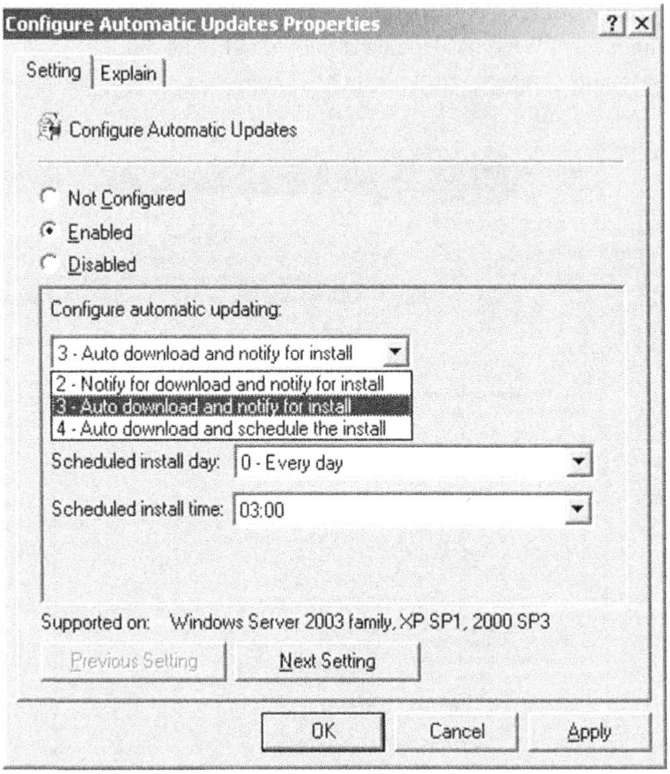

Figure 3.7: Configure Automatic Updates.

Once enabled, you have to choose from three options (2, 3 or 4) for the notification behavior. If 4 is chosen, then the update can be scheduled. This is the primary configuration for client settings. The other major setting is the next setting, Specify intranet Windows update service location. This allows you to tell the client the server from which to download updates, and also where to send statistics relating to downloads. See Figure 3.8.

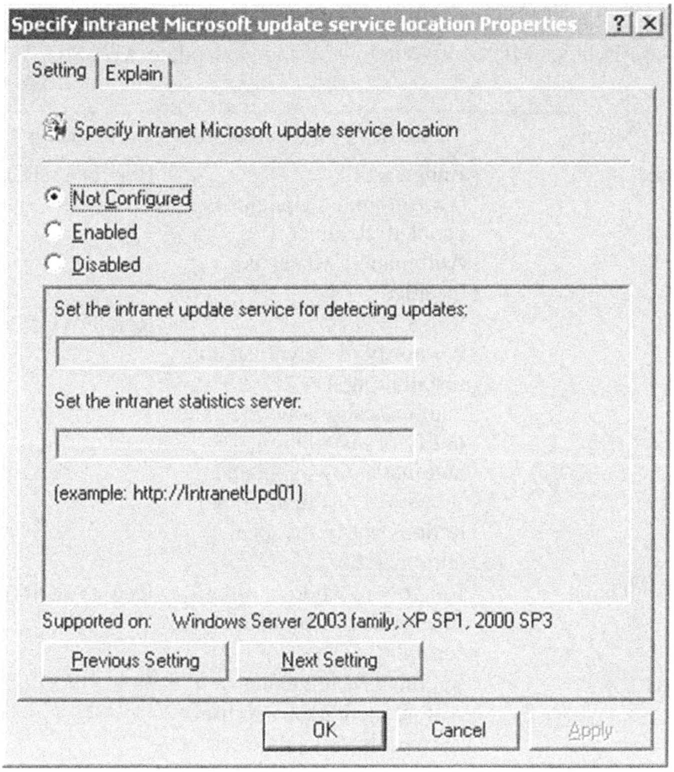

Figure 3.8: Specify SUS Server.

3.2.3 Configure Software Updates on Earlier Operating Systems

For earlier Windows operating systems, Group Policy will not be effective. For Windows NT, Microsoft recommends using the System Policy editor. For all down level, clients use registry edits. Use these edits with caution because they can cause serious problems on a machine. The registry settings are stored in

HKLM\Software\Policies\Microsoft\Windows\WindowsUpdate\AU. See Table 3.1 and 3.2 below.

<table>
<tr><th>Entry Name</th><th>Value Range and Meanings</th><th>Data Type</th></tr>
<tr><td>NoAutoUpdate</td><td>Range = 0|1
0 = Automatic Updates is enabled (default), 1 = Automatic Updates is disabled.</td><td>Reg_DWORD</td></tr>
<tr><td>AUOptions</td><td>Range = 2|3|4
2 = notify of download and installation, 3 = automatically download and notify of installation, 4 = automatic download and scheduled installation. All options notify the local administrator.</td><td>Reg_DWORD</td></tr>
<tr><td>ScheduledInstallTime</td><td>Range = n; where n = the time of day in 24-hour format (0–23).</td><td>Reg_DWORD</td></tr>
<tr><td>UseWUServer</td><td>Set this to 1 to enable Automatic Updates to use the Windows Update server as specified in WUServer.</td><td>Reg_DWORD</td></tr>
<tr><td>ScheduledInstallDay</td><td>Range = 0|1|2|3|4|5|6|7
0 = every day; 1 through 7 = the days of the week from Sunday (1) to Saturday (7).</td><td>Reg_DWORD</td></tr>
<tr><td>RescheduleWaitTime</td><td>Range = n; where n = time in minutes (1–60).</td><td>Reg_DWORD</td></tr>
<tr><td>NoAutoRebootWithLoggedOnUsers</td><td>0 to 1; set this value to 1 if you want logged on users to choose whether or not to reboot their system.</td><td>Reg_DWORD</td></tr>
</table>

Table 3—1: Entry Name—Range and Meanings.

To specify the server running SUS that you want your clients and servers to connect to for their Windows updates, you need to add two entries to the registry in the subkey HKLM\Software\Policies\Microsoft\Windows\WindowsUpdate. For the required entries, see Table 3.2.

Entry Name	Values	Data Type
WUServer	The HTTP name for the Windows Update intranet server (for example, http://intranetsus).	Reg_SZ
WUStatusServer	The HTTP name for the Windows Update intranet server (for example, http://intranetsus).	Reg_SZ

Table 3—2: Entry Name—Values.

Pop Quiz 3.2

Pop Quiz 3.2 Questions

1.What two steps are needed to install Software Update Services on a Windows Server 2003?

2. What is the Security.inf template used for on a Windows Server 2003?

3. Where are the client SUS files for Windows 2000 client machine?

4. What is the WUServer registry key used for on older Window client machines?

5. Does a local or group policy setting take precedence on a Windows Server 2003?

Pop Quiz 3.2 Answers

1. Download the software from the Microsoft site and then run the update configuration.
2. The Security.inf template represents the default security settings applied during installation of the operating system, including the file permissions for the root of the system drive.
3. Client components for SUS are contained in Windows 2000 SP3 as an msi file. Also, Windows XP SP 1, and in all Windows 2003 installations.
4. WUServer is used to enable Automatic Updates on the client server. Set the key to 1 to allow the client to use the Windows Update server for updates.
5. Group Policy settings always take precedence over local settings.

3.3 Monitor Network Protocol Security

For this Microsoft exam, there are two main areas of monitoring that you need to be familiar with: IPSec and Kerberos authentication. The IPSec snap-in for mmc provides a complete monitoring tool for IPSec issues, while for Kerberos authentication, there are numerous tools. First, we will look at the IPSec Monitor.

3.3.1 The IP Security Monitor Microsoft Management Console (MMC) Snap-in

The IPSec Monitor snap-in for mmc provides extensive monitoring and troubleshooting capabilities for the network administrator. You can view details about the IPSec process, and also examine IPSec policies in effect both locally and in the domain. See Figure 3.9.

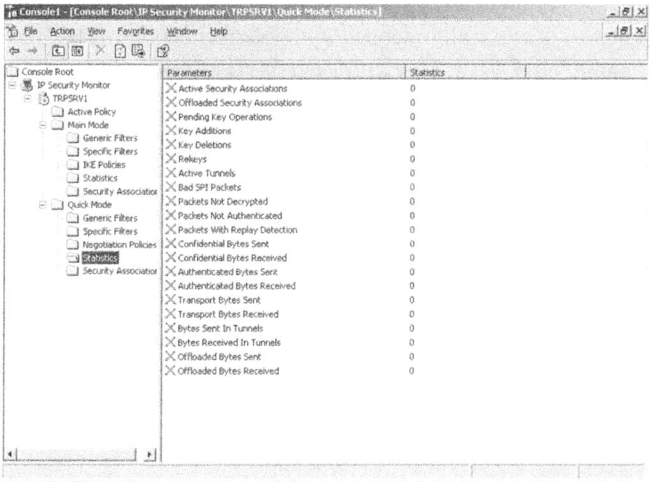

Figure 3.9: IpSec Monitor Snap-in for mmc.

The first node, Active Policy, shows information relating to the active IPSec policy currently in effect. The other nodes allow for advanced troubleshooting of the IPSec process.

3.3.2 Kerberos Support Tools

Auditing logon events and viewing with Event Viewer can provide some insight into Kerberos issues. The Microsoft Windows 2000 Resource Kit provided a troubleshooting tool, kerbtray.exe. Kerbtray allows you to see the ticket-granting process, and is also considered an advanced tool for network support.

3.4 Troubleshoot Network Protocol Security

Troubleshooting in this area can be extensive, but for this discussion, we will only look at two tools: Event Viewer and Network Monitor.

3.4.1 Event Viewer

Event Viewer is one of the best-known tools in Microsoft's Administrative Tools folder. For troubleshooting network protocol security, this centers on the configuration of auditing, and the subsequent examination of the security log. As we noted above, auditing account logon events can give us information about Kerberos issues. For Kerberos-related troubleshooting, some of the more common problems are Event 672—Authentication service ticket successful, Event 673—A ticket granting service ticket was granted, Event 675—Pre-authentication failed; user typed in wrong password and Event 678—An account was successfully mapped to a domain account. If the server is running RRAS and is being used as a remote access server, then auditing can be used to troubleshoot access issues.

3.4.2 Network Monitor

Network Monitor is a very advanced tool, as is any packet analysis utility. Captured traffic can be analyzed for a wide variety of purposes. Even Microsoft concedes that most administrators will need to send packet captures to an expert for analysis.

Chapter 3: Review Questions

1. Which of the following does the Layer Two Tunneling Protocol use with Internet Protocol security (L2TP/IPSec) in 2003?

A. User-level PAP authentication methods over a connection that is encrypted with IPSec

B. User-level PPP authentication methods over a connection that is encrypted with IPSec

C. User-level SLIP authentication methods over a connection that is encrypted with IPSec

D. User-level CHAP authentication methods over a connection that is encrypted with IPSec

---

2. Which of the following is recommended for secure VPN authentication in Windows 2003?

A. L2TP/IPSec

B. PPTP

C. SLIP

D. CHAP

3. What is the proper syntax to register the Houston remote access server in the bluesky domain?

A. netsh ras add registeredserver bluesky houston

B. netsh ras add registeredserver bluesky

C. netsh ras add registeredserver houston

D. netsh registeredserver bluesky houston

---

4. The Windows Server 2003 family supports which of the following authentication methods for dial-up networking?

A. CHAP, PAP, and SPAP

B. EAP-TLS and EAP-MD5 Challenge

C. SPOP and POP

D. MS-CHAP and MS-CHAP v2

E. POP and CHOP

5. If you have a DHCP server on your private network, how many addresses can the VPN server lease at a time from the DHCP server to assign to remote clients?

A. 10 addresses

B. 50 addresses

C. 100 addresses

D. 20 addresses

---

6. What are the two different modes in which a WLAN operates in Windows 2003?

A. Hyper Point Infrastructure WLAN

B. Access Point Infrastructure WLAN

C. Peer-to-peer (ad hoc) WLAN

D. Client/server WLAN

7. An 802.11a network can interoperate with which of the following wireless network standards?

A. 802.11b and 802.11g

B. 802.11b only

C. 802.11g only

D. Neither 802.11b nor 802.11g

---

8. With which of the following can PEAP be configured?

A. SPAP

B. MS-CHAP v2

C. SLIP

D. TLS

E. PAP

9. Which of the following statements are true regarding EAP-MS-CHAP v2?

A. It uses password-based credentials for server authentication.

B. It uses certificates for server authentication.

C. It uses password-based credentials for client authentication.

D. It uses certificates for client authentication.

E. It provides mutual authentication.

---

10. Which of the following is the recommended solution if you have multiple RAS servers in a 2003 environment?

A. Configure a single server with IAS as a RADIUS server.

B. Configure the remote access servers as RADIUS clients.

C. Administer the access policies of all the access servers separately.

D. Set up a VPN administrator.

Chapter 3: Review Answers

1. Which of the following does the Layer Two Tunneling Protocol use with Internet Protocol security (L2TP/IPSec) in 2003?

   A. User-level PAP authentication methods over a connection that is encrypted with IPSec

***B. User-level PPP authentication methods over a connection that is encrypted with IPSec**

   C. User-level SLIP authentication methods over a connection that is encrypted with IPSec

   D. User-level CHAP authentication methods over a connection that is encrypted with IPSec

Explanation: The Windows Server 2003 family uses two types of tunneling (encryption) protocols for secure communication. The first is Point-to-Point Tunneling Protocol (PPTP). It employs user-level PPP authentication methods and Microsoft Point-to-Point Encryption (MPPE) for data encryption. The second is Layer Two Tunneling Protocol with Internet Protocol security (L2TP/IPSec). It employs user-level PPP authentication methods over a connection that is encrypted with IPSec. IPSec requires host authentication using the Kerberos protocol, shared secret or computer-level certificates.

---

2. Which of the following is recommended for secure VPN authentication in Windows 2003?

***A. L2TP/IPSec**

   B. PPTP

   C. SLIP

   D. CHAP

Explanation: Microsoft recommends using L2TP/IPSec with certificates for secure VPN authentication.

3. What is the proper syntax to register the Houston remote access server in the bluesky domain?

***A. netsh ras add registeredserver bluesky houston**

B. netsh ras add registeredserver bluesky

C. netsh ras add registeredserver houston

D. netsh registeredserver bluesky houston

Explanation: To register the Houston remote access server in the blueskydomain, at a command prompt, type netsh ras add registeredserver bluesky houston.

---

4. The Windows Server 2003 family supports which of the following authentication methods for dial-up networking?

***A. CHAP, PAP, and SPAP**

***B. EAP-TLS and EAP-MD5 Challenge**

C. SPOP and POP

***D. MS-CHAP and MS-CHAP v2**

E. POP and CHOP

Explanation: The Windows Server 2003 family supports the following authentication methods for dial-up networking: CHAP, PAP, SPAP, MS-CHAP, MS-CHAP v2, EAP-TLS and EAP-MD5 Challenge.

5. If you have a DHCP server on your private network, how many addresses can the VPN server lease at a time from the DHCP server to assign to remote clients?

***A. 10 addresses**

B. 50 addresses

C. 100 addresses

D. 20 addresses

Explanation: If you have a DHCP server on your private network, the VPN server can lease 10 addresses at a time from the DHCP server and assign those addresses to remote clients. If you do not have a DHCP server on your private network, the dial-up server can automatically generate and assign IP addresses to remote clients. You must specify the range from which the remote access server will assign IP addresses.

---

6. What are the two different modes in which a WLAN operates in Windows 2003?

A. Hyper Point Infrastructure WLAN

***B. Access Point Infrastructure WLAN**

***C. Peer-to-peer (ad hoc) WLAN**

D. Client/server WLAN

Explanation: A WLAN operates in two different modes, which are defined by the Institute of Electrical and Electronics Engineers (IEEE) 802.11. The first mode is an Access Point Infrastructure WLAN; with it, wireless stations (devices with radio network cards or external modems) connect to wireless access points that function as bridges between the stations and the existing network backbone. For example, wireless users within a corporate or campus building can access network resources as if they were connected with a network cable. The second is a peer-to-peer (ad hoc) WLAN. In a peer-to-peer network, wireless clients communicate directly with each other without the use of cables. For example, several users within a limited area, such as a conference room, can form a temporary network to each other without using access points. Although they can communicate and share resources with each other, they cannot access network resources that are not part of their peer-to-peer network.

7. An 802.11a network can interoperate with which of the following wireless network standards?

A. 802.11b only

***B. 802.11b and 802.11g**

C. 802.11g only

D. Neither 802.11b nor 802.11g

Explanation: 802.11a cannot interoperate with either 802.11b or 802.11g.

---

8. With which of the following can PEAP be configured?

A. SPAP

***B. MS-CHAP v2**

C. SLIP

***D. TLS**

E. PAP

Explanation: PEAP can be configured with TLS or MS-CHAP v2. PEAP-TLS is the recommended authentication mechanism, because it provides the strongest authentication and key determination method. A certificate is required on the network access server for MS-CHAP v2. Certificates are required for both client and network access servers for PEAP-TLS.

9. Which of the following statements are true regarding EAP-MS-CHAP v2?

A. It uses password-based credentials for server authentication.

***B. It uses certificates for server authentication.**

***C. It uses password-based credentials for client authentication.**

D. It uses certificates for client authentication.

***E. It provides mutual authentication.**

Explanation: EAP-MS-CHAP v2 provides mutual authentication and uses certificates for server authentication and password-based credentials for client authentication.

---

10. Which of the following is the recommended solution if you have multiple RAS servers in a 2003 environment?

***A. Configure a single server with IAS as a RADIUS server.**

***B. Configure the remote access servers as RADIUS clients.**

C. Administer the access policies of all the access servers separately.

D. Set up a VPN administrator.

Explanation: IAS performs centralized authentication, authorization, auditing and accounting of connections for VPN, dial-up and wireless connections. If you have more than one remote or wireless access server, rather than administer the access policies of all the access servers separately, you can configure a single server with IAS as a RADIUS server and configure the remote access servers as RADIUS clients.

Implementing, Managing, and Maintaining Routing and Remote Access

The objective of this chapter is to provide the reader with an understanding of the following:

Configure Routing and Remote Access user authentication.

- Configure remote access authentication protocols.
- Configure Internet Authentication Service (IAS) to provide authentication for Routing and Remote Access clients.
- Configure Routing and Remote Access policies to permit or deny access.

Manage remote access.

- Manage packet filters.
- Manage Routing and Remote Access routing interfaces.
- Manage devices and ports.
- Manage routing protocols.
- Manage Routing and Remote Access clients.

Manage TCP/IP routing.

- Manage routing protocols.
- Manage routing tables.
- Manage routing ports.

Implement secure access between private networks.

Troubleshoot user access to remote access services.

- Diagnose and resolve issues related to remote access VPNs.
- Diagnose and resolve issues related to establishing a remote access connection.
- Diagnose and resolve user access to resources beyond the remote access server.

Troubleshoot Routing and Remote Access routing.

- Troubleshoot demand-dial routing.
- Troubleshoot router-to-router VPNs.

Chapter 4: Managing Routing and Remote Access

Introduction:

In this section, we are going to explore RRAS, the Routing and Remote Access Service. RRAS is most commonly used as a remote access service (the RAS part), whether that is dial-up or VPN. What is often overlooked, however, is the routing functionality that Microsoft has included with the service. Any computer with 2 NICs that is running Windows Server 2003 can be used as a full-featured router, either at the edge of the network or somewhere inside—perhaps serving as the router for a new subnet. In fact, when you think about the remote access side of the service, you can think of that as a router as well. In essence, dial-up users (modem, VPN, ISDN, etc.) are dialing in to a router, which has server functionality.

Getting Ready Questions

1. How can one computer have more than one IP address?

2. How can you see the routing table?

3. If you want users within your network to be able to use FTP to get files from the Internet, but not allow users from the Internet to use FTP to get files from your network, what would you configure?

4. What authentication protocol would be appropriate for wireless clients?

5. Which account or accounts have Remote Access Permission (Dial-in or VPN) by default?

Getting Ready Answers

1. With multiple NICs, or even with one NIC, multiple IP addresses can be assigned using the Advanced button on TCP/IP properties.
2. Either the Route Print command or using the Routing and Remote Access utility.
3. An inbound filter on Port 21
4. PEAP
5. None

Routing Overview

Now, you are probably familiar with the term router, and may have an idea what a router is, but we are going to start by building a foundation and work up from there. That said, let's start by looking at what a router is and what it does.

A router is defined as an intermediate system that forwards packets between interconnected networks. The router may be a hardware router or a software router.

A hardware router is one whose primary function is routing, typically using a proprietary operating system optimized for that purpose. A hardware router may also include firewall, remote access and/or bridging functionality. A hardware router typically does not use magnetic or optical storage, but rather stores configuration information in non-volatile RAM.

A software router is typically a multipurpose device, such as a server class computer running a network operating system like Windows Server 2003. Windows Server 2003 supports routing with the RRAS, or Routing and Remote Access Service. RRAS is an effective interior router (routing between internal IP networks) for businesses large and small, as well as a very good border router and remote access server.

So far, so good, right? But what about the reason to implement a router in the first place? Well, the main reason to implement a router is to subdivide a broadcast domain. As you may recall, there are a couple of other intermediate systems used in networking—the hub, the bridge and the switch. You can think of a switch as a multiport bridge, since they perform essentially the same function. All of those intermediate systems have something in common—they allow computers to communicate with each other. They have something else in common—broadcast traffic sent from one port will go to all other ports. If you segment a network by placing a router between two switches, then a broadcast packet, such as an ARP request, will only go to all end systems on one switch, instead of both. This results in a greater amount of bandwidth available for data transmission. The end result, then, is a greater efficiency in data transmission when you segment a network using a router, even when the network is fully switched.

Now, you are probably wondering how a router knows where to send a packet, right? A hub is an OSI layer 1 device and just broadcasts to every active port, having no logic to tell it what to do with a packet. A switch is an OSI layer 2 device and uses the MAC address, like a bridge does, forwarding packets to the port associated with the destination MAC address. Routers, on the other hand, are OSI layer 3 devices and use the network information in the packet. Routers compare the destination network address with their routing table to determine where to send the packet. Routers may have static or manually configured routing tables, or they may have dynamically configured routing tables. Dynamic routing tables are populated with a routing protocol, such as RIP or OSPF. RRAS supports a number of routing protocols, which we will cover in detail later.

RRAS Overview

Windows Server 2003 RRAS is always installed, and in fact cannot be removed. In order to use RRAS, you must first enable it. To do this, you can either navigate to the Routing and Remote Access object in Administrative Tools, or you can type rrasmgmt.msc in the run dialogue box. I prefer the keyboard method, but either approach works just fine. Note that you can manage RRAS on all servers from a single console, which need not even be installed on a server!

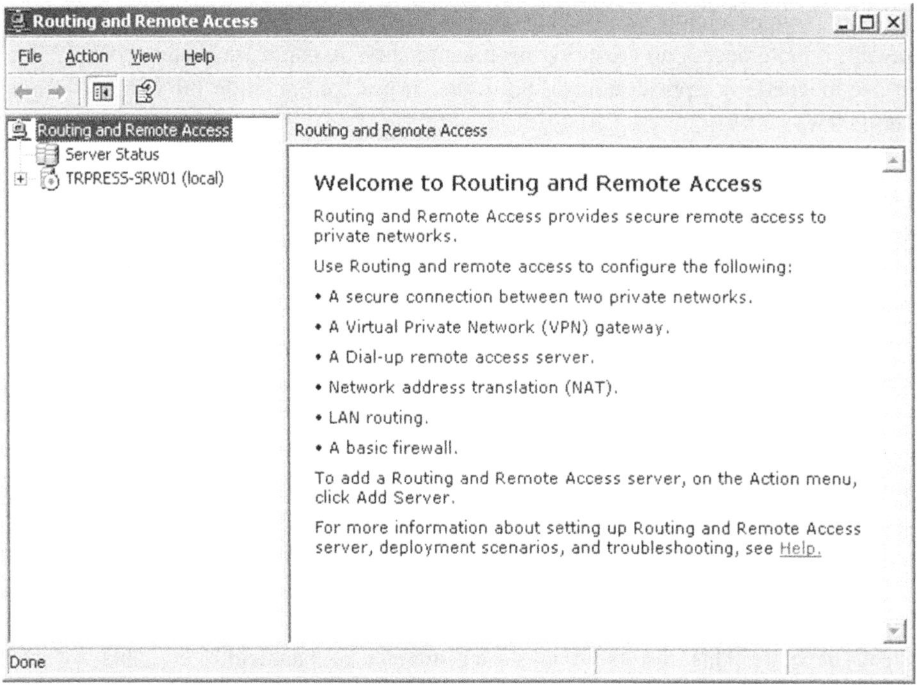

Figure 4-1: RRAS Management Console.

Now, since you will typically be configuring RRAS on a server with two or more NICs (network interface cards), it is a good idea to rename each interface with a meaningful name before you enable and configure RRAS. Renaming an interface is very easy. Open the Network Connections console and choose an interface. From there you can either use the file menu, the context menu or you can wait a moment after choosing the interface and then click again. However you choose to rename the interfaces is up to you, but it is a very good idea on any computer with two or more interfaces.

In figure 4.2, you see two LAN interfaces, but a routing interface can be any network interface. This includes, but is not limited to, PSTN, ISDN, xDSL and T-carrier. The key element is that a routing interface is a network connection over which packets are routed.

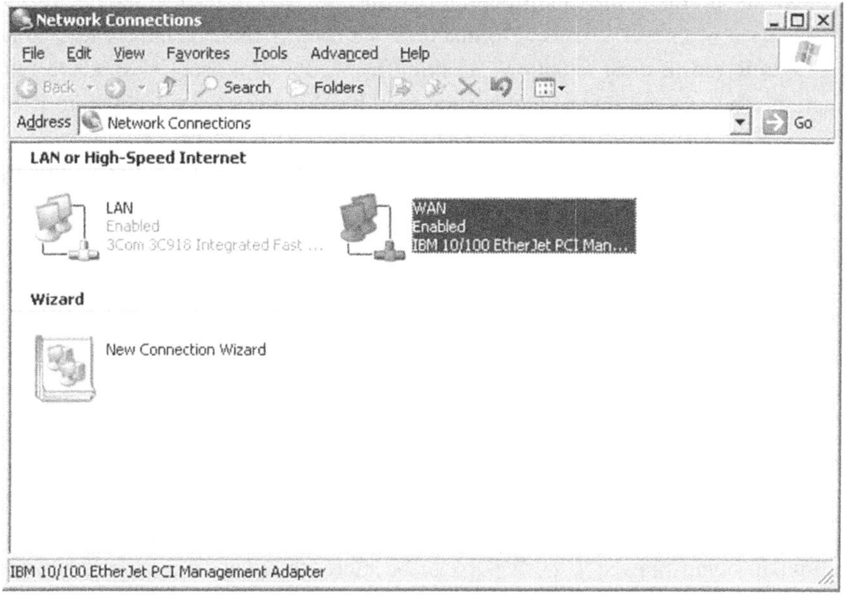

Figure 4-2: Network Connections console with interfaces renamed LAN and WAN

A common implementation is RRAS as a NAT server connecting to the public Internet. In that scenario, Windows Server 2003 will have one interface connected to the internal network, and some form of Internet connection—often a demand dial interface such as a PSTN modem or an ISDN interface.

4.1 Manage TCP/IP Routing

So far, we have explored what a routing interface is. As mentioned earlier, there are two other elements needed—the routing protocol and the routing table itself. A routing protocol is used whenever you want to maintain the routing tables dynamically, which is definitely preferred in most situations. Routing protocols allow routers to share routing information. The two routing protocols supported by Windows Server 2003 are RIP and OSPF.

RIP, or Routing Information Protocol, is used in smaller networks. It does not scale well, but is very simple to implement. RIP is available in two versions, v.1 and v.2. Both use a routing table. RIPv.1 broadcasts its full table to its neighboring routers, while RIPv.2 can be configured to multicast instead of broadcast. Windows Server 2003 only supports RIPv.2, so you will need to ensure that all other routers also support version 2 if you plan to use RIP. Typically, RIP is used in networks with less than 50 servers, and less than 15 connected networks.

OSPF, or Open Shortest Path First, is known as a link state protocol. OSPF maintains a database of link states rather than a routing table and, rather than advertising its full database to all neighbors, it only sends change messages. Because of this, it is a far more efficient routing protocol from the perspective of processor overhead and bandwidth utilization. Its main drawback is that it can be more complex to configure—though a default configuration on a network using entirely Windows Server 2003 can be quite effective. If, however, you have a mix of hardware routers and software routers running Windows 2000 Server or Windows Server 2003, you will need to be careful to configure all of the routers so that they properly communicate with each other.

4.1.1 Manage Routing Tables

The third element is the routing table itself. Every computer connected to a network has a routing table for that interface. This is true whether the interface is a modem or a T-3 connection.

In figure 4.3, you see the results of typing **route print** from the command console. This shows you the protocol version (in this case IPv4), the interfaces (MS Loopback, 3Com 3C918 and IBM 10/100 EtherJet), the MAC address in hexadecimal and then the routing table itself.

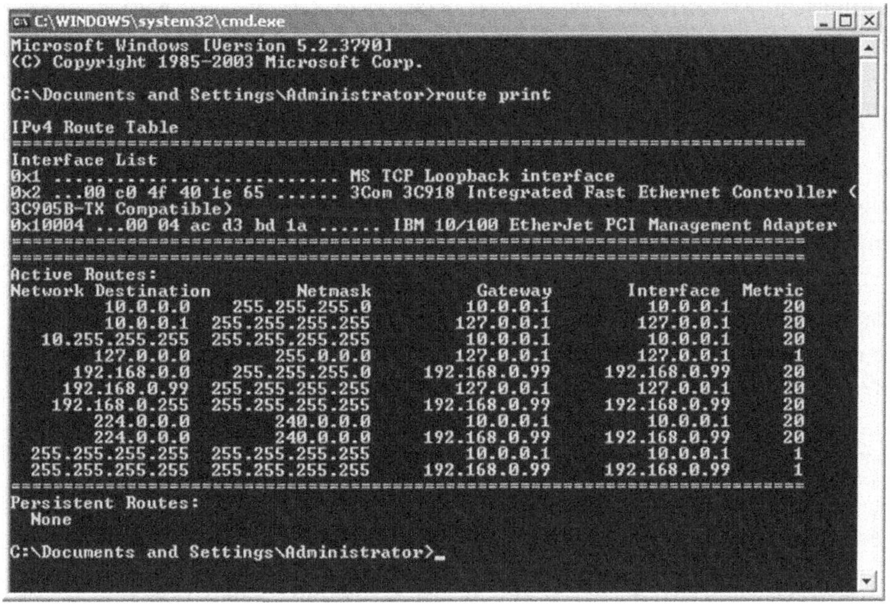

```
C:\WINDOWS\system32\cmd.exe
Microsoft Windows [Version 5.2.3790]
(C) Copyright 1985-2003 Microsoft Corp.

C:\Documents and Settings\Administrator>route print

IPv4 Route Table
===========================================================================
Interface List
0x1 ........................... MS TCP Loopback interface
0x2 ...00 c0 4f 40 1e 65 ...... 3Com 3C918 Integrated Fast Ethernet Controller (
3C905B-TX Compatible)
0x10004 ...00 04 ac d3 bd 1a ...... IBM 10/100 EtherJet PCI Management Adapter
===========================================================================
===========================================================================
Active Routes:
Network Destination        Netmask          Gateway       Interface  Metric
          10.0.0.0    255.255.255.0         10.0.0.1        10.0.0.1     20
          10.0.0.1  255.255.255.255        127.0.0.1       127.0.0.1     20
    10.255.255.255  255.255.255.255         10.0.0.1        10.0.0.1     20
         127.0.0.0        255.0.0.0        127.0.0.1       127.0.0.1      1
       192.168.0.0    255.255.255.0     192.168.0.99    192.168.0.99     20
      192.168.0.99  255.255.255.255        127.0.0.1       127.0.0.1     20
     192.168.0.255  255.255.255.255     192.168.0.99    192.168.0.99     20
         224.0.0.0        240.0.0.0         10.0.0.1        10.0.0.1     20
         224.0.0.0        240.0.0.0     192.168.0.99    192.168.0.99     20
   255.255.255.255  255.255.255.255         10.0.0.1        10.0.0.1      1
   255.255.255.255  255.255.255.255     192.168.0.99    192.168.0.99      1
===========================================================================
Persistent Routes:
  None

C:\Documents and Settings\Administrator>_
```

Figure 4-3: Example of a Routing Table.

The routing table section shows the active routes, with 5 columns of information. First is the destination network, followed by the netmask for that destination. Next you have the gateway, which is the IP address for the interface used to access that destination, followed by the IP address of the interface that is using that gateway address. Last you find the metric. The metric is the value deducted from the time to live for the packet. Every packet has a TTL, or time to live, so that it does not just keep going. Every routing interface will have a cost or metric, which will be deducted from the TTL for the packet. If the TTL runs out before the packet reaches its destination, it will be destroyed and a time-out message will be returned to the sending host.

The purpose of a routing table is to allow the IP portion of the TCP/IP suite to determine the best path for a data transmission. Bear in mind that all IP hosts will have a routing table—not just routers.

There are three types of entries in a routing table. These are the Network Route, Host Route and Default Route.

A network route is a path to a specific network. For example, if there was a 10.0.1.0 network which the server in figure 4.3 was part of, it may have a network route of:

Destination	Netmask	Gateway	Interface	Metric
192.168.0.0	255.255.255.0	10.0.1.1	10.0.1.1	2

Which can be read as "to get to network 192.168.0.0 with subnet mask 255.255.255.0, use address 10.0.1.1 and deduct 2 from the TTL for the packet."

A host route is an entry that shows the exact path to an IP host, rather than a network ID. In place of the network ID, the host address would be listed.

A default route is used when there are no entries in the routing table that match up to either the destination host or the destination network ID. Essentially, IP looks for either a host or network route, and if it does not find an entry, it sends the packet on to a default router, which hopefully has more information on how to get to the destination.

Uses for RRAS Information:
Windows Server 2003 RRAS is typically enabled on a multi-role server. In smaller networks, it may be a file and print server that is also routing between connected networks. It may also be used to connect remote offices over the Internet or via a demand-dial connection. Finally, RRAS is often used as a remote access server for end-user VPN access to the internal network over the Internet.

4.1.1.1 Enabling RRAS

Remember that RRAS is always present with Windows Server 2003—in order to use it, you need to enable it.

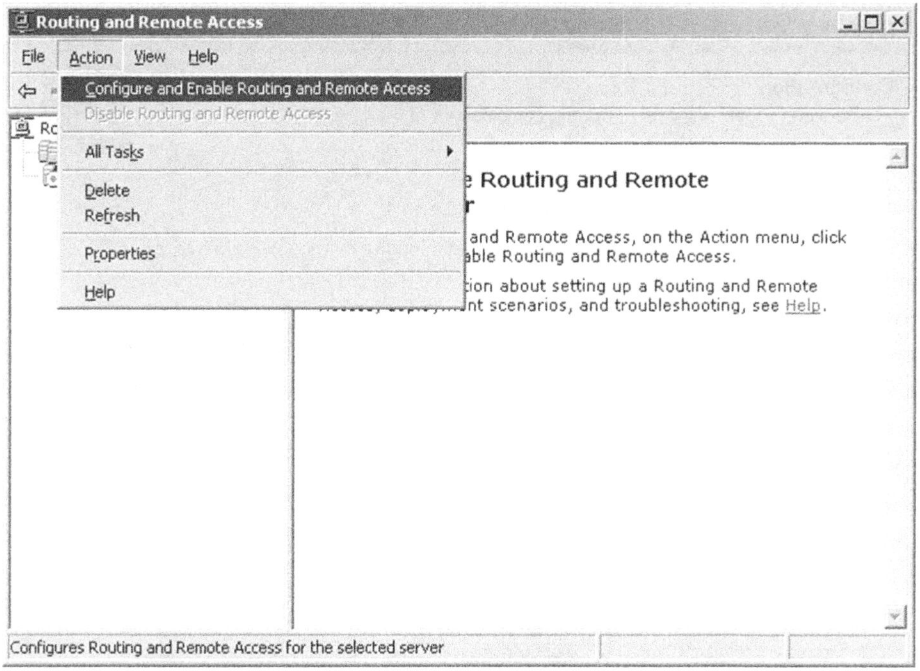

Figure 4-4: Enabling RRAS.

As you see in figure 4.4, all you need to do is choose **Configure and Enable Routing and Remote Access** from the **Action** menu of the RRAS management console. You will be presented with a splash screen, which is the beginning of the wizard from which you choose from one of several options (see figure 4.5).

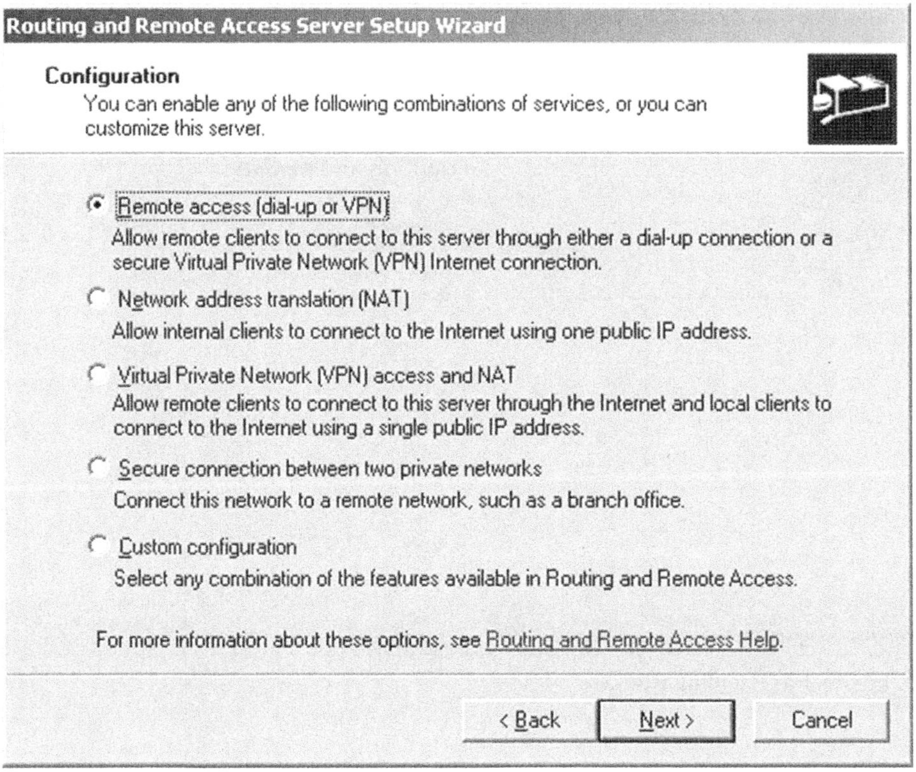

Figure 4-5: RRASSetup.

When you first install Windows Server 2003, you will also be presented with a "Manage your Server" page, from which you can choose a variety of roles for a server—including one of several RRAS roles. For the certification exam, you may want to get familiar with both methods of enabling and configuring RRAS.

Once you have enabled RRAS, you can further configure it with routing protocols, packet filters and remote access policies. Remote Access Policies will be covered later in this section. First, however, we are going to look at how to add routing protocols and then packet filters.

4.1.2 and 4.1.3 Managing Routing Protocols

There are 3 steps involved in configuring a routing protocol. First, you must add the protocol itself, and then you must add at least one interface for the protocol. You can add as many interfaces as you want to a given routing protocol, or at least as many as you have. Once you have added the interface or interfaces to the protocol, you then can perform any additional configuration necessary for your networking environment.

Let's start by looking at how you install a routing protocol.

Starting in the RRAS Management console, lets configure this server for LAN routing. To do this, you would choose the custom configuration option. On the next screen, you will choose the LAN Routing checkbox only. After Windows Server 2003 enables and configures the server as a LAN router, you will see the following:

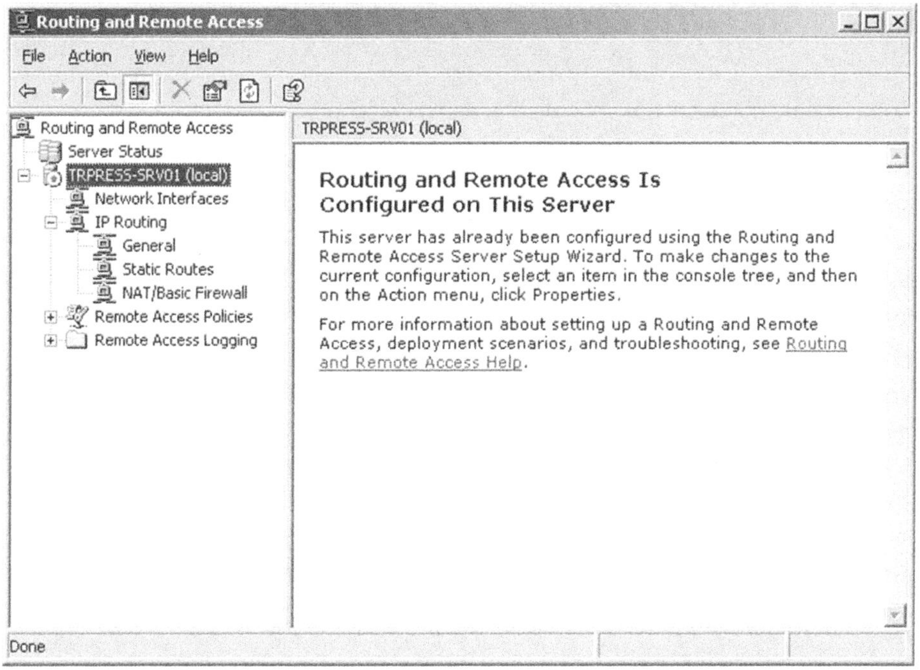

Figure 4-6: RRASLAN.

Now, to add a routing protocol, you click on General, then either right-click or click on the **Action** menu and choose **New Routing Protocol** (Figure 4.7).

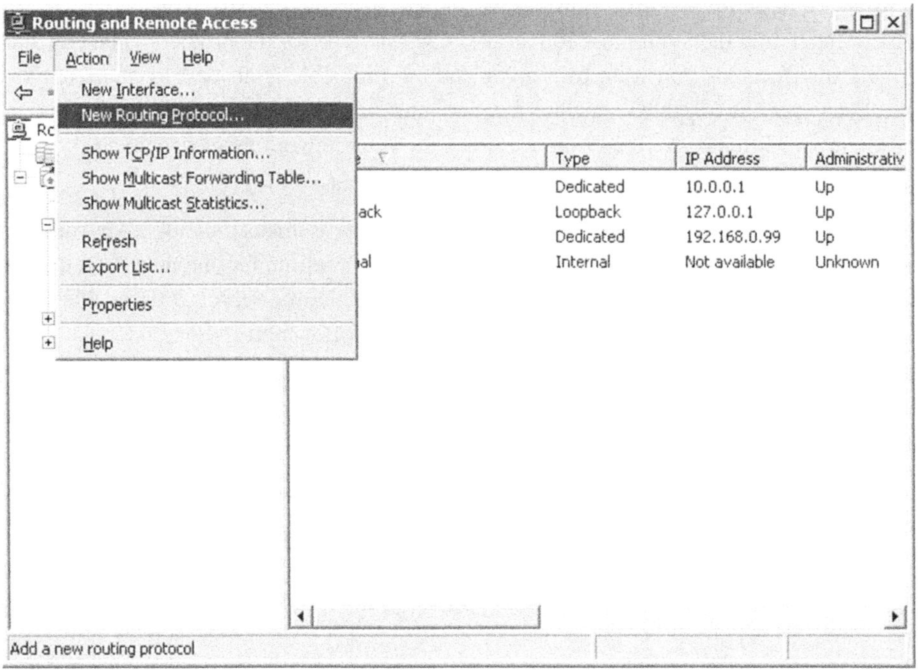

Figure 4-7: RRASNewRouting.bmp

After clicking on **New Routing Protocol**, the following dialog box appears:

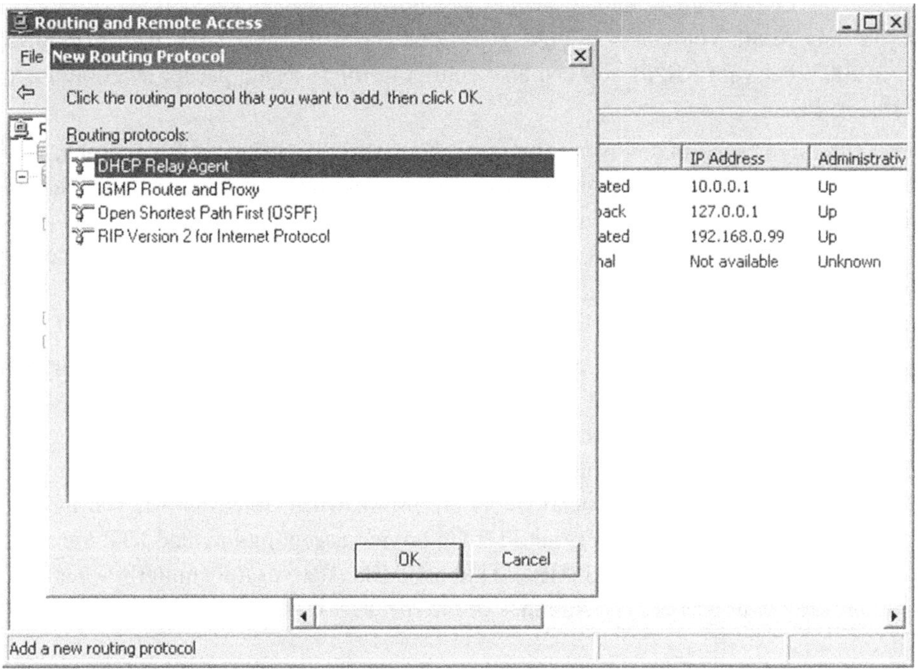

Figure 4-8: RRASNewRoutingChoice.

As you can see, you have the option of installing and configuring the DHCP Relay Service, IGMP Router and Proxy (used for multicast), Open Shortest Path First (OSPF) and RIPv.2.

Once you have installed the routing protocols needed, they will be listed in the IP Routing section for that server. After they are installed, you will need to add an interface to the protocol, and may then need to perform additional configuration. Adding an interface is similar to the other actions you have performed. Either right-click on the routing protocol or select the protocol and click on the **Action** menu, then choose **Add Interface**. You will be presented with a dialog box that shows the names of the interfaces as they are listed in the Network Connections dialog box—which is why I suggest renaming them before you enable and configure RRAS!

After you add the interface or interfaces for the routing protocol, you will be presented with the properties page for that protocol. Here you can configure it as needed.

4.1.4 Configuring Packet Filters

As you may recall, you can configure TCP/IP filters at the host level with Windows Server 2003, but with RRAS you can also configure filters at the packet level on a per interface basis.

Packet filtering is used to control traffic through a router. By using packet filtering, you can prevent attacks on your internal network by blocking the protocol and ports that are vulnerable. Packet filtering affects all traffic through an interface, so before you implement filters make sure that the protocol and port is not needed by a service. In addition to preventing attacks, you can also improve network performance by only allowing necessary traffic.

There are two settings you can choose when implementing packet filtering. You can either allow all traffic except that specified, or you can prevent all except that specified. In either case, when you implement packet filtering, the router will drop any traffic that does not meet the conditions you specify. You can also configure packet filtering as either inbound or outbound. Inbound filters are useful when, for example, you have a Web server that is only serving FTP and HTTP, but not accepting inbound FTP transfers or allowing inbound SMTP/POP3 traffic. Outbound filters are useful similarly when you want to restrict your users to certain kinds of Internet access, such as only HTTP and not FTP.

You can also configure multiple conditions within a filter, or you can configure multiple filters for an interface. When you configure multiple conditions within a filter, then a logical AND is performed, whereby all conditions must be met for the packet to be allowed. On the other hand, if you configure multiple inbound OR outbound filters, then a logical OR operation is performed, whereby the packet must meet at least one of the allow conditions on one of the filters in order to pass. It is possible, however, to configure inbound and outbound filters where all packets will be dropped because the filters are contradictory.

To configure packet filters, you start with the RRAS Management console. You need to expand the IP Routing section, click on General, and then click on the interface that you wish to configure packet filters on. From there, you can either right-click and choose properties or click on the **Action** menu and choose properties.

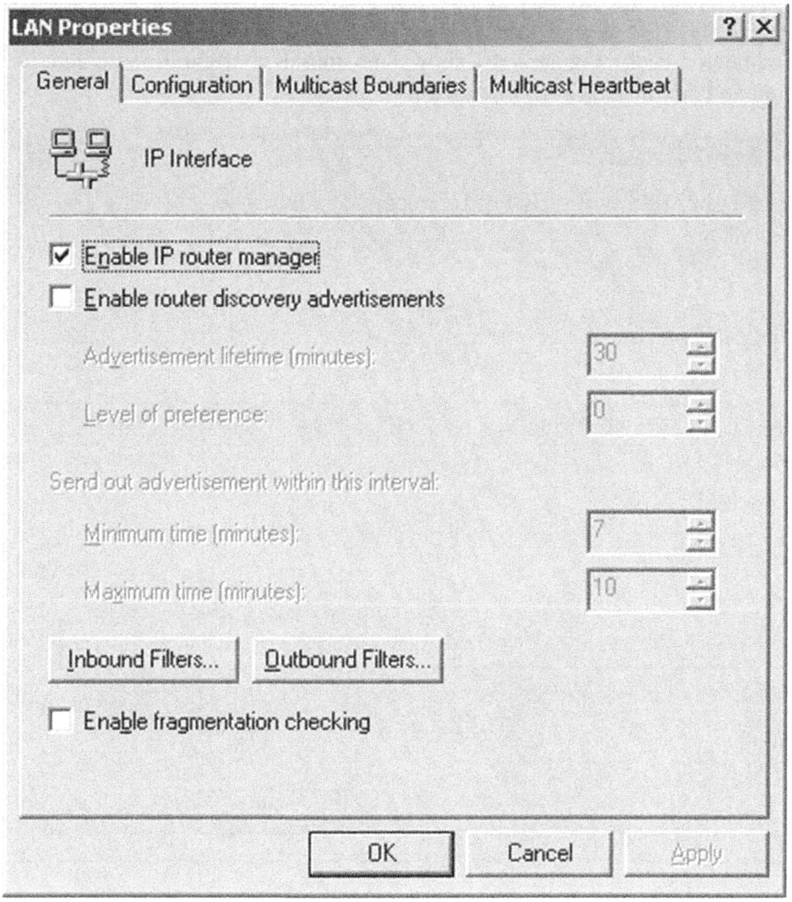

Figure 4-9: RRASLANProperties.

On the general tab, you choose either inbound or outbound filters. The configuration method is the same for each. Figure 4.10 shows the initial configuration screen for inbound filters on the LAN interface for this server.

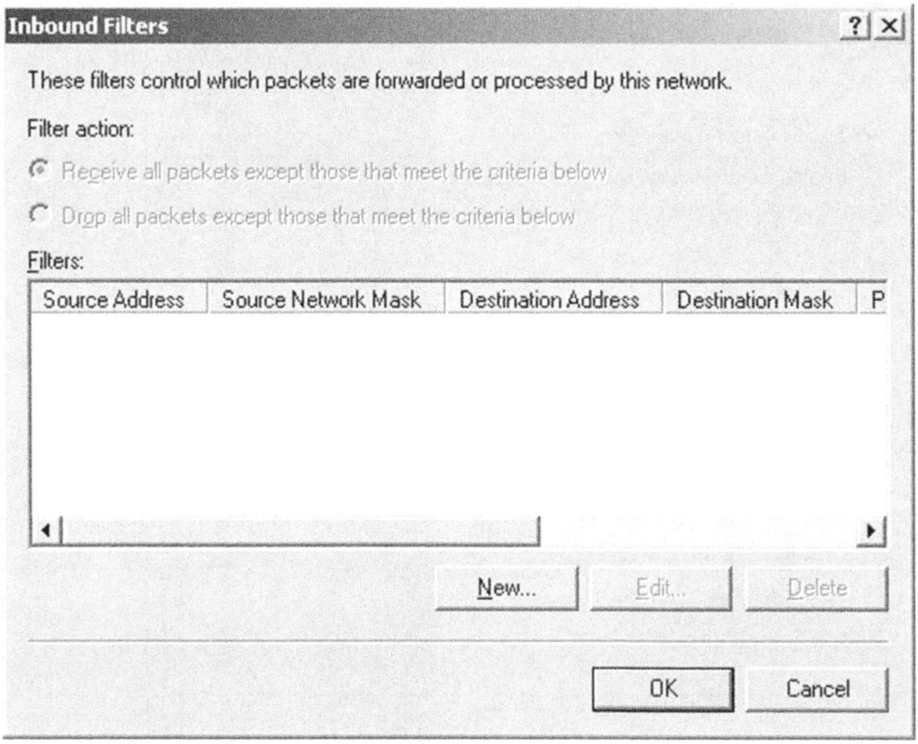

Figure 4-10: RRASLANinbound.

When you click on **New**, you will see the Add IP Filter dialog box. There you can configure the source and destination networks, and the protocol to filter. After you choose the protocol, you will then be able to configure a source and destination port, or a type and code in the case of ICMP traffic. Figure 4.11 shows you the protocol options available to you.

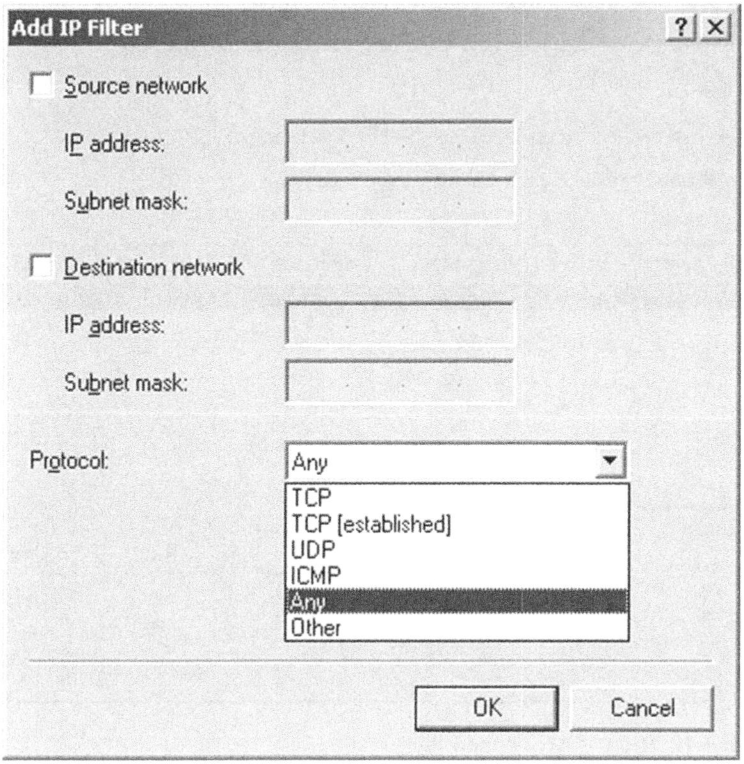

Figure 4-11: RRASLANinboundadd.

Filtering ICMP traffic is useful, for example, when you do not want an ICMP Echo Request (ping or tracert) to pass through your router. This is used both when a demand dial interface is configured and you only want actual data streams to instantiate the demand dial connection, and when you want to limit the exposure of your internal computers to probes from the public Internet.

After you have configured the protocol or protocols for the filter, you then need to define whether this will be an allow or an exclusion. Remember that you can either block all except, or allow all except. For this reason, packet filters are often referred to as using an exception list.

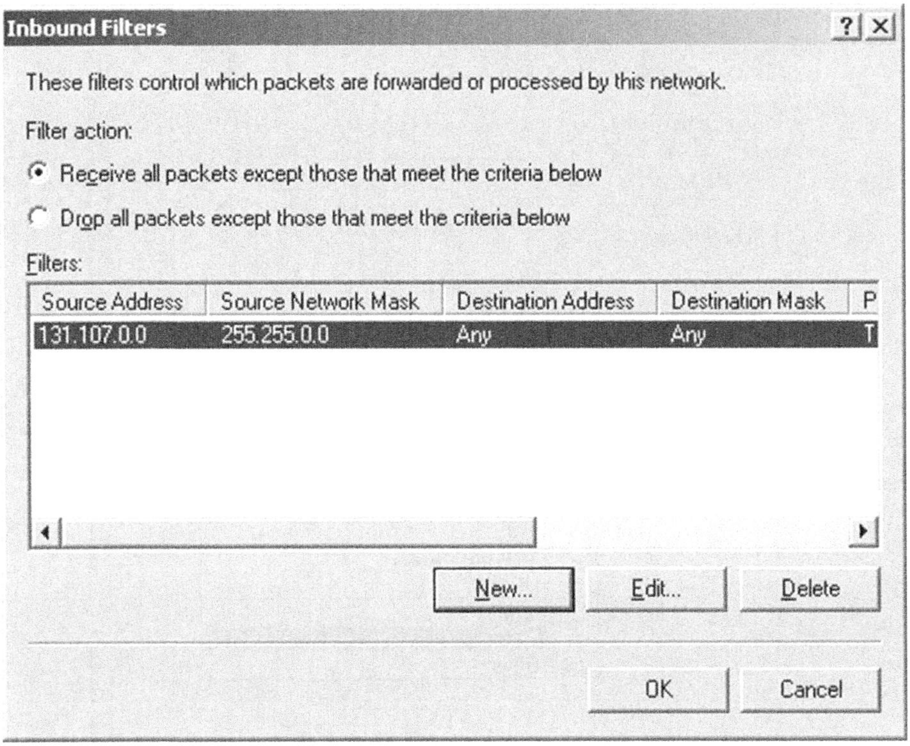

Figure 4-12: RRASLANinboundfilters.

When you have finished configuring filters, click on OK to return to the properties page for the interface, and OK again to apply the changes and close the properties page.

Pop Quiz 4.1

Pop Quiz 4.1 Questions

1. You know that RRAS is installed on your Windows Server 2003 but you cannot use the service. What do you need to do to troubleshoot this?
2. What can you do to stop Ping traffic across your router?
3. What is the first step to configuring a Routing Protocol?
4. What is the second step to configuring a Routing Protocol?
5. What is the third and final step to configuring a Routing Protocol?

Pop Quiz 4.1 Answers

1. Enable the service from the RRAS Management Console. Right-click and choose Action, then enable the service.
2. Use Packet Filtering.
3. Add the protocol to RRAS.
4.Add a minimum of one interface for the protocol in the RRAS console.
5. Configure the interfaces for use in the RRAS console.

4.2 Configure and Manage Remote Access

Now that we have explored the routing side of RRAS, lets dig in to the more commonly used aspect—providing network access to remote users or remote networks.

As you know, in any network environment, there are users who use computers directly connected to the LAN or Local Area Network. In some enterprises, there are users who are not directly connected to the LAN, but rather access network resources remotely. These users will either use an existing Internet connection to make a VPN or Virtual Private Networking connection to the LAN, or they will use a WAN technology to connect. In addition, some businesses have many locations connected to each other in the same way that remote users connect. In either case, a connection will need to be made between the remote computer or network and a remote access service connected to the LAN.

4.2.1 Remote Access Service Overview

The Windows Server 2003 RRAS service can be used to provide this access, by choosing the VPN/Remote Access role or by configuring VPN/Remote Access in the Configure and Enable Routing and Remote Access wizard.

As is the case with configuring routing, it is a good idea to practice both methods. Using the wizard gives you more immediate granularity, but you can always go back and fine-tune your configuration after setting up the basics.

It is very important that you work from the minimum permissions needed principle when implementing remote access, as it opens a door to the world through which unscrupulous people may attempt to gain unauthorized access. So, only enable what is needed—don't just open everything up because that is easier!

In a Windows Server 2003 remote access solution, there are many components that you need to configure. The obvious ones are the remote access service itself, and the clients that connect. In addition to this, however, you may need to support wireless clients, and you may need to configure Active Directory elements as well.

Before we get too far in, it is important to point out that every user who gains access to a network via the remote access server will need to have some kind of user account for authentication purposes. If that user account is local to the remote access server, then it can be configured to either allow/deny remote access OR control access through remote access policy. If, however, the remote access server is a member of a domain and the account used is a domain account, then certain conditions need to be met in order to control access through remote access policy.

That said, lets look at what the elements are in a remote access solution using Windows Server 2003 in more detail.

4.2.2 Remote Access Solution Elements

There are 4 main components to a remote access solution using Windows Server 2003. Your solution may not include all of these elements with all variations, but you should be familiar with all the variations for the certification exam.

Every solution has a Network Access Server. This is a computer, usually server class, on which Windows Server 2003 has been installed and on which RRAS has been configured to provide remote access.

Every solution also has Network Access Clients. These are either the end user computers or the network access servers on the remote network that are used to access the local network. The client may be VPN, dial-up or even wireless using 802.1x. Each has unique security needs that you will need to configure and support.

Every solution will have an authorization service, which is separate and distinct from the authentication service. Authorization is performed on the Network Access Server, while authentication may be handled elsewhere.

Every solution will need some form of authentication service, whether it is handled by the Network Access Server locally, uses Active Directory, EAP/TLS (for smart cards) or other certificate based authentication, or has some other form of authentication.

4.2.3 The Network Access Server

The Network Access Server is the gateway by which access to the internal network from the outside world happens. This is the computer running Windows Server 2003 RRAS configured as VPN/Network Access. There are a few things you need to know about how and what access will be available. First, you need to know whether clients will only be accessing resources on the network access server or will be going beyond the NAS to the internal network (this requires routing). In addition, you need to know how addressing will be handled—will it be a DHCP server or will you be using an address pool on the server? You need to consider the authentication methods, whether it is local to the server, using Active Directory, or using some other method such as RADIUS (Remote Authentication Dial-In User Service). You will need to know or define logging, but ONLY implement logging if you will regularly review the logs. If you are not going to review the logs, then simply don't make them. Finally, you need to know how PPP or the VPN protocol needs to be configured. Remember that the protocol is the common language that allows the computers on each end to communicate.

All of that information will be asked for in the wizard used for setting up a VPN/Remote Access server, so it is best to get it ahead of time. If you need to, you can always modify the port properties for the appropriate server after the wizard is complete.

4.2.4 Network Access Clients

Network access clients come in one of three flavors:

- VPN client using PPTP or L2TP
- Dial-up client
- Wireless client.

A VPN client, as mentioned earlier, establishes a session with the network access server using an existing connection to the public Internet. There are two protocols available for use, either PPTP (point-to-point tunneling protocol) or L2TP (layer 2 tunneling protocol). L2TP is more secure and is an Internet standard, though it does have limitations. Currently, only Windows 2000 or later operating systems support L2TP. In addition, not all NAT (network address translation) implementations support L2TP. PPTP is an older protocol, but also one that operating systems as early as Windows 95 support. It is somewhat less secure, but it is a viable option in a mixed computing environment.

Dial-up clients are the good old stand by. They are typically slower than a VPN connection in today's world of high-speed Internet access, but they are secure because a connection is made directly between the network access client and server. Typical dial-up connections include a modem (PSTN or POTS) or an ISDN adapter. VPN clients are a subset of dial-up, because a similar method is used to configure them on the client side, but you should consider VPN to be its own distinct access method.

Wireless clients are the newcomers to the network access client family. A wireless connection may be an infrared connection, but is more typically a WiFi or 802.1x implementation. Many different types of devices may be wireless clients, such as cell phones, PDAs and laptop or notebook computers with wireless network adapters installed.

4.2.5 Network Access Authentication and Authorization

As mentioned above, there is both an authentication process and an authorization process. Authentication means that the credentials of the user attempting the connection are validated. Those credentials may be local to the server, exist in Active Directory, or be handled through the RADIUS Server portion of the Internet Authentication Service. If the credentials are authenticated, the Network Access Server then proceeds to the Authorization phase where policies (if any) are checked and/or where permissions are evaluated. Only when both the authentication and authorization phases pass will access be allowed.

4.2.6 Network Access Authentication Methods

When it comes to the authentication side of the process, you have many options available to you. Always choose the strongest method that does not pose an undue burden on the network and your users.

The recommended method for authentication is smart cards, which use a certificate based system.

In order to use that method, however, you need to have a PKI (public key infrastructure) in place, install a computer certificate on the server providing remote access, configure the Smart Card or other TLS (transport layer security) EAP (extensible authentication protocol) in the remote access policy, be able to USE remote access policies, and configure Smart Card authentication on all remote access clients that will use that method. Sounds like a lot? It is—but when you consider that it is by far the most secure access method, it is easily worth it.

In addition to EAP/TLS, the following authentication methods are supported:

- CHAP
- PAP
- SPAP
- MS-CHAP
- MS-CHAPv2
- PEAP
- MD-5 Challenge.

CHAP stands for Challenge Handshake Authentication Protocol. It is probably the most widely supported, though not all that secure.

PAP stands for Password Authentication Protocol. A major drawback to this method is that the passwords are sent in plain text, which means that anyone with a sniffer between the client and the server can capture the password.

SPAP stands for Shiva Password Authentication Protocol, and is used by Shiva LANRover systems primarily. The password is encrypted, though lightly.

MS-CHAP stands for Microsoft Challenge Handshake Authentication Protocol. It is supported by Microsoft clients only, and then only from Windows 95 and up.

MS-CHAPv2 is the later version of the Microsoft Challenge Handshake Authentication Protocol, and is the default for Windows 2000 and later operating systems.

PEAP is Protected Extensible Authentication Protocol. It is used with 802.1x wireless systems. Of note is that access is granted based on user identity, rather than on a certificate. It also improves the encryption security for wireless networks.

MD-5 Challenge is Message Digest-5, and is used by EAP systems to provide authentication using standard name/password combinations.

You keep seeing this EAP character, too! EAP is Extensible Authentication Protocol, and extensible is just that. It provides a framework or infrastructure on which custom authentication solutions, such as PEAP, can be developed and implemented.

Now that we have covered the authentication protocols that can be used, lets explore the network access methods themselves. Remember that we have three methods to work from:

- Dial-up
- VPN
- Wireless.

Pop Quiz 4.2

Pop Quiz 4.2 Questions

1. What can be done to block network attacks on a Windows Server 2003?
2. Name three network Access clients.
3. If you want to implement a SMART Card-based authentication method, what do you have to have in place first?
4. Which authentication method is supported by Windows 2000 clients and higher?
5. What does the acronym RADIUS stand for on a Windows Server 2003?

Pop Quiz 4.2 Answers

1. Packet filtering is used to control traffic through a router so it can be a security defense against network attacks.
2. The three network access clients are: VPN, VPN Client using PPTP or L2TP or a dial up client.
3. You need to have a PKI (public key infrastructure) in setup, install a computer certificate on the server providing the remote access, configure the Smart Card or other TLS (transport layer security) EAP (extensible authentication protocol) in the remote access policy, be able to USE remote access policies, and configure Smart Card authentication on all remote access clients that will use that method.
4. MS-CHAPv2 is the default authentication method and is supported by Windows 2000 and Windows XP client operating systems.
5. The RADIUS acronym stands for Remote Authentication Dial-In User Service and is used for remote access on a Windows Server 2003.

4.3 Troubleshoot Routing and Remote Access Routing

4.3.1 Troubleshoot Demand-dial Routing

As mentioned before, the dial-up method is the good old stand by. Typically, you will either use a POTS (plain old telephone service)/PSTN (public switched telephone service) modem or an ISDN adapter for point-to-point dial-up connections. This is the same method you use if you connect to the Internet using a modem and, depending on the DSL service, can be the method used there as well.

From a hardware standpoint, the requirements on the client and server side are identical. To make an ISDN connection, both ends must have an ISDN adapter and ISDN service. For POTS, you need standard analog modems and a live phone line to plug into.

The password and data encryption requirements are typically non-existent, though you can encrypt both. It usually isn't done, however, both because of the connect speeds and because of the fairly robust native security—that security being native when the network access server performs the authentication.

The process of making a connection is pretty basic. The client initiates the connection, the server answers if possible, the server then authenticates and authorizes the client and the client has access either to the server or the entire network depending on configuration.

4.3.2 Troubleshoot Router-to-Router VPNs

Starting way back in the Windows 95 days, it became possible to make a virtual private connection to a remote network over the public Internet. This opened up the potential for telecommuters and remote workers, both of which save companies a considerable amount of money in terms of required office space.

Before we get into the support requirements, let's take a look at how a VPN connection works. First, the client and server need a connection to the Internet. That connection can be temporary such as a dial-up Internet connection on the client side, or it can be a more permanent connection such as DSL or cable 'modem.' I put modem in quotes because a modem is a device used to convert the digital signal from a computer into analog. ISDN, xDSL and cable systems that provide high-speed Internet access are all digital systems, so those devices cannot technically be called modems—no analog to convert to. You will find, however, that the DSL and cable interfaces are called modems, and often ISDN adapters are referred to as modems too.

Once a connection to the Internet is established, the client makes a new dial-up type connection over that existing connection to the VPN server. Instead of a phone number, though, either a host name or IP address is used. Using a host name allows for load balancing or round robin, which can be useful in higher volume environments.

So far, we have covered the client, server, the Internet (or other Transit Connection) and the VPN connection, or tunnel. It is important to understand that what is happening with a VPN connection. A tunnel is made inside which the data is transmitted. Another way to think of it is that the data is encapsulated.

In addition to the elements listed above, there is the tunneling protocol. As with any network communication method, a common protocol must be used so that both ends can communicate. With Windows Server 2003, you have two options—PPTP or L2TP. While L2TP was developed out of PPTP, you cannot use one to connect with the other.

As with any other remote access method, there are the elements of authorization and authentication. Once you have passed the authentication and authorization phases, data can flow over the existing VPN tunnel.

The most common use for a VPN connection is and has been remote user access to the network. Recently, however, companies have been turning to VPN to establish the data links between offices. The reason for this is primarily cost, since a dedicated line between offices at the same data rate is usually far more expensive than using the existing Internet connection in a slightly different way.

Care should be taken when using VPN to ensure that the ISP supports the use of the preferred tunneling protocol. I have had issues in the past where PPTP was not supported over a given vendor because they were using one of the protocol/port combinations used by a particular VPN implementation. As a result we were forced to roll back to a previous version.

4.3.3 Implementing and Supporting the Wireless Access Method

Well, it took us a while, but we have now caught up with current technology—and what is likely the future of network access.

Wireless access has been around for quite some time, but has only recently become standardized enough and fast enough for general uses. What has been around for quite some time is infrared, but it never really caught on beyond providing peripheral device access for laptop/notebook type computers. A few years ago, an emerging system called BlueTooth came on the scene, and you could say that with that the future of radio frequency-based wireless had come of age. Since then, we have been through a number of standards, the end result, at the time of this writing, being the 802.11 protocol set.

One challenge with the current wireless access methods is the lack of inherent security, but Microsoft and others are addressing that with a layer between the access method itself and the data transmission.

Windows XP and Windows Server 2003 have built-in extensive support for the 802.11 protocol set. There are a number of protocols associated with what has come to be known as WiFi (for Wireless Fidelity). 802.11 is the overall family. 802.11b was the first standard ratified, and provides data rates up to 11Mbps—as long as you are the only wireless device on that particular WAP. 802.11a came later, but offers a data rate up to 54Mbps. 802.11g is fairly new on the scene, and was intended as a replacement for both **A** and **B.** Its data rate is the same as **A**, though its range is less. It can, however, connect with either the 802.11a or 802.11b system.

One significant advantage to implementing a wireless network is speed of implementation—another is portability. While a traditional LAN requires you to pull cable, and potentially lots of it, a WLAN or Wireless LAN only requires a WAP or Wireless Access Point as a service concentrator.

In addition to the WiFi family, there is the 802.1x protocol. Primarily used for WLANs, it can also be used for traditional wired LANs. One key advantage to implementing 802.1x is that authentication occurs before access is granted. On the flip side, it requires a larger investment, both in terms of hardware and infrastructure. 802.1x can use either certificate-based or password-based authentication methods. There are a number of authentication protocols you can use with 802.1x, falling into two main families.

EAP	PEAP
EAP-TLS	PEAP-TLS
EAP-MS-CHAP v2	PEAP-MS-CHAP v2

Table 4—1: EAP MS-CHAP v2 AND PEAP MS-CHAP v2.

EAP-MS-CHAP v2 can be used with passwords, while the other methods are certificate based. With PEAP-MS-CHAP v2, certificates are required on the network access server, while PEAP-TLS needs certificates on both the network access server and on the client.

[Tip] Microsoft has a number of whitepapers on their Web site that will enhance your results both on the certification exam and in job performance. For wireless, see "Microsoft Wireless LAN Deployment and Best Practices." A good place to start when searching for whitepapers and other technical documentation is www.microsoft.com/technet.

So far, we have looked at a number of authentication protocols that can be used with RRAS. Next we are going to explore Remote Access Policies and then the Internet Authentication Service.

4.4 Configure Routing and Remote Access User Authentication

4.4.1 Configure Remote Access Authentication Protocols

As you may recall, I earlier said that there are two conditions under which you can configure user accounts to control access through remote access policies. One is when the account used for access is local to the network access server, and the other is when the domain account is part of a domain in the proper functional level. When a domain is in mixed mode, meaning domain controllers from NT4, Windows 2000 and Windows Server 2003 are supported, the domain accounts can not be configured to control access through remote access policy. In that case, the button itself will be dimmed, as will the associated configuration options. All that you will be able to do in that case is define on a case-by-case basis whether remote access is allowed or denied, with the default condition being denied.

When you CAN use remote access policies, however, life as a RAS admin is very nice! In order to use control access through remote access policy for domain accounts, the domain must either be in Windows 2000 Native or Windows Server 2003 mode. With remote access policies, you can control access based on the time of day, day of the week, type of computer, group membership and so on. The possibilities, while not truly endless, sometimes seem that way!

In addition, there is also the Dial-in permissions that you will need to configure. So, before we get into remote access policies, lets take a look at the dial-in permissions tab of a user account.

Figure 4.13 is a local user account, showing the dial-in tab of the account properties.

As you can see, there are five areas that you can configure.

Under Remote Access Permission (Dial-in or VPN), you can allow, deny or control access through remote access policy.

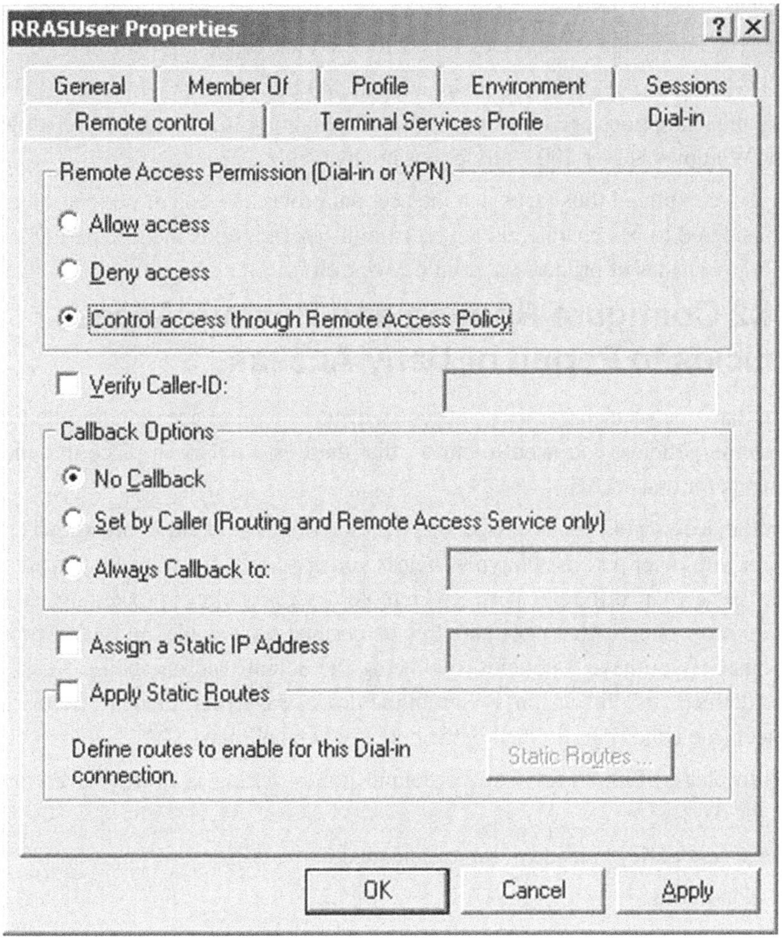

Figure 4-13: RRAS User Dial-in.

You can also use caller ID to verify that the number being used to make the connection is the same as what is configured in the account properties. This option is very secure, though limits users to a single set of computers in their home or a mobile computer with a built in cellular modem.

Under callback options, you can either set no callback, have the caller set the callback number or always callback to a particular number. Set by caller is not used for security, but rather to allow the user to reverse the charges.

Always callback to can be used as a security method, however, as access will not be granted until the network access server calls back the computer and it responds on the number configured in the user account.

You can assign a static address to a caller, which will override the settings in a remote access policy if one is used.

Likewise, you can assign static routes for a caller in their account properties.

Note that when the account is a domain account and the mode is Windows 2000 Mixed, only the callback options and allow or deny are available. If the domain is Windows 2000 Native or Windows Server 2003, all options are available.

What we have explored thus far is just the account properties side of permissions. This is really considered to be separate, however, from the permissions that are part of a remote access policy (shades of printers vs. print devices, eh?).

4.4.2 Configure Routing and Remote Access Policies to Permit or Deny Access

Once you have defined that a user account will have remote access controlled through remote access policies, you need to ensure that there is a policy in place that meets the requirements for that access.

With remote access policies, access is very cut and dried. You either are allowed, or you are not. As with other permission types, unless you are explicitly allowed, you are denied. What is somewhat different between remote access policy processing and other permission processing is that once an allow determination is made, no further processing occurs. Thus, if you have 3 policies, two being the default and one being a custom that you have defined, and the custom is first in the processing order, then any access attempt which meets the conditions defined in the policy will be allowed.

[Light bulb please] Remember that the default policy setting is to deny everyone at all times of the day!

A remote access policy is made of three elements:

- Conditions
- Permissions
- Profile.

Conditions are policy elements that include settings such as time of day, calling station ID, day of week and even the groups that a user is a member of. When processing a policy, condition is evaluated first. If the conditions for a policy are not met, then processing moves to the next policy in the processing order. If it is the last policy in the processing order, then the result is an implicit deny because the calling station did not meet any of the conditions of access. When conditions for a policy ARE met, the policy processing moves to the next stage—permissions evaluation.

Permissions are policy elements that are evaluated as soon as a condition is met. For example, the conditions on the second default remote access policy are that the everyone group, at all times of the day, on all days of the week, is denied access. So, if a user attempts a connection with the default remote access policy unmodified, they will meet the conditions of everyone group, time of day and day of week. As a result, policy processing will determine the permission applied under those conditions and in this case deny access.

[Light bulb please] Remember that once an allow or a deny is reached, no further processing occurs!

Figure 4.14 is the second default remote access policy. This is where you would edit or add conditions, edit the profile and define grant or deny remote access permission.

In the conditions section, you can add as many separate conditions as you would like. Remember that policy processing is an AND operation in a single policy, and an OR operation between policies. In Figure 4.15 are the conditions that can be set.

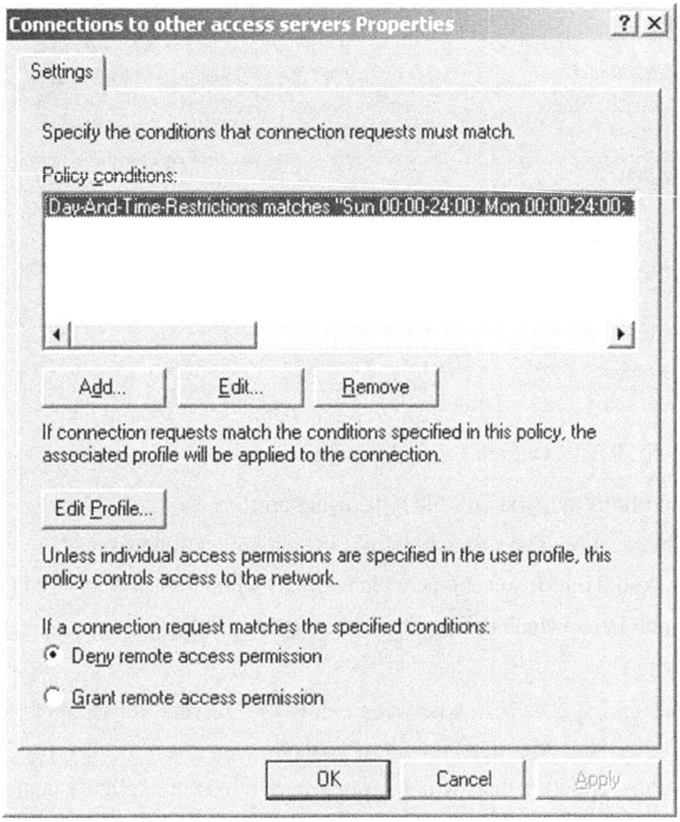

Figure 4-14: RRAS Default Policy2.

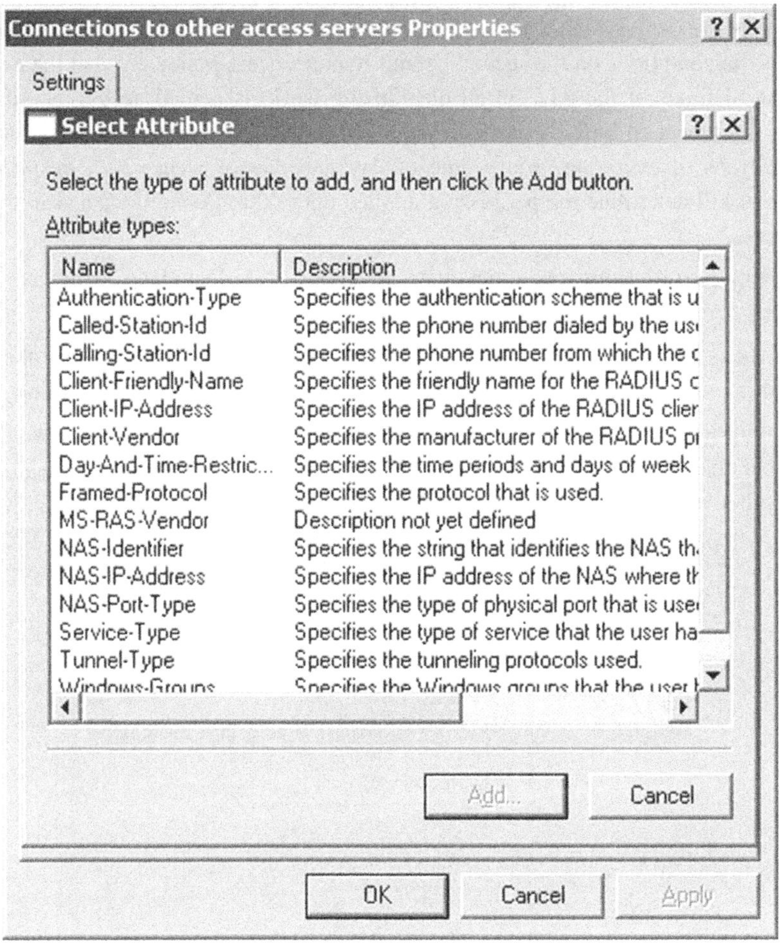

Figure 4-15: RRAS Default Policy2 Conditions.

Some key conditions that you will likely be using are:

- Authentication-Type, which defines the authentication protocol.
- Day-And-Time-Restrictions, which defines when access is allowed OR denied.
- Tunnel-Type, which defines the tunneling protocol.

If you are configuring a VPN link between two RRAS servers, for example, you must be sure that both are using the same tunneling protocol.

Windows-Groups, which defines which groups are allowed or explicitly denied access.

A remote access profile can be used to override the settings on the network access server, placing restrictions in a number of areas as shown below:

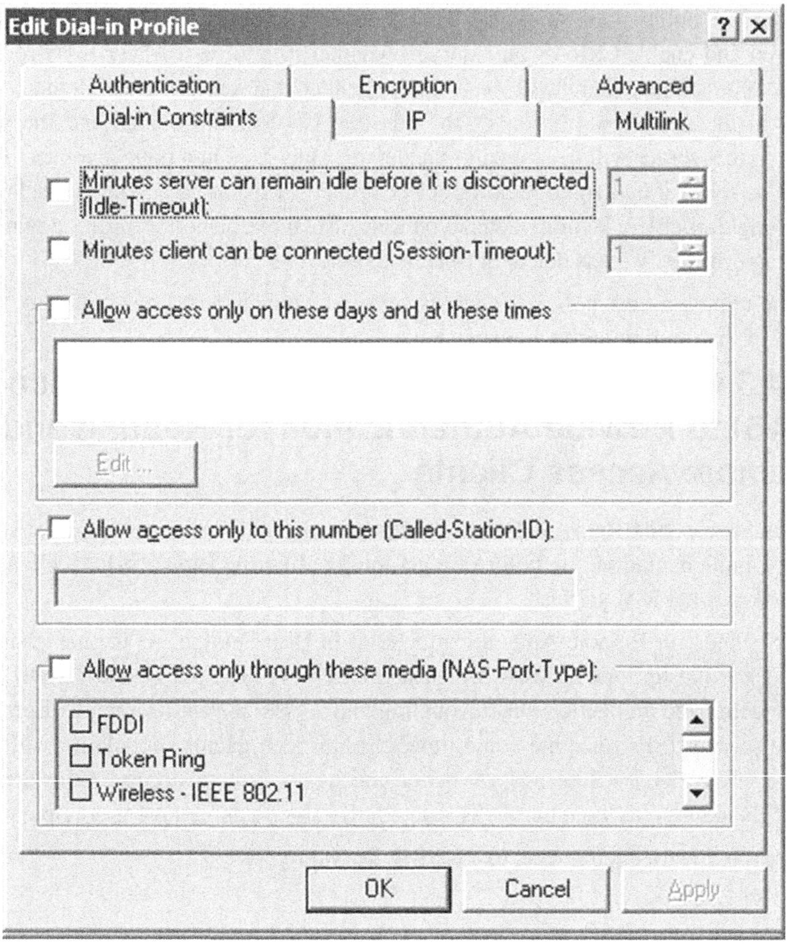

Figure 4-16: RRAS Default Policy2 Profile.

As you can see, just on the Dial-in Constraints tab there is a number of configuration options. You will find that some condition elements are duplicated here. Since the conditions and permissions are processed before the profile, you may find that some contradictory settings still work. What you should do, however, is make the setting in one place or the other. If, for example, you want to control access based on time, then set that as a condition rather than a profile element. Remember that conditions and permissions are evaluated first, while the profile is applied only after an access attempt is authorized.

Configuring a policy is done using the RRAS Management console. Once you have configured and enabled RRAS on a server, whether it is to be used for LAN routing or Remote Access/VPN, there will be a section under that server called Remote Access Policies in the tree view portion of the console. Choose that object, and the policies defined on that server will be shown in the details pane. To edit a policy, you can double-click on it, select it and right-click, or select properties from the action menu. From the context (right-click) or action menu, you can also move a policy up or down in the processing order, as well as delete or rename a policy.

When the remote access policies object is selected, you can add a new policy or modify the view of that portion of the management console.

4.4.3 Configure Internet Authentication Service (IAS) to Provide Authentication for Routing and Remote Access Clients

Windows Server 2003 IAS, or Internet Authentication Service, is an industry standard RADIUS implementation. So, before we get into configuring IAS for RRAS clients, let's take a look at what RADIUS is.

RADIUS stands for Remote Authentication Dial-In User Service. As the name suggests, it is used for dial-up type access—which includes VPN. The purpose of RADIUS is to provide centralized authentication, accounting and access control for remote users. It has been in use with ISPs for quite some time, but has been gaining popularity with use in corporate networks as a means of better managing remote access. Consider using RADIUS in medium to large networks with a fairly significant remote user population.

There are three main components to a RADIUS solution:

- RADIUS Server
- RADIUS Client
- RADIUS Proxy.

These names are not quite as self-explanatory as they seem! It is very important that you differentiate between the client and server components. That said, let's look at each of the components.

A **RADIUS Server** is a server that handles authentication and accounting services. The server or servers use a centralized database that can be a Kerberos realm, a flat file or a directory service. When using a file-based system, keep in mind that all RADIUS servers need to use the same file so that access is consistent. It is, after all, a means for centralized authentication!

A **RADIUS client** is an RRAS server—the server that actually provides the access. When an access attempt is made, the RADIUS client will send the authentication request to the configured RADIUS server or servers, rather than checking its local database. This can also be a WAP, or a RADIUS proxy. Anything that falls in the realm of remote access can be a RADIUS client, providing it has the necessary hardware and software/firmware.

A **RADIUS client** is similarly an access server, but one that is configured as a go-between. Often this is used in solutions where there are multiple RADIUS servers that a RADIUS client can use. By pointing the RADIUS client to the RADIUS proxy, you can offload logic processing on the client to the proxy, thereby freeing up resources for what the client does best—providing access.

Now let's look at **IAS** itself. Note that while RRAS is installed automatically, IAS is not. To install it, you must choose Internet Authentication Service from the Network Services portion of Add Windows Components in Add/Remove Programs. One of the biggest advantages to using IAS is centralized policies. When using remote access policies, they are stored on each RRAS server. If you have a couple of remote access servers, it is not too big of a deal to duplicate policies. If you have a large number of them, however, things can get kind of rough! IAS can solve this for you because you can use the IAS server as the central policy holder. Bear in mind that if you do configure RRAS to use an IAS server, any policy on the RRAS server will no longer be used.

In addition, if your IAS server is a domain member, it will use domain credentials only, which provides a single sign on solution.

The authentication processing flow, when using RADIUS/IAS, is only slightly more complicated than that of a more traditional Windows solution. First, the user instantiates the access attempt with the network access server—which is also the RADIUS/IAS client. Then the client sends the authentication request to the RADIUS/IAS server or proxy, as the case may be. From there, either the proxy forwards the request to the server or the server uses its configured database to process the authentication request. If the server is a domain member, then it will send the authentication request to a domain controller. After authentication occurs or fails, the server responds to the client request with either an access-accept or an access-reject.

If there are policies in place on the server, then the same processing method that you learned earlier applies. The authentication occurs, then the conditions are evaluated. Once there is a matching set of conditions, the permissions for that condition are evaluated. Once the permissions are determined to be allow, the profile (if any) is added to the mix, after which the information is returned to the client.

While this seems like a lot of overhead, it doesn't really add that much time to an access request and in the long run will save you time by providing a centralized management infrastructure for RRAS administration.

In order to use Active Directory, an IAS server must be authorized in Active Directory—much the same way a DHCP or RIS server is. If you do, as part of the process, the IAS Server computer account will be added to the RAS and IAS Servers security group. Don't remove them, because these groups have the necessary rights to access Active Directory user information.

Figure 4.17 shows the IAS console. As you may notice, this IAS server is not configured to process requests for any RADIUS clients, as there are no clients configured yet.

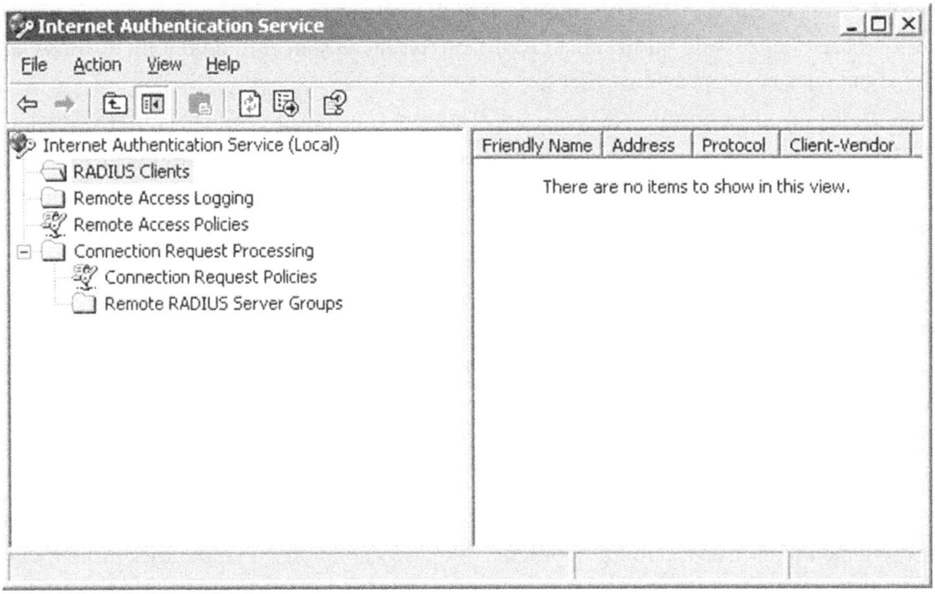

Figure 4-17: IAS Console.

Adding a client is done much the same way you have done everything else so far. Right-click on RADIUS clients or choose it, then click on the Action menu. From there, you choose to add a client.

When adding a RADIUS client, you need to specify (in order):

1. On the first screen of the wizard, you will configure:

   a. Client Friendly Name – this is the name you will have this IAS server display in the IAS console.

   b. Client Address – this can be either the IP address or DNS name of the client.

2. On the second screen of the wizard, you will configure:

   a. Client Vendor – you have a drop down list where you choose the RADIUS client vendor. The default is standard, but you can specify a different vendor if necessary.

b. Shared Secret/Confirm Shared Secret – this is where you configure the password that a RADIUS client will use so that it can be authenticated by the IAS server. The shared secret can be up to 255 characters long, and as with any password longer is more secure.

c. Request must contain the Message Authenticator attribute – here you can choose whether or not the RADIUS client includes a digital signature for PAP, CHAP and MS-CHAP authentication. IAS always requires the signature for EAP authentication, so if you are using EAS make sure to check this option.

On the RRAS server providing network access, or any other server type performing the same function, you will need to configure it to point to the IAS server you just configured. To do that with RRAS, click on the server name of the RRAS server, then either right-click or action and then properties. Click on the security tab, and instead of Windows Authentication change it to RADIUS. Once you have chosen RADIUS for authentication (and optionally accounting as well), you will need to configure the RADIUS server(s) to use. To do this, you will click on configure and then add. Fill in the IP address, configure the shared secret, and you are good to go!

[Light bulb please] Important! After configuring RRAS to use RADIUS for authentication, you will need to restart the service. Click on action, restart to restart the RRAS service.

Chapter 4: Review Questions

1. Which of the following statements accurately describe RIP?

A. RIP doesn't dynamically build routing tables.

B. Routers connected to RIP interfaces receive routing table announcements.

C. The routers that receive RIP announcements then compile their own routing table.

D. RIP dynamically builds routing tables.

E. Routers connected to RIP interfaces don't receive routing table announcements.

---

2. Which of the following steps are necessary when adding a routing interface to a protocol in Server 2003?

A. In the Manage Your Server console tree, right-click the routing protocol to which you want to add an interface, and then click New Interface.

B. In the Routing and Remote Access console tree, right-click the routing protocol to which you want to add an interface, and then click New Interface.

C. In the New Interface dialog box, select the appropriate interface, and then click OK.

D. In the New RIP Interface dialog box, select the appropriate interface, and then click OK.

3. Which of the following would allow clients on one subnet or network segment to connect to clients on another subnet or network segment?

A. Manually entering different default gateways on each of the clients

B. Manually entering different subnet masks on each of the clients

C. Setting up a server that connects the network segments to enable IP routing

D. Setting up a server that uses the same IP addresses on both interfaces

---

4. Which of the following protocol combinations would be the most secure for use with dial-in and Windows 2003 computers?

A. L2TP and IPSec

B. L2TP and MPPE

C. MS-CHAP v2 and MPPE

D. EAP-CHAP and MPPE

5. Which of following will allow you to encrypt business traffic from the client or customer to the Web site?

A. SSL (Secure Socket Layer)

B. Integrated Windows Authentication

C. Digest authentication

D. EFS (Encrypting File System)

---

6. Which of the following commands will allow you to view the routing table in Windows 2003?

A. route print

B. nbtstat -r

C. netstat -r

D. route view

7. You need to use your Windows Server 2003 computer to route packets between two networks. You have properly configured the IP Forwarding box, assigned the network cards an IP address to share and created a static route for each network to which you need to route. What else will you need to do to use this computer as a router?

A. Assign each of the network cards a unique default gateway.

B. Assign each of the network cards a unique subnet mask.

C. Assign the network cards valid IP addresses. They cannot share the same IP address.

D. Nothing, it is configured properly.

---

8. If a RRAS server isn't configured, what color arrow will it have next to it?

A. Black

B. Green

C. Blue

D. Yellow

E. Red

9. How can you make a new network connection?

A. Right-click My Network Places to bring up Network and Dial-up Connections. Select the Make New Connection icon.

B. Right-click My Computer to bring up Network and Dial-up Connections. Select the Make New Connection icon.

C. Left-click My Network Places to bring up Network and Dial-up Connections. Select the Make New Connection icon.

D. Left-click My Computer to bring up Network and Dial-up Connections. Select the Make New Connection icon.

---

10. The Internet Authentication Service includes which of the following?

A. Clients

B. Remote Access Policies

C. Remote Access Logging

D. Remote Access Switching

11. Which of the following services is not available with IIS?

A. DHCP

B. FTP

C. NNTP

D. SNMP

E. DNS

---

12. With IIS, what kind of sites can we set up?

A. SMTP sites

B. Web sites

C. DHCP sites

D. DNS sites

E. FTP sites

13. Which of the following is a requirement for RIS?

A. You need only two local computers.

B. Member server with CD images of RIP Prep images.

C. You need a DC (Domain Controller).

D. You need only a local computer.

---

14. How do you raise the domain functional level to Windows 2003 on a domain controller?

A. Open Active Directory Domains and Trusts. Right-click the appropriate domain, and then click Raise Domain Functional Level. In the Raise Domain Functional Level dialog box, select Windows Server 2003, and then click Raise.

B. Open Computer Management. Right-click the appropriate domain, and then click Raise Domain Functional Level. In the Raise Domain Functional Level dialog box, select Windows Server 2003, and then click Raise.

C. Open My Computer. Right-click the appropriate domain, and then click Raise Domain Functional Level. In the Raise Domain Functional Level dialog box, select Windows Server 2003, and then click Raise.

D. Open Active Directory Domains and Trusts. Double-click the appropriate domain, and then click Raise Domain Functional Level. In the Raise Domain Functional Level dialog box, select Windows Server 2003, and then click Raise.

15. With what messages can a RADIUS server respond?

A. Encryption message

B. Access-Reject message

C. Access-Accept message

D. Decryption message

Chapter 4: Review Answers

1. Which of the following statements accurately describe RIP?

A. RIP doesn't dynamically build routing tables.

***B. Routers connected to RIP interfaces receive routing table announcements.**

***C. The routers that receive RIP announcements then compile their own routing table.**

***D. RIP dynamically builds routing tables.**

E. Routers connected to RIP interfaces don't receive routing table announcements.

Explanation: RIP dynamically builds routing tables by announcing the contents of its routing table to its configured interfaces. Routers connected to those interfaces receive these announcements and use them to build the appropriate routing tables. The routers that receive the announcements then compile their own routing table, which is then transmitted to other routers. This process continues in a manner that should provide each configured router with the routes from each of the other routers.

---

2. Which of the following steps are necessary when adding a routing interface to a protocol in Server 2003?

A. In the Manage Your Server console tree, right-click the routing protocol to which you want to add an interface, and then click New Interface.

***B. In the Routing and Remote Access console tree, right-click the routing protocol to which you want to add an interface, and then click New Interface.**

***C. In the New Interface dialog box, select the appropriate interface, and then click OK.**

D. In the New RIP Interface dialog box, select the appropriate interface, and then click OK.

Explanation: To add a routing interface to a protocol, access the Routing and Remote Access console. In the Routing and Remote Access console tree, right-click the routing protocol to which you want to add an interface, and then click New Interface. In the New Interface dialog box, select the appropriate interface, and then click OK. If applicable, complete any configuration required for the interface. To view installed and configured routing interfaces in the Routing and Remote Access console, click Routing Interfaces in the console tree.

3. Which of the following would allow clients on one subnet or network segment to connect to clients on another subnet or network segment?

A. Manually entering different default gateways on each of the clients

B. Manually entering different subnet masks on each of the clients

***C. Setting up a server that connects the network segments to enable IP routing**

D. Setting up a server that uses the same IP addresses on both interfaces

Explanation: Enabling IP routing will allow IP packets to be routed to either subnet. Different default gateways and subnet masks on each client will only hinder or halt communication between the clients. The same is true if there aren't different IP addresses for each interface on the server being used as a router.

---

4. Which of the following protocol combinations would be the most secure for use with dial-in and Windows 2003 computers?

***A. L2TP and IPSec**

B. L2TP and MPPE

C. MS-CHAP v2 and MPPE

D. EAP-CHAP and MPPE

Explanation: L2TP is required for IPSec and IPSec needs to be used by both the client and the server. MS-CHAP v2 and MPPE are good but aren't as secure as L2TP and IPSec. EAP-TLS is supported by Windows 2003, but not EAP-CHAP.

5. Which of following will allow you to encrypt business traffic from the client or customer to the Web site?

***A. SSL (Secure Socket Layer)**

B. Integrated Windows Authentication

C. Digest authentication

D. EFS (Encrypting File System)

Explanation: Of the choices available, SSL is the only choice for secure transport of data on the Internet (because of its ability to encrypt data).

---

6. Which of the following commands will allow you to view the routing table in Windows 2003?

***A. route print**

B. nbtstat -r

***C. netstat -r**

D. route view

Explanation: To view the IP routing table on a computer running Windows Server 2003, type 'route print' at the command prompt. You can also use the netstat -r command.

7. You need to use your Windows Server 2003 computer to route packets between two networks. You have properly configured the IP Forwarding box, assigned the network cards an IP address to share and created a static route for each network to which you need to route. What else will you need to do to use this computer as a router?

A. Assign each of the network cards a unique default gateway.

B. Assign each of the network cards a unique subnet mask.

***C. Assign the network cards valid IP addresses. They cannot share the same IP address.**

D. Nothing, it is configured properly.

Explanation: IP addresses on the same network have to be unique.

---

8. If a RRAS server isn't configured, what color arrow will it have next to it?

A. Black

B. Green

C. Blue

D. Yellow

***E. Red**

Explanation: If a RRAS server isn't configured, it will have a red arrow next to it.

9. How can you make a new network connection?

***A. Right-click My Network Places to bring up Network and Dial-up Connections. Select the Make New Connection icon.**

B. Right-click My Computer to bring up Network and Dial-up Connections. Select the Make New Connection icon.

C. Left-click My Network Places to bring up Network and Dial-up Connections. Select the Make New Connection icon.

D. Left-click My Computer to bring up Network and Dial-up Connections. Select the Make New Connection icon.

Explanation: To make a new network connection, right-click My Network Places to bring up Network and Dial-up Connections. Select the Make New Connection icon.

---

10. The Internet Authentication Service includes which of the following?

***A. Clients**

***B. Remote Access Policies**

***C. Remote Access Logging**

D. Remote Access Switching

Explanation: Clients, Remote Access Logging and Remote Access Policies are all available in Internet Authentication Service.

11. Which of the following services is not available with IIS?

A. DHCP

B. FTP

C. NNTP

D. SNMP

***E. DNS**

Explanation: IIS supports FTP, NNTP, WWW and NNTP.

---

12. With IIS, what kind of sites can we set up?

A. SMTP sites

***B. Web sites**

C. DHCP sites

D. DNS sites

***E. FTP sites**

Explanation: FTP sites and Web sites can be set up with IIS.

13. Which of the following is a requirement for RIS?

A. You need only two local computers.

***B. Member server with CD images of RIP Prep images.**

***C. You need a DC (Domain Controller).**

D. You need only a local computer.

Explanation: You need a DC (Domain Controller) or a member server with CD images of RIP Prep images when using RIS.

---

14. How do you raise the domain functional level to Windows 2003 on a domain controller?

***A. Open Active Directory Domains and Trusts. Right-click the appropriate domain, and then click Raise Domain Functional Level. In the Raise Domain Functional Level dialog box, select Windows Server 2003, and then click Raise.**

B. Open Computer Management. Right-click the appropriate domain, and then click Raise Domain Functional Level. In the Raise Domain Functional Level dialog box, select Windows Server 2003, and then click Raise.

C. Open My Computer. Right-click the appropriate domain, and then click Raise Domain Functional Level. In the Raise Domain Functional Level dialog box, select Windows Server 2003, and then click Raise.

D. Open Active Directory Domains and Trusts. Double-click the appropriate domain, and then click Raise Domain Functional Level. In the Raise Domain Functional Level dialog box, select Windows Server 2003, and then click Raise.

Explanation: To raise the domain functional level to Windows 2003, open Active Directory Domains and Trusts. Right-click the appropriate domain, and then click Raise Domain Functional Level. In the Raise Domain Functional Level dialog box, select Windows Server 2003, and then click Raise.

15. With what messages can a RADIUS server respond?

A. Encryption message

***B. Access-Reject message**

***C. Access-Accept message**

D. Decryption message

Explanation: A RADIUS server receives and processes connection requests or accounting messages from RADIUS clients or RADIUS proxies. In the case of connection requests, the RADIUS server processes the list of RADIUS attributes in the connection request. Based on a set of rules and the information in the user account database, the RADIUS server either authenticates and authorizes the connection and sends back an Access-Accept message or sends back an Access-Reject message.

Maintaining a Network Infrastructure

The objective of this chapter is to provide the reader with an understanding of the following:

Monitor network traffic. Tools might include:

- **Network Monitor**
- **System Monitor.**

Troubleshoot connectivity to the Internet.

Troubleshoot server services.

- **Diagnose and resolve issues related to service dependency.**
- **Use service recovery options to diagnose and resolve service-related issues.**

Chapter 5: Maintaining a Network Infrastructure

Getting Ready Questions

1. What kind of address is associated with a frame?

2. On the toolbar of System Manager, what icon would you click on to add a counter?

3. If you wanted to highlight a trace in System Monitor, what would you click after you selected the counter in the bottom frame?

4. For a remote computer with an IP address of 192.168.0.100, what command would you enter to get its machine name, MAC address and domain or workgroup?

5. What command would you use to see the mapped network drives on your computer?

Getting Ready Answers

1. MAC address
2. The Plus Sign icon
3. Cntl-H
4. Nbtstat –a 192.168.0.100
5. Net use

5.1 Monitor Network Traffic

Network Monitor allows you to gather information for analysis. The results of that analysis will help you to prevent, diagnose and solve a variety of network problems.

5.1.1 Network Monitor

By configuring Network Monitor in different fashions, you can gather specific information. Triggers can be set up so that when certain incidents occur, Network Monitor will start or stop capturing information. As well, you can set up filters to separate out what type of information Network Monitor captures or displays. These filters can be configured to capture frames based on criteria such as source address, destination address or protocol.

> **Note:** Network Monitor on Server 2003 can capture frames that are sent to or from the computer on which it is installed. If you want to capture frames that are sent to or from a remote computer, you must use the full version of Network Monitor that comes with Microsoft Systems Management Server. This version can capture frames sent to or from any computer on which the Network Monitor driver is installed. The Network Monitor driver can be installed through the Windows Components Wizard in Control Panel.

The information that Network Monitor provides comes from the network traffic itself, which is divided into frames. Each frame contains the following information:

- **Source address** – The address of the network adapter from which the frame originated.
- **Destination address** – The address of the network adapter that is meant to receive the frame. This address can also specify a group of network adapters.
- **Header information** – Information specific to each protocol used to send the frame.
- **Data** – The information (or a portion of it) being sent.

Every computer on a network segment receives frames transmitted on that segment. The network adapter in each computer processes only those frames that are addressed specifically to it. The rest of the frames, with the exception of broadcast and multicast frames, are dropped.

By default, Network Monitor is not installed on Server 2003. To install, use the **Add/Remove Windows Components** section of **Add/Remove Programs** under **Control Panel**.

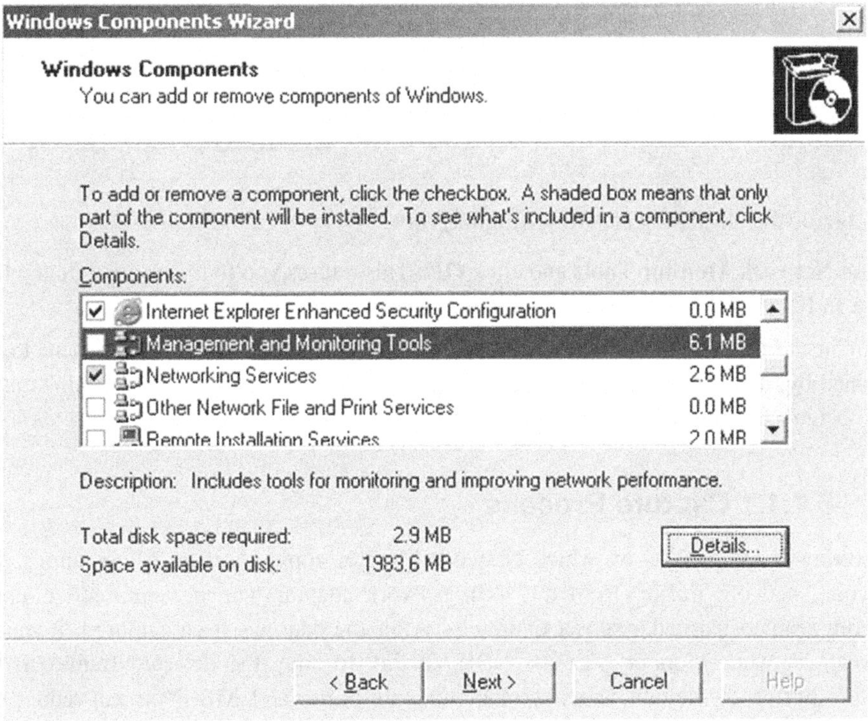

Figure 5-1: Windows Components Wizard.

Highlight Management and Monitoring Tools and click Details. The dialog box in Figure 5.2 appears.

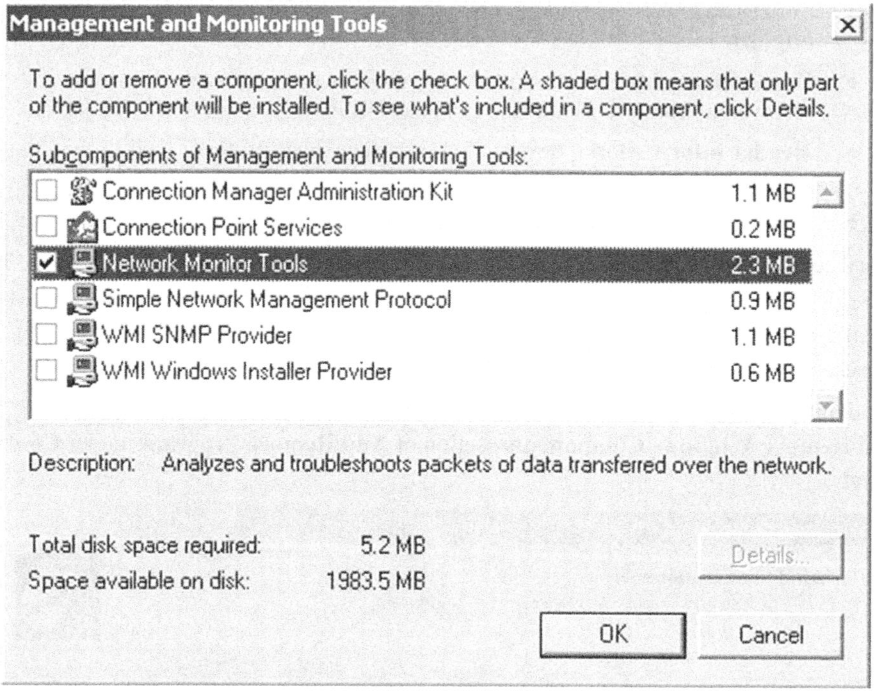

Figure 5-2: Installing Network Monitor Tools.

Select **Network Monitor Tools** and click **OK**. This returns you to the original dialog box show in Figure 5.1. Clicking **Next** will continue the installation process.

After installing Network Monitor, it can be used to capture all the frames sent to, or retained by, the network adapter of the computer on which it is installed. Administrators can design a capture filter so that only certain frames are captured.

5.1.1.1 Capture Process

Capturing is the process by which Network Monitor copies frames. All incoming and outgoing network traffic (from the local network adaptor) can be captured or, using filtering, only a particular subset of frames. After the data has been captured, it can be viewed. Network Monitor uses the NDIS facility to copy the detected frames to the capture buffer. By default, the size of the capture buffer is 1 MB. You can reduce the amount of data you capture by shrinking the capture buffer.

While Network Monitor is capturing frames from the network, statistics about these frames appear in the Capture window. There are four panes in the Capture Window:

- **Graph** – A graphical representation of frames sent to or from the local computer.
- **Session Statistics** – Statistics about current individual sessions.
- **Station Statistics** – Statistics about frames sent to or from the computer running Network Monitor.
- **Total Statistics Summary** – Statistics about frames sent to or from the local computer since the capture process began.

The steps to capture network frames are as follows:

- To start Network Monitor, click Start | Control Panel | Administrative Tools | Network Monitor.
- If prompted, select the local network from which you want to capture data by default.
- On the Capture menu, click Buffer Settings, and then set the buffer and frame size as appropriate.
- On the Capture menu, click Start.

> Note: To run Network Monitor, you must be a member of the Administrators group on the local computer, or you must have been delegated the appropriate authority. If the computer is joined to a domain, members of the Domain Admins group may be able to perform this procedure.

5.1.2 System Monitor

System Monitor and Performance Logs and Alerts are both found in the Performance Console in Server 2003. Performance can be found under Administrative Tools in Control Panel.

System Monitor allows you to view real time performance of your server. You can capture this data in a log as well, so that you can view it at a later time. When you first open System Monitor, you will notice that nothing is being tracked. This is because you must first set counters to monitor the particular process in which you are interested. These counters will be displayed on the screen.

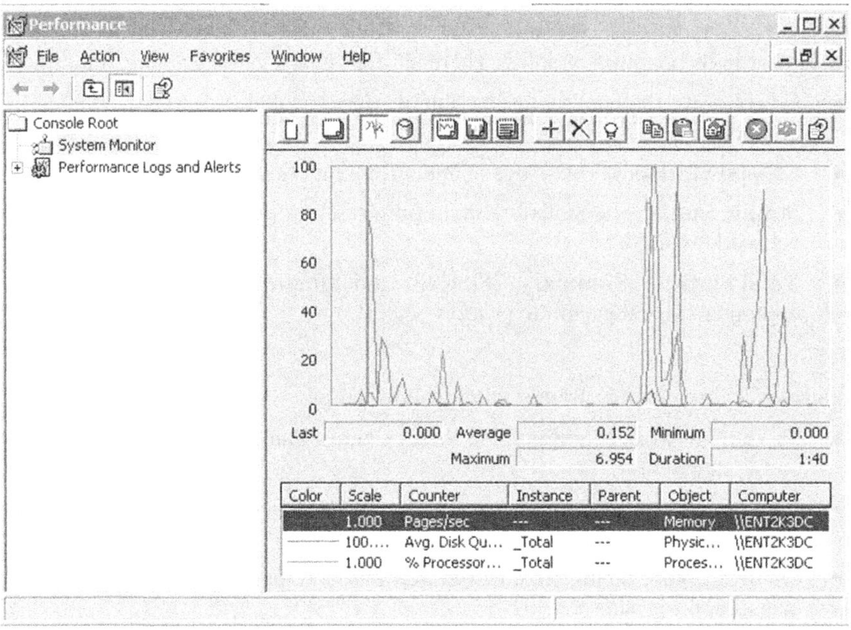

Figure 5-3: System Monitor.

There are three views available to you in System Monitor:

- **Chart** – (The default view) allows you to view a small number of counters over a set period of time.
- **Histogram** – (Bar chart) allows you to view a large number of counters as a snapshot.
- **Report** – Allows you to view the counters in text format in real time.

Using the Performance Logs and Alerts will allow you to create counter and trace logs, as well as define alerts. You can use this tool to collect logged data that can be used for detailed analysis and record keeping.

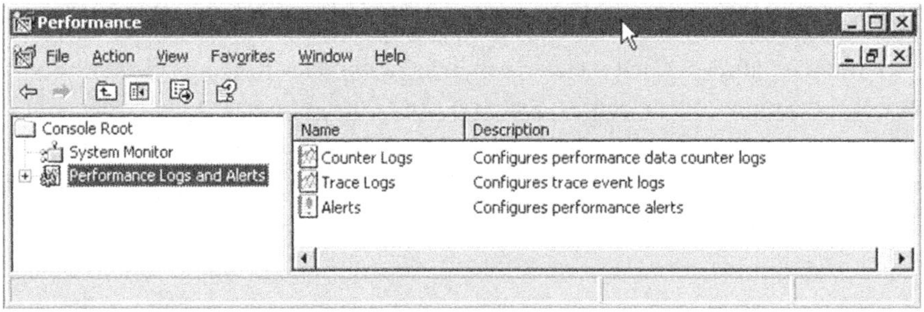

Figure 5-4: Performance Logs and Alerts.

The three logs available to you through Performance Logs and Alerts are:

- **Counter logs** – record data about hardware usage and activity on a system. You can configure logging to occur on a regular basis, or on-demand. As an administrator, you should plan how often to collect data, based on the type of results you need to obtain.

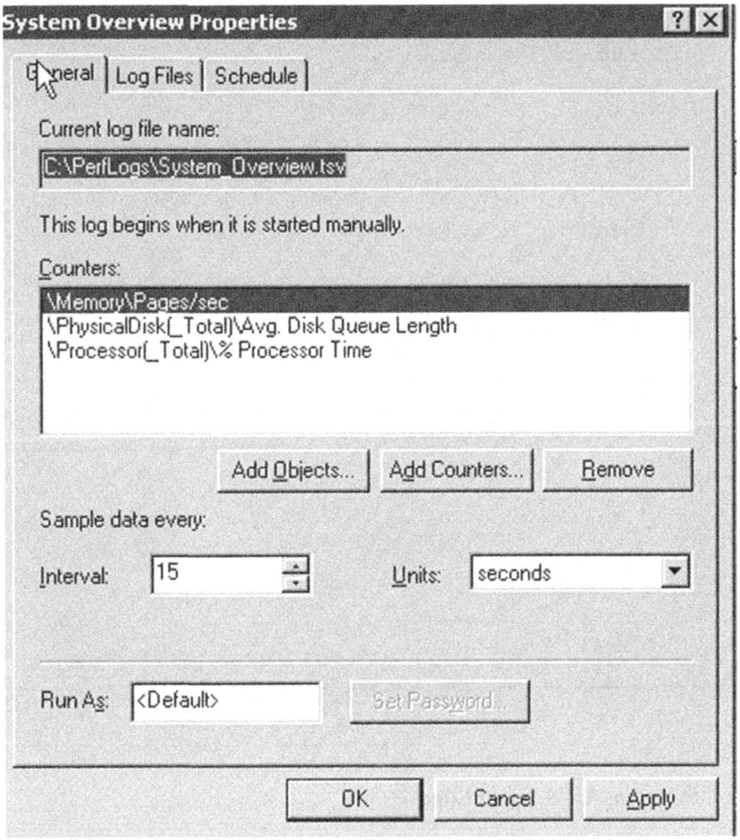

Figure 5-5: Setting Up a Counter Log.

- **Trace logs** – measure data on a continuous basis.

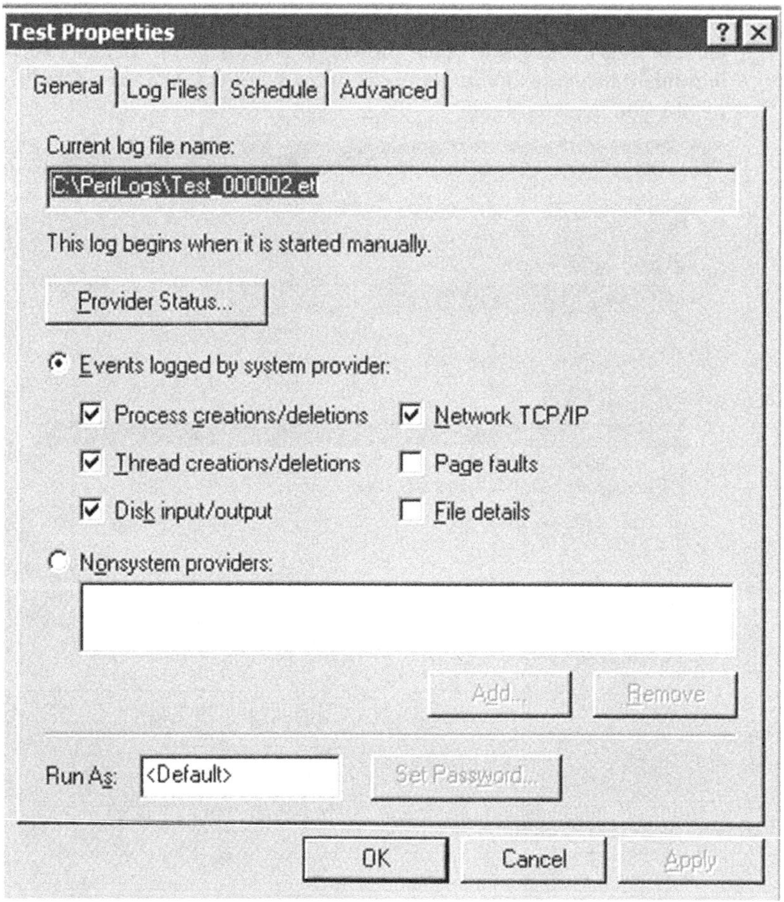

Figure 5-6: Setting Up a Trace Log.

- **Alerts** – are messages that are sent to the system administrator when a specific counter exceeds, or falls below, a predetermined setting.

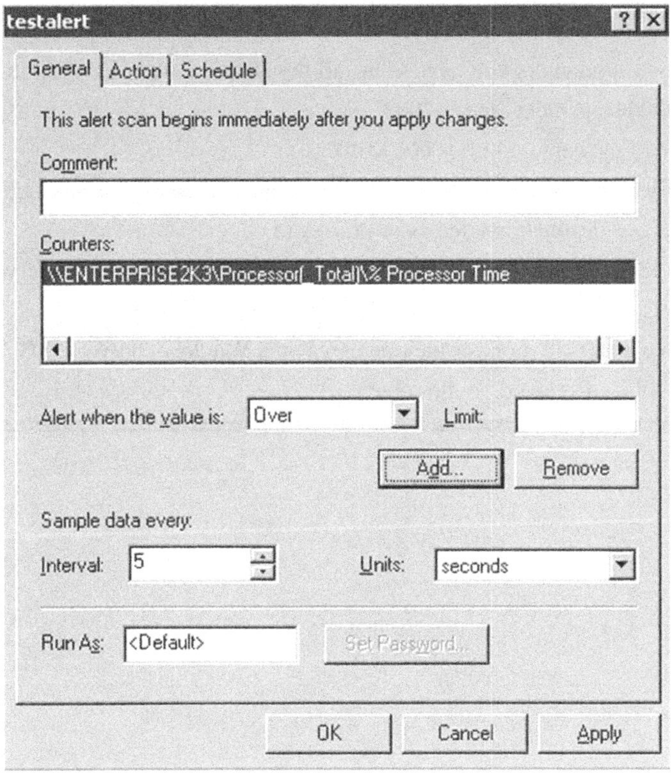

Figure 5-7: Setting Up An Alert.

Pop Quiz 5.1

Pop Quiz 5.1 Questions

1. What can be used to monitor network traffic on a remote computer?
2. What is the default size buffer of a capture using Network Monitor?
3. What type of criteria can be used to capture network traffic with filters?
4. What utility can be used to capture real time network statistics on a Windows Server 2003?
5. What do you have to do to begin captures using System Monitor on a Windows Server 2003?

Pop Quiz 5.1 Answers

1. For remote computers you have to install the Network Monitor version included in Systems Management Server 2003.
2. The size of the capture buffer is 1 MB3.
3. These filters can be configured to capture frames based on criteria such as source address, destination address or protocol
4. System Monitor allows you to view real time performance of your server. Capture this data in a log so that you can view it at a later time
5. First set counters to monitor the processes on a Windows Server 2003. These counters will be displayed on the screen.

5.2 Troubleshoot Connectivity to the Internet

If you want to troubleshoot a TCP/IP networking problem, first check the TCP/IP configuration of the computer that is experiencing the problem.

5.2.1 Ipconfig.exe

Ipconfig.exe will give you the current TCP/IP configuration on the system. To run this command, use the following steps:

- Click **Start**, click **Run**, type **cmd** in the Open box and then press **Enter**.
- At the command prompt, type **ipconfig**, and then press **Enter**. This command returns your computer's DNS suffix, IP address, subnet mask and default gateway. If you want more detailed information, such as the IP address configured for DNS and WINS, type **ipconfig /all** instead at the command prompt.
- Confirm that your computer has the appropriate settings for DNS and WINS servers, an available IP address, the correct subnet mask, the correct default gateway and the correct host name.

5.2.2 Nbtstat.exe

NetBIOS over TCP/IP resolves NetBIOS names to IP addresses. TCP/IP provides many choices for NetBIOS name resolution, including local cache lookup, WINS server query, broadcast, DNS server query and LMHOSTS and HOSTS lookup. Nbtstat.exe is a handy tool for troubleshooting NetBIOS name resolution problems. You can use the Nbtstat.exe command to eliminate or amend preloaded entries.

The following lists common Nbtstat commands and the reasons why you may use them in your troubleshooting process.

> **NOTE**: Nbtstat switches are frequently case sensitive. Make sure you use the upper or lowercase switch as indicated in the list.

- To list the NetBIOS table of the local computer, type nbtstat -n at the command prompt, and then press Enter. This returns the NetBIOS local name table, which will specify whether each name is a unique name or a group name and whether the name is registered or unregistered on the network.
- To list the contents of the NetBIOS name cache, type nbtstat -c at the command prompt, and then press Enter. This command displays the NetBIOS name cache, which contains name-to-address mappings for other computers.
- To clear the contents of the name cache and reload it from the LMHOSTS file (if one is used), type nbtstat -R at the command prompt, and then press Enter.

- To display the name table of a remote computer, type nbtstat -a RemoteComputerName (where RemoteComputerName is the NetBIOS computer name of the remote computer) at the command prompt, and then press Enter.
- To display a list of client and server connections, type nbtstat -s at the command prompt, and then press Enter. This command lists the current NetBIOS sessions and their status, including statistics, as shown in the following example.

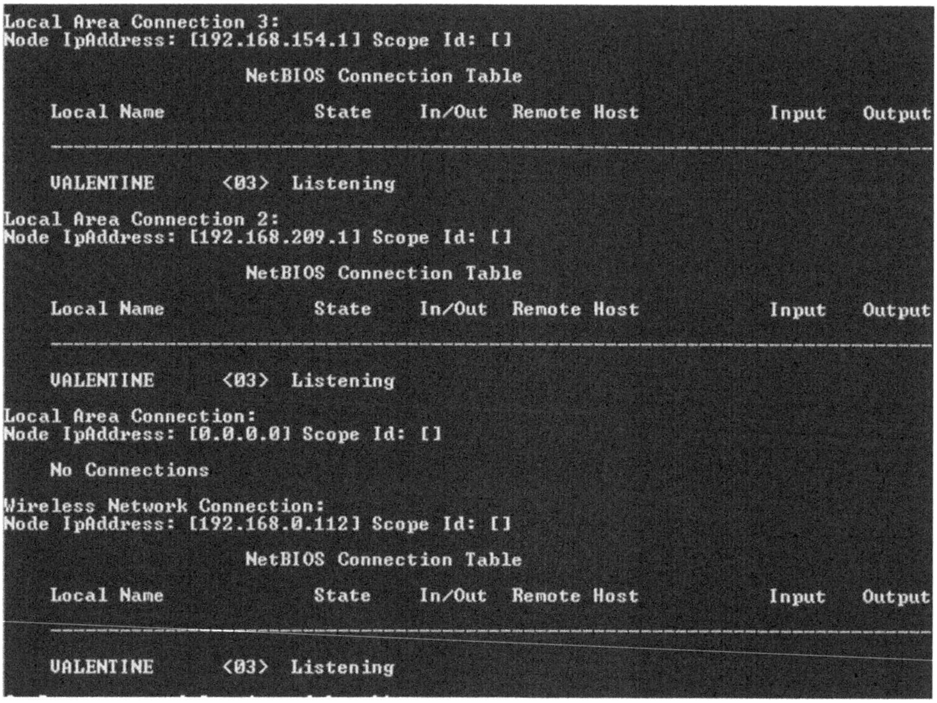

Figure 5-8: NBTSTAT –s.

> **NOTE**: To see additional switches for Nbtstat.exe, type **nbtstat /?** at the command prompt.

5.2.3 PING and TRACERT

If you cannot connect to a remote server, there are two helpful tools that can be used—PING and TRACERT. Use PING to verify that a host computer can connect to the TCP/IP network and network resources. Use TRACERT to examine the route taken to a destination.

Let's first look at the PING command. You can use PING as a troubleshooting tool to successively test connectivity to different network resources. The steps taken to "ping" a network host directly are as follows:

- Click **Start**, click **Run**, type **cmd** in the **Open** box and then press **Enter**.
- Type one of the following lines (Figure 5.9 or Figure 5.10), and then press **Enter**, where *IPAddressOfRemoteHost* is the IP address of the computer that you want to connect to, and *HostName* is the name of the computer that you want to connect to:

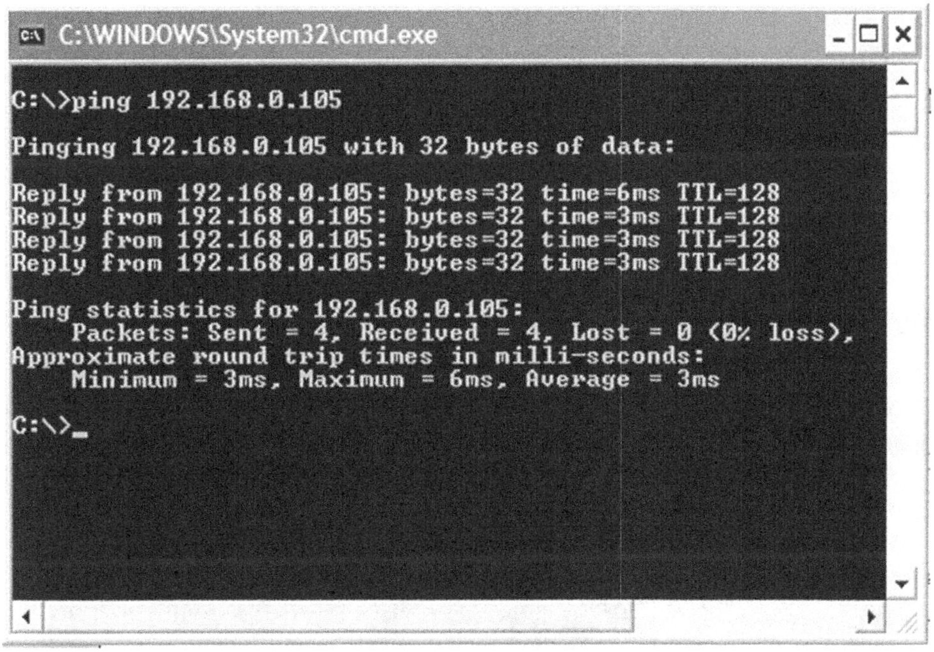

Figure 5-9: Ping IP Address of Remote Host.

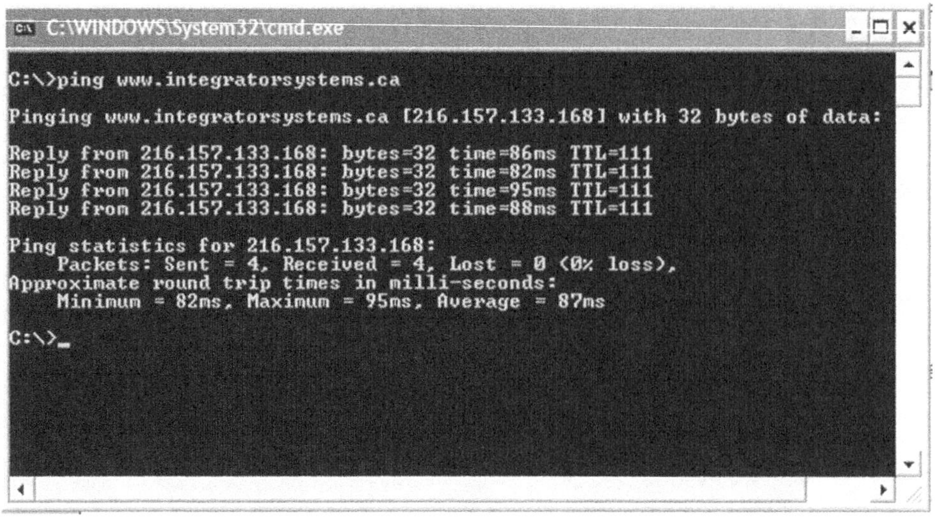

Figure 5-10: Ping Hostname of Remote Host.

If you receive a similar response as to those shown in Figure 5.9 and Figure 5.10 above, the server is available on the network. If you cannot contact the resource, you can troubleshoot the connection by using the PING command to test connectivity to various network resources:

- Ping the loopback address to verify that TCP/IP is installed and working correctly on the local computer (**ping loopback** or **ping 127.0.0.1**).

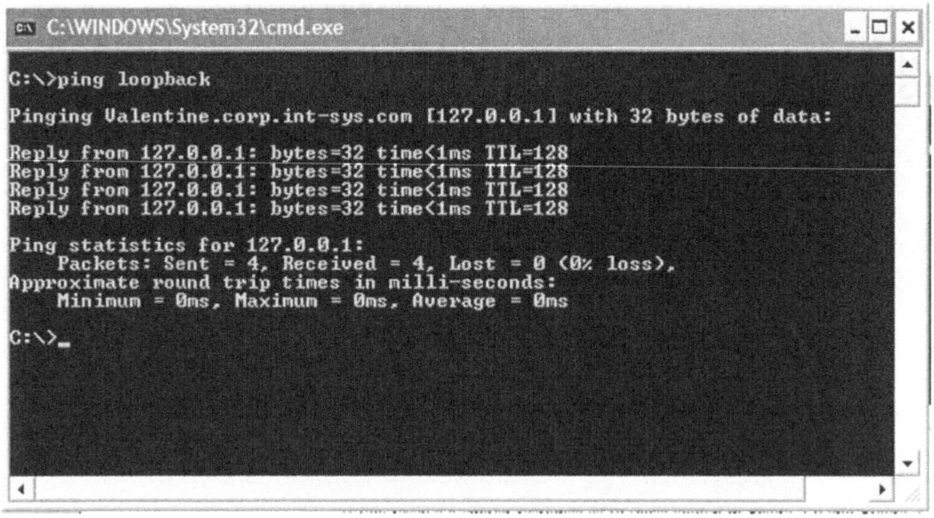

Figure 5-11: Ping Loopback.

- Ping the IP address of the local computer to verify that it was added to the network correctly

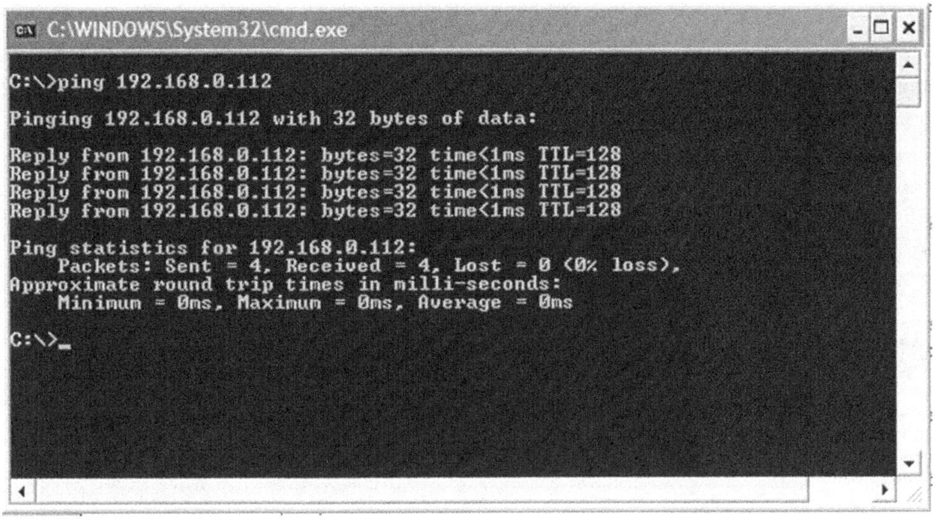

Figure 5-12: Ping Local IP Address.

- Ping the IP address of the default gateway to verify that the gateway is functional and it is possible to connect to a local host on the local network. Use IPCONFIG /ALL to determine the address of the default gateway.

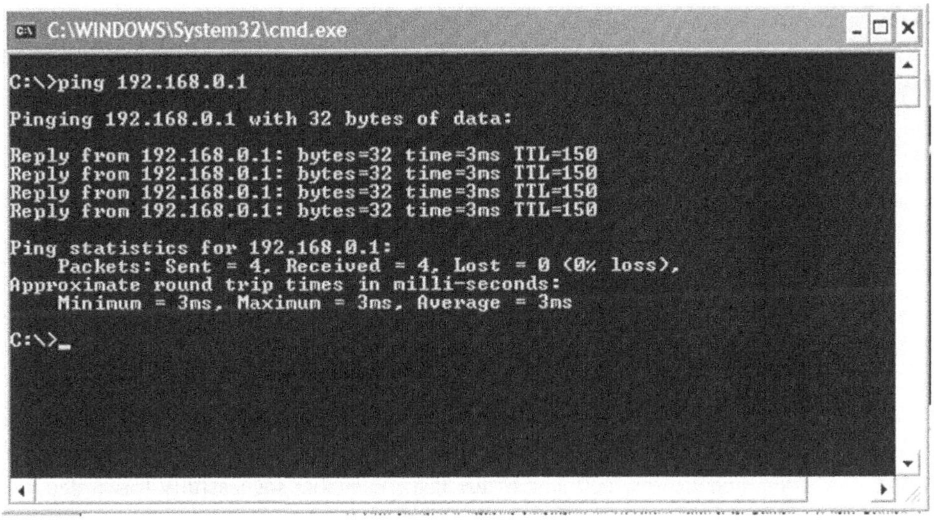

Figure 5-13: Ping IP Address of Default Gateway.

- Ping the IP address of another remote host to verify that you can communicate through a router.

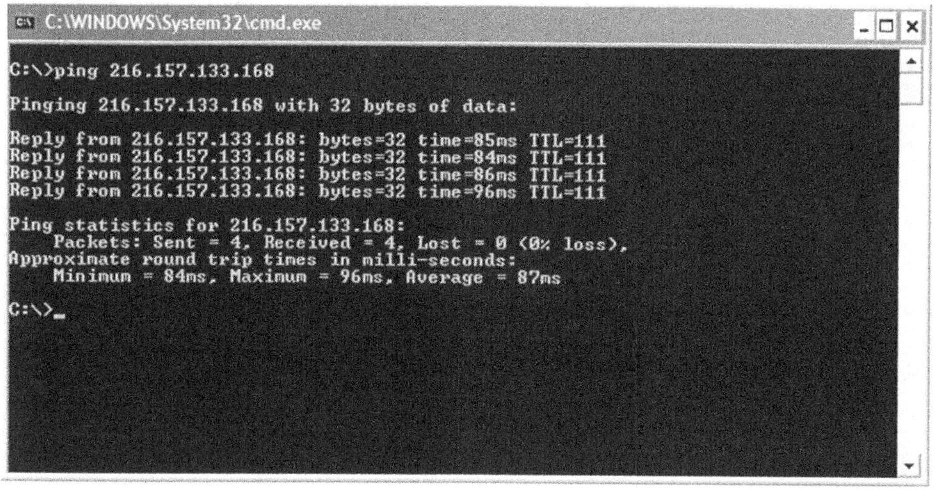

Figure 5-14: Ping IP Address of Different Remote Host.

> NOTE: To see additional switches for Ping, type ping /? at the command prompt.

Many organizations block the return of ICMP (ping) packets as a security measure. As a result, if you try to ping a resource, you may not receive a response to the PING or TRACERT message (Figure 5.16). So if you can contact the network resource directly, but always receive "Request Timed Out" when you ping the same resource, chances are the PING packets are being blocked.

If you can ping a resource by using its IP address but not by its host name, the problem is probably caused by a name resolution problem, rather than by a network connectivity issue. Make sure that the computer is configured with the correct DNS or WINS address, and that the DNS or WINS servers are available.

Tracert.exe is, as its name suggests, a route-tracing utility that you can use to establish what is the network path to a destination. The TRACERT command shows the series of IP routers that are used to deliver packets from your computer to the destination and shows how long it takes for each hop. If packets cannot reach the destination, the TRACERT command returns the name of the last router that successfully forwarded the packets.

To determine the path that a packet takes on the network and where that path may be ending:

- Click **Start**, click **Run**, type **cmd** in the **Open** box and then press **Enter**.
- At the command prompt, type **tracert** ***IPAddressOfRemoteHost***, and then press **Enter**.
- Examine the results that appear in the window to determine the length of time that the packet took to reach each network segment and the point at which the connection may stop working.

> NOTE: To see additional options of the Tracert.exe tool, type tracert /? at the command prompt.

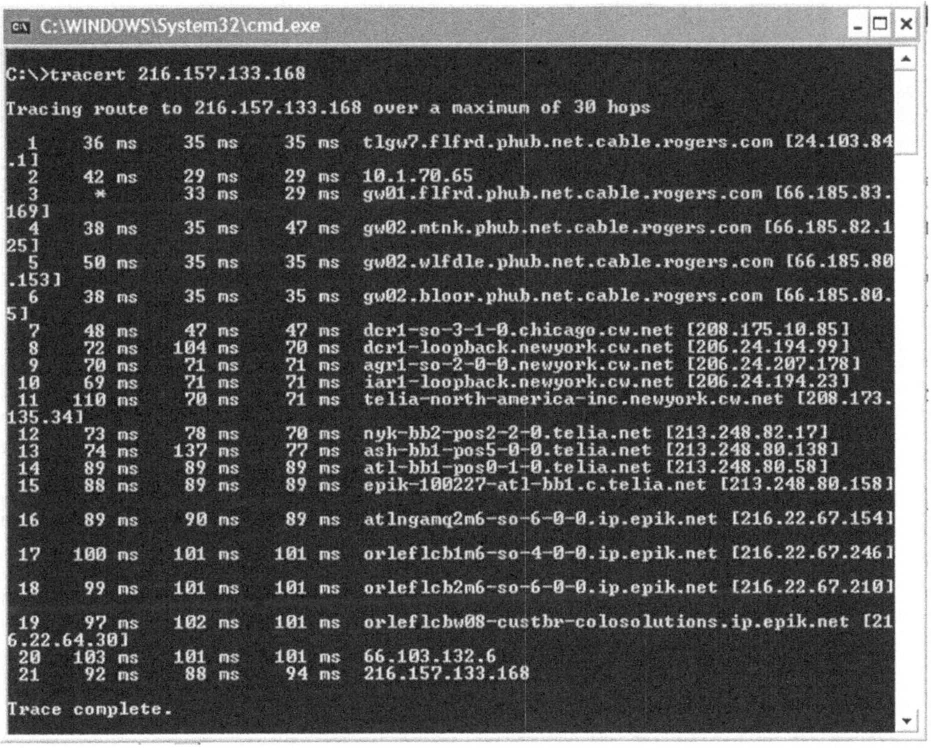

Figure 5-15: Successful Tracert.

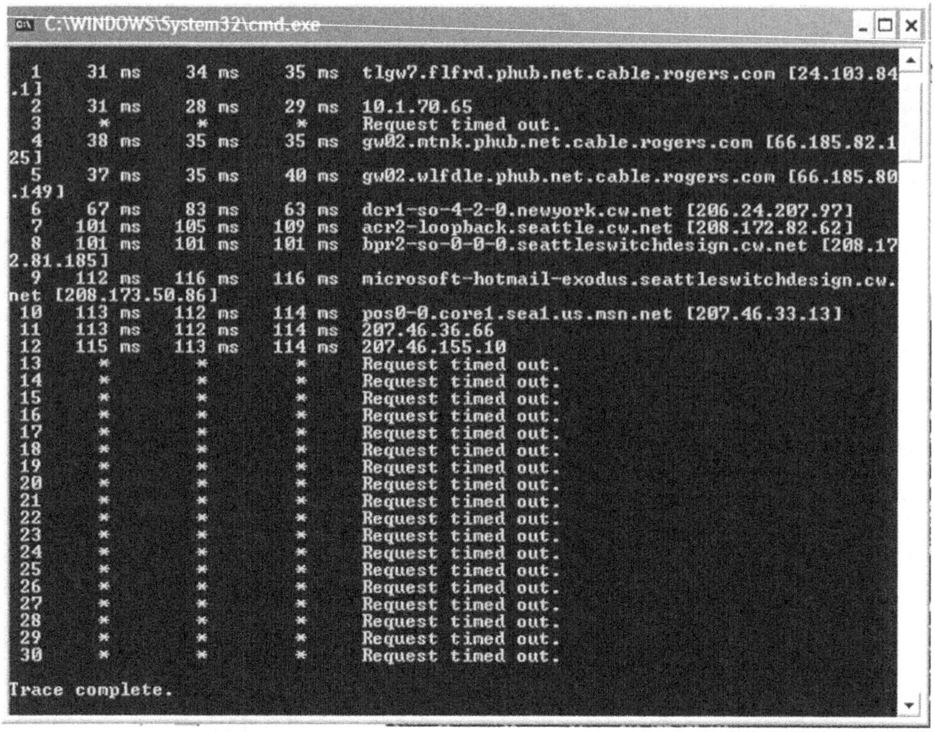

Figure 5-16: Unsuccessful Tracert.

5.2.4 NET VIEW

You are also able to test connections by using the NET VIEW command. To do this you will also start at the command prompt.

Click **Start**, click **Run**, type **cmd** in the **Open** box and then press **Enter**.

At the command prompt, type **net view *ComputerName***, and then press **Enter**, where *ComputerName* is the NETBIOS name of the computer that you want to connect to. A list of the file and print shares on that computer is produced by creating a temporary NetBIOS connection (Figure 5.17). If no file or print shares are shown as available on the computer, you receive a "There are no entries in the list" message.

If the **NET VIEW** *ComputerName* command does not work and you receive a "**System error has occurred**" error message, follow these steps:

1. Verify that you entered the name of the remote computer correctly.
2. Verify that the computer is functioning.
3. Verify that the File and Printer Sharing for Microsoft Networks service is running on the remote computer.
4. Use the PING command to verify that all the routers between the local computer and the remote computer are operational.

If the NET VIEW *ComputerName* command does not work, type **NET VIEW *IPAddressOfRemoteComputer***, and then press **Enter**. Alternately, if the NET VIEW *IPAddressOfRemoteComputer* command works, but the NET VIEW *ComputerName* command does not work, the computer name may be resolving to the wrong address. Check the WINS and DNS settings.

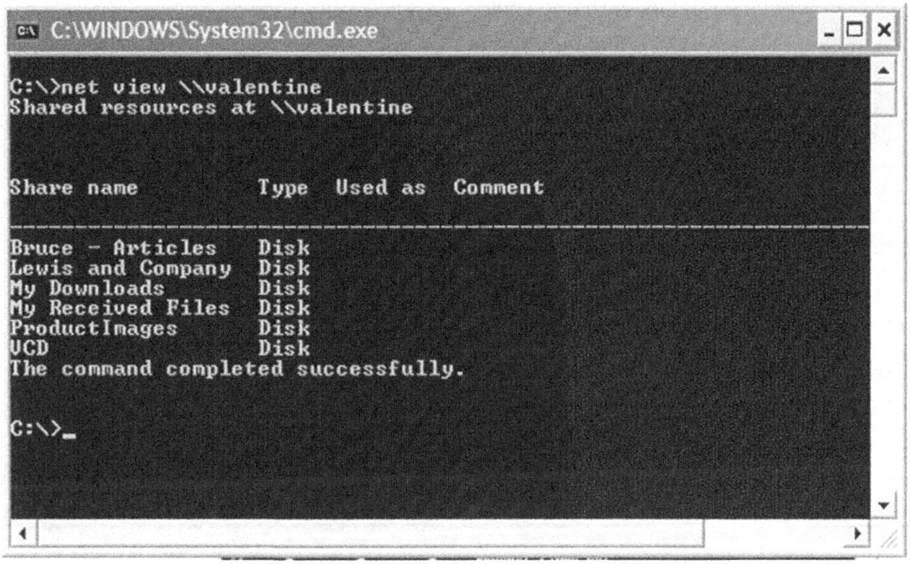

Figure 5-17: Net View Command.

Pop Quiz 5.2

Pop Quiz 5.2 Questions

1. If you need to view current TCP/IP settings at the prompt, what command can be used?
2. To troubleshoot NetBIOS over TCP/IP, what command can you use at the prompt?
3. You are having trouble accessing a router and want to view the destination path at the prompt, what command can you use?
4. To view a listing of client and server connections at the prompt, which two utilities can be used?
5. You received the following error when using netview, "System Error has occurred," what can you do to troubleshoot this error?

Pop Quiz 5.2 Answers

1. IPCONFIG is used to give you current TCP/IP settings. Use the command at the prompt by typing ipconfig then enter. Switches can be viewed to give you additional options with the command.
2. Nbtstat.exe is used at the command prompt for troubleshooting NetBIOS name resolution problems. Make sure you use the switches correctly; they are case sensitive.
3. Use tracert at the command to view the destination path used by a packet. Type tracert at the command prompt to view packet destinations.
4. To display a list of client and server connections, type nbtstat -s or netview at the command prompt press Enter
5. If you receive the error "System error has occurred" uses these steps: Check the computer name, check if the machine is powered on, check that the File and Printer Sharing for Microsoft Networks service is on and use the PING command to check router connectivity between the two computers.

NOTE: To see additional switches for Net View, type net view /? at the command prompt.

5.3 Troubleshoot Server Services

The control of system services has been appreciably enhanced in Windows 2003 using the Services Snap-in for the MMC. Most significantly, each time a service fails, the following recovery options are available:

- Take No Action.
- Restart the Service.
- Run a File.
- Reboot the Computer.

5.3.1 Diagnose and Resolve Issues Related to Service Dependency

Of note, the Run a File option is especially effective, since it may be used with a WSH (Windows Scripting Host) script file to send an e-mail notice to the administrator and document a custom event to the System event log before the service is restarted.

Administrators now also have access to service dependency information and can use the Services Snap-in to manage services on remote computers.

There are some notable benefits. Downtime is noticeably reduced because a failed service can be restarted automatically. As well, being able to perform advanced logging and execute administrative scripts allows administrators the chance to be involved more quickly with problem resolution, with more information at hand. As a final point, the ability to easily control services remotely will help the administrators responsible for a large number of distributed servers.

5.3.2 Use Service Recovery Options to Diagnose and Resolve Service-related Issues

Recovery Console

Recovery Console is an extremely powerful tool that should be used only by an experienced administrator that understands the implications of its use. Improper handling of Recovery Console can, rather than solving the problems, instead cause further harm to your system. It should be emphasized that you make sure all data is backed-up before using this tool, as your hard drive may be formatted as part of the recovery.

> **Note**: You must be an administrator to use the Recovery Console.

Using the Recovery Console, you can:

- Enable and disable services
- Format drives
- Read and write data on a local drive (including drives formatted as NTFS)
- Perform many other administrative tasks.

There are two ways to start the Recovery Console. If you cannot start your computer, Recovery Console can be run from the Server 2003 setup CD. You can also be proactive and install Recovery Console on your computer, so that if something does happen that stops you from starting Server2003, you can choose Recovery Console as an option from the boot menu. To install the Recovery Console, insert the Server 2003 installation CD and run the command ***D*:\I386\WINNT32 /CMDCONS**, where ***D*:** represents your CDROM drive.

Recovery Console provides a command line utility during the startup process. You can use this utility to make system changes when Server 2003 doesn't start. Many different tasks can be performed using Recovery Console without even starting Server 2003. A list of all commands that can be performed is shown in Table 5.1.

Attrib	Changes the attributes of a file or directory.
Batch	Executes the commands specified in the text file.
Bootcfg	Boot file (boot.ini) configuration and recovery
ChDir (Cd)	Displays the name of the current directory or changes the current directory.
Chkdsk	Checks a disk and displays a status report.
Cls	Clears the screen.
Copy	Copies a single file to another location.
Delete (Del)	Deletes one or more files.
Dir	Displays a list of files and subdirectories in a directory.
Disable	Disables a system service or a device driver.
Diskpart	Manages partitions on your hard drives.
Enable	Starts or enables a system service or a device driver.
Exit	Exits the Recovery Console and restarts your computer.
Expand	Extracts a file from a compressed file.
Fixboot	Writes a new partition boot sector onto the specified partition.
Fixmbr	Repairs the master boot record of the specified disk.
Format	Formats a disk.
Help	Displays a list of the commands you can use in the Recovery Console.
Listsvc	Lists the services and drivers available on the computer.
Logon	Logs on to a Windows installation.
Map	Displays the drive letter mappings.
Mkdir	Creates a directory.
More	Displays a text file.
NetUse	Connects a network share to a drive letter.
Rename (Ren)	Renames a single file.
Rmdir (Rd)	Deletes a directory.
Set	Displays and sets environment variables.
Systemroot	Sets the current directory to the systemroot directory of the system you are currently logged on to.
Type	Displays a text file.

Table 5—1: Recovery Console Commands.

Chapter 5: Review Questions

1. Which of the following commands will show you the hops to a destination?

A. IIS

B. Pathping

C. Ping

D. Arp

E. Tracert

---

2. If you need to find out the capability of a network client, which of the following will send the lengthy results of the client network capability test to netdiag.log?

A. Ipconfig /release

B. Nbtstat -RR

C. Nslookup

D. Netdiag /l

3. What does TRACERT allow you to discover?

A. Renew IP address

B. Time associated with each hop

C. Refresh IP address

D. Number of hops to the destination

E. Release IP address

---

4. The first thing you should do to verify that TCP/IP has initialized correctly is:

A. Ping your IP address.

B. Ping the DNS server.

C. Ping the loopback address.

D. Ping your host name.

5. Which of the following is true after installing Certificate Services?

A. The computer cannot join a domain.

B. The computer cannot be used.

C. The computer cannot be renamed.

D. The computer cannot be removed from a domain.

---

6. Which of the following is not a type of CA (Certificate Authority)?

A. Enterprise Root CA

B. Stand alone distributed CA

C. Stand alone Root CA

D. Enterprise Subordinate CA

7. Where can we install Terminal services?

A. In the Add/Remove Programs applet in Control Panel

B. In the Internet Options applet in Control Panel

C. In the Fax applet in Control Panel

D. In the Regional Options applet in Control Panel

---

8. What options do we have when setting up Terminal Services?

A. Remote Administration Mode

B. Application Demonstration Mode

C. Remote Demonstration Mode

D. Application Server Mode

9. List the default Subnet Mask for a Class A Network.

A. 255.0.0.0

B. 255.255.255.0

C. 255.255.255.0

D. 255.255.0.0

---

10. List the default Subnet Mask for a Class B Network.

A. 255.255.255.0

B. 255.0.0.0

C. 255.255.0.0

D. 255.255.255.0

11. List the Subnet Mask (in dotted-decimal notation) for a Class C Network in which one bit is being borrowed to create subnets.

A. 255.255.255.224

B. 255.255.255.128

C. 255.255.255.192

D. 255.255.255.252

---

12. List the Subnet Mask (in dotted-decimal notation) for a Class C Network in which three bits are being borrowed to create subnets.

A. 255.255.255.128

B. 255.255.255.252

C. 255.255.255.192

D. 255.255.255.224

13. List the Subnet Mask (in dotted-decimal notation) for a Class C Network in which six bits are being borrowed to create subnets.

A. 255.255.255.128

B. 255.255.255.192

C. 255.255.255.252

D. 255.255.255.248

---

14. List the Subnet Mask (in dotted-decimal notation) for a Class B Network in which two bits are being borrowed to create subnets.

A. 255.255.224.0

B. 255.255.192.0

C. 255.255.252.0

D. 255.255.240.0

15. List the Subnet Mask (in dotted-decimal notation) for a Class B Network in which five bits are being borrowed to create subnets.

A. 255.255.248.0

B. 255.255.192.0

C. 255.255.224.0

D. 255.255.252.0

---

16. You have a network address of 196.119.203.0 with a subnet mask of /27. What is the network address of the third usable subnet?

A. 196.119.203.255

B. 196.119.203.0

C. 196.119.203.96.

D. 196.119.203.64

17. You have a network address of 196.119.203.0 with a subnet mask of /27. How many usable subnets can you create with this networking scheme?

A. 2 subnets

B. 16 subnets

C. 26 subnets

D. 6 subnets

---

18. You have a network address of 196.119.203.0 with a subnet mask of /27. How many usable hosts can you create with this networking scheme?

A. 16 hosts

B. 180 hosts

C. 260 hosts

D. 20 hosts

19. You have a network address of 199.154.99.0 and a subnet mask of 255.255.255.240. How many usable hosts can you create with this network address and subnet mask?

A. 120 hosts

B. 22 hosts

C. 255 hosts

D. 196 hosts

---

20. You have a network address of 213.15.40.0 and a subnet mask of /29. What is the network address of the fourth usable subnet?

A. 213.15.40.16

B. 213.15.40.32

C. 213.15.40.8

D. 213.15.40.242

21. You have a network address of 213.15.40.0 and a subnet mask of /29. With this network address and subnet mask, how many usable subnets can you create?

A. 3 subnets

B. 130 subnets

C. 225 subnets

D. 30 subnets

---

22. You have a network address of 213.15.40.0 and a subnet mask of /29. With this network address and subnet mask, how many usable hosts can you create?

A. 180 hosts

B. 80 hosts

C. 225 hosts

D. 3 hosts

23. You have a network address of 135.53.0.0 and a subnet mask of 255.255.252.0. What is the network address of the forty-fifth usable subnet?

A. 135.53.112.0

B. 135.53.180.0

C. 135.53.180.1

D. 135.53.80.0

---

24. You have a network address of 135.53.0.0 and a subnet mask of 255.255.252.0. What is the host range of the forty-fifth usable subnet?

A. 135.53.180.1–135.53.183.24

B. 135.53.180.1–135.53.183.25

C. 135.53.180.1–135.53.183.12

D. 135.53.180.1–135.53.183.254

25. You have a network address of 135.53.0.0 and a subnet mask of 255.255.252.0. How many usable hosts can you create with this network scheme?

A. 200 hosts

B. 12 hosts

C. 12,000 hosts

D. 63,364 hosts

---

26. Summarize the following addresses:

192.168.4.0 /24, 192.168.5.0 /24, 192.168.6.0 /24, 192.168.7.0 /24.

A. 192.168.4.0 /24

B. 192.168.4.0 /22

C. 192.168.4.0 /12

D. 192.168.4.0 /28

Chapter 5: Review Answers

1. Which of the following commands will show you the hops to a destination?

A. IIS

***B. Pathping**

C. Ping

D. Arp

***E. Tracert**

Explanation: Tracert and Pathping will both show the hops to a destination. Pathping will also show the packet loss at each hop.

---

2. If you need to find out the capability of a network client, which of the following will send the lengthy results of the client network capability test to netdiag.log?

A. Ipconfig /release

B. Nbtstat -RR

C. Nslookup

***D. Netdiag /l**

Explanation: Nbtstat -RR will release and refresh the name registration at the WINS server. Ipconfig /flushdns gets rid of any cached DNS information. Ipconfig /release and /renew will allow a client to get a fresh IP address and other information, such as a subnet mask and a default gateway. Nslookup (with the host name) will give you the IP address of the host. Netdiag /l will send the lengthy results of the client network capability test to netdiag.log.

3. What does TRACERT allow you to discover?

A. Renew IP address

***B. Time associated with each hop**

C. Refresh IP address

***D. Number of hops to the destination**

E. Release IP address

Explanation: Tracert counts the hops to a destination and the time for each hop. It does not release or renew IP addresses, which is done with IPCONFIG. When clients on networks separated by firewalls or routers and the Internet cannot ping each other, use the tracert command from the local computer to discover how far the packet can travel.

---

4. The first thing you should do to verify that TCP/IP has initialized correctly is:

A. Ping your IP address.

B. Ping the DNS server.

***C. Ping the loopback address.**

D. Ping your host name.

Explanation: The first thing you should do to verify that TCP/IP has initialized correctly is ping the loopback address, then your IP, your host name, and then DNS server (for this particular scenario).

5. Which of the following is true after installing Certificate Services?

***A. The computer cannot join a domain.**

B. The computer cannot be used.

***C. The computer cannot be renamed.**

***D. The computer cannot be removed from a domain.**

Explanation: After installing Certificate Services, the computer cannot be renamed, join a domain, or be removed from a domain.

---

6. Which of the following is not a type of CA (Certificate Authority)?

A. Enterprise Root CA

***B. Stand alone distributed CA**

C. Stand alone Root CA

D. Enterprise Subordinate CA

Explanation: The following are types of CA you can set up: Enterprise Root CA, Enterprise Subordinate CA, Stand-alone Root CA, and Stand-alone Subordinate CA.

7. Where can we install Terminal services?

***A. In the Add/Remove Programs applet in Control Panel**

B. In the Internet Options applet in Control Panel

C. In the Fax applet in Control Panel

D. In the Regional Options applet in Control Panel

Explanation: We can install Terminal services in the Add/Remove Programs applet in Control Panel.

---

8. What options do we have when setting up Terminal Services?

***A. Remote Administration Mode**

B. Application Demonstration Mode

C. Remote Demonstration Mode

***D. Application Server Mode**

Explanation: Remote Administration Mode and Application Server Mode are the options we have when setting up Terminal Services.

9. List the default Subnet Mask for a Class A Network.

***A. 255.0.0.0**

B. 255.255.255.0

C. 255.255.255.0

D. 255.255.0.0

Explanation: The default Subnet Mask for a Class A Network is 255.0.0.0.

---

10. List the default Subnet Mask for a Class B Network.

A. 255.255.255.0

B. 255.0.0.0

***C. 255.255.0.0**

D. 255.255.255.0

Explanation: The default Subnet Mask for a Class B Network is 255.255.0.0.

11. List the Subnet Mask (in dotted-decimal notation) for a Class C Network in which one bit is being borrowed to create subnets.

A. 255.255.255.224

***B. 255.255.255.128**

C. 255.255.255.192

D. 255.255.255.252

Explanation: The Subnet Mask (in dotted-decimal notation) for a Class C Network in which one bit is being borrowed to create subnets is 255.255.255.128.

---

12. List the Subnet Mask (in dotted-decimal notation) for a Class C Network in which three bits are being borrowed to create subnets.

A. 255.255.255.128

B. 255.255.255.252

C. 255.255.255.192

***D. 255.255.255.224**

Explanation: The Subnet Mask (in dotted-decimal notation) for a Class C Network in which three bits are being borrowed to create subnets is 255.255.255.224.

13. List the Subnet Mask (in dotted-decimal notation) for a Class C Network in which six bits are being borrowed to create subnets.

A. 255.255.255.128

B. 255.255.255.192

***C. 255.255.255.252**

D. 255.255.255.248

Explanation: The Subnet Mask (in dotted-decimal notation) for a Class C Network in which six bits are being borrowed to create subnets is 255.255.255.252.

---

14. List the Subnet Mask (in dotted-decimal notation) for a Class B Network in which two bits are being borrowed to create subnets.

A. 255.255.224.0

***B. 255.255.192.0**

C. 255.255.252.0

D. 255.255.240.0

Explanation: The Subnet Mask (in dotted-decimal notation) for a Class B Network in which two bits are being borrowed to create subnets is 255.255.192.0.

15. List the Subnet Mask (in dotted-decimal notation) for a Class B Network in which five bits are being borrowed to create subnets.

***A. 255.255.248.0**

B. 255.255.192.0

C. 255.255.224.0

D. 255.255.252.0

Explanation: The Subnet Mask (in dotted-decimal notation) for a Class B Network in which five bits are being borrowed to create subnets is 255.255.248.0.

---

16. You have a network address of 196.119.203.0 with a subnet mask of /27. What is the network address of the third usable subnet?

A. 196.119.203.255

B. 196.119.203.0

***C. 196.119.203.96.**

D. 196.119.203.64

Explanation: You have a network address of 196.119.203.0 with a subnet mask of /27. The network address of the third usable subnet is 196.119.203.96. The host range of the third usable subnet is 196.119.203.97 - 196.119.203.126. The broadcast address of the third usable subnet is 196.119.203.127. You can create 6 usable subnets and 180 usable hosts using this addressing scheme.

17. You have a network address of 196.119.203.0 with a subnet mask of /27. How many usable subnets can you create with this networking scheme?

    A. 2 subnets

    B. 16 subnets

    C. 26 subnets

***D. 6 subnets**

Explanation: You have a network address of 196.119.203.0 with a subnet mask of /27. The network address of the third usable subnet is 196.119.203.96. The host range of the third usable subnet is 196.119.203.97–196.119.203.126. The broadcast address of the third usable subnet is 196.119.203.127. You can create 6 usable subnets and 180 usable hosts using this addressing scheme.

---

18. You have a network address of 196.119.203.0 with a subnet mask of /27. How many usable hosts can you create with this networking scheme?

    A. 16 hosts

***B. 180 hosts**

    C. 260 hosts

    D. 20 hosts

Explanation: You have a network address of 196.119.203.0 with a subnet mask of /27. The network address of the third usable subnet is 196.119.203.96. The host range of the third usable subnet is 196.119.203.97–196.119.203.126. The broadcast address of the third usable subnet is 196.119.203.127. You can create 6 usable subnets and 180 usable hosts using this addressing scheme.

19. You have a network address of 199.154.99.0 and a subnet mask of 255.255.255.240. How many usable hosts can you create with this network address and subnet mask?

A. 120 hosts

B. 22 hosts

C. 255 hosts

***D. 196 hosts**

Explanation: You have a network address of 199.154.99.0 and a subnet mask of 255.255.255.240. The network address of the sixth usable subnet is 199.154.99.96. The host range of the sixth usable subnet is 199.154.99.97–199.154.99.110. The broadcast address of the sixth usable subnet is 199.154.99.111. You can create 14 usable subnets and 196 usable hosts by using this addressing scheme.

---

20. You have a network address of 213.15.40.0 and a subnet mask of /29. What is the network address of the fourth usable subnet?

A. 213.15.40.16

***B. 213.15.40.32**

C. 213.15.40.8

D. 213.15.40.242

Explanation: You have a network address of 213.15.40.0 and a subnet mask of /29. The network address of the fourth usable subnet is 213.15.40.32. The host range of the fourth usable subnet is 213.15.40.33–213.15.40.38. The broadcast address of the fourth usable subnet is 213.15.40.39. With this network address and subnet mask you can create 30 usable subnets and 180 usable hosts.

21. You have a network address of 213.15.40.0 and a subnet mask of /29. With this network address and subnet mask, how many usable subnets can you create?

A. 3 subnets

B. 130 subnets

C. 225 subnets

***D. 30 subnets**

Explanation: You have a network address of 213.15.40.0 and a subnet mask of /29. The network address of the fourth usable subnet is 213.15.40.32. The host range of the fourth usable subnet is 213.15.40.33–213.15.40.38. The broadcast address of the fourth usable subnet is 213.15.40.39. With this network address and subnet mask you can create 30 usable subnets and 180 usable hosts.

---

22. You have a network address of 213.15.40.0 and a subnet mask of /29. With this network address and subnet mask, how many usable hosts can you create?

***A. 180 hosts**

B. 80 hosts

C. 225 hosts

D. 3 hosts

Explanation: You have a network address of 213.15.40.0 and a subnet mask of /29. The network address of the fourth usable subnet is 213.15.40.32. The host range of the fourth usable subnet is 213.15.40.33–213.15.40.38. The broadcast address of the fourth usable subnet is 213.15.40.39. With this network address and subnet mask you can create 30 usable subnets and 180 usable hosts.

23. You have a network address of 135.53.0.0 and a subnet mask of 255.255.252.0. What is the network address of the forty-fifth usable subnet?

A. 135.53.112.0

***B. 135.53.180.0**

C. 135.53.180.1

D. 135.53.80.0

Explanation: You have a network address of 135.53.0.0 and a subnet mask of 255.255.252.0. The network address of the forty-fifth usable subnet is 135.53.180.0. The host range of the forty-fifth usable subnet is 135.53.180.1–135.53.183.254. The broadcast address of the forty-fifth usable subnet is 135.53.183.255. Using this addressing scheme, you can create 62 usable subnets and 63,364 usable hosts.

---

24. You have a network address of 135.53.0.0 and a subnet mask of 255.255.252.0. What is the host range of the forty-fifth usable subnet?

A. 135.53.180.1–135.53.183.24

B. 135.53.180.1–135.53.183.25

C. 135.53.180.1–135.53.183.12

***D. 135.53.180.1–135.53.183.254**

Explanation: You have a network address of 135.53.0.0 and a subnet mask of 255.255.252.0. The network address of the forty-fifth usable subnet is 135.53.180.0. The host range of the forty-fifth usable subnet is 135.53.180.1–135.53.183.254. The broadcast address of the forty-fifth usable subnet is 135.53.183.255. Using this addressing scheme, you can create 62 usable subnets and 63,364 usable hosts.

25. You have a network address of 135.53.0.0 and a subnet mask of 255.255.252.0. How many usable hosts can you create with this network scheme?

A. 200 hosts

B. 12 hosts

C. 12,000 hosts

***D. 63,364 hosts**

Explanation: You have a network address of 135.53.0.0 and a subnet mask of 255.255.252.0. The network address of the forty-fifth usable subnet is 135.53.180.0. The host range of the forty-fifth usable subnet is 135.53.180.1–135.53.183.254. The broadcast address of the forty-fifth usable subnet is 135.53.183.255. Using this addressing scheme, you can create 62 usable subnets and 63,364 usable hosts.

---

26. Summarize the following addresses: 192.168.4.0 /24, 192.168.5.0 /24, 192.168.6.0 /24, 192.168.7.0 /24.

A. 192.168.4.0 /24

***B. 192.168.4.0 /22**

C. 192.168.4.0 /12

D. 192.168.4.0 /28

Explanation: Summarize the following addresses: 192.168.4.0 /24, 192.168.5.0 /24, 192.168.6.0 /24, 192.168.7.0 /24.These addresses can be summarized into 192.168.4.0 /22.

List of Figures and Tables

I Listing of all Figures

II Listing of all Tables

Glossary

A

AC-3

The coding system used by Dolby Digital. A standard for high quality digital audio that is used for the sound portion of video stored in digital format.

Accelerated Graphics Port (AGP)

A type of expansion slot that is solely for video cards. Designed by Intel and supported by Windows 2000, AGP is a dedicated bus that provides fast, high-quality video and graphics performance.

Access control entry (ACE)

An entry in an access control list (ACL) containing the security ID (SID) for a user or group and an access mask that specifies which operations by the user or group are allowed, denied, or audited.

See also *access control list*; *access mask*; *security descriptor*.

Access control list (ACL)

A list of security protections that apply to an entire object, a set of the object's properties, or an individual property of an object. There are two types of access control lists: discretionary and system.

See also *access control entry*; *discretionary access control list*; *security descriptor*; *system access control list*.

Access mask

A 32-bit value that specifies the rights that are allowed or denied in an access control entry (ACE) of an access control list (ACL). An access mask is also used to request access rights when an object is opened.

See also *access control entry*.

Access token

A data structure containing security information that identifies a user to the security subsystem on a computer running Windows 2000 or Windows NT. An access token contains a user's security ID, the security IDs for groups that the user belongs to, and a list of the user's privileges on the local computer.

See also *privilege*; *security ID*.

Accessibility

The quality of a system incorporating hardware or software to engage a flexible, customizable user interface, alternative input and output methods, and greater exposure of screen elements to make the computer usable by people with cognitive, hearing, physical, or visual disabilities.

Accessibility status indicators

Icons on the system status area of the taskbar of the Windows desktop that let the user know which accessibility features are activated.

Accessibility Wizard

An interactive tool that makes it easier to set up commonly used accessibility features by specifying options by type of disability, rather than by numeric value changes.

ACPI

See *Advanced Configuration and Power Interface.*

Active Accessibility

A core component in the Windows operating system that is built on COM and defines how applications can exchange information about user interface elements.

Active Directory

The directory service included with Windows 2000 Server. It stores information about objects on a network and makes this information available to users and network administrators. Active Directory gives network users access to permitted resources anywhere on the network using a single logon process. It provides network administrators with an intuitive hierarchical view of the network and a single point of administration for all network objects.

See also *directory*; *directory service*.

ActiveX

A set of technologies that enable software components to interact with one another in a networked environment, regardless of the language in which the components were created.

Administrator

See *system administrator*.

Advanced Configuration and Power Interface (ACPI)

An open industry specification that defines power management on a wide range of mobile, desktop, and server computers and peripherals. ACPI is the foundation for the OnNow industry initiative that allows system manufacturers to deliver computers that will start at the touch of a keyboard. ACPI design is essential to take full advantage of power management and Plug and Play in Windows 2000. Check the manufacturer's documentation to verify that a computer is ACPI-compliant.

See also *Plug and Play*.

Advanced Power Management (APM)

A software interface (designed by Microsoft and Intel) between hardware-specific power management software (such as that located in a system BIOS) and an operating system power management driver.

Advertisement

In Windows 2000, the Software Installation snap-in generates an application advertisement script and stores this script in the appropriate locations in Active Directory and the Group Policy object.

Allocation unit

In file systems an allocation unit is the smallest amount of disk space that can be allocated to hold a file. All file systems used by Windows 2000 organize hard disks based on allocation units. The smaller the allocation unit size, the more efficiently a disk stores information. If no allocation unit size is specified during formatting, Windows 2000 chooses default sizes based on the size of the volume and the file system used. These defaults are selected to reduce the amount of space lost and the amount of fragmentation on the volume. Also called cluster.

American Standard Code for Information Interchange (ASCII)

A standard single byte character-encoding scheme used for text-based data. ASCII uses designated 7-bit or 8-bit number combinations to represent either 128 or 256 possible characters. Standard ASCII uses 7 bits to represent all uppercase and lowercase letters, the numbers 0 through 9, punctuation marks, and special control characters used in U.S. English. Most current x86 systems support the use of extended (or “high”) ASCII. Extended ASCII allows the eighth bit of each character to identify an additional 128 special symbol characters, foreign-language letters, and graphic symbols.

See also *Unicode*.

Answer file

A text file that you can use to provide automated input for unattended installation of Windows 2000. This input includes parameters to answer the questions required by Setup for specific installations. In some cases, you can use this text file to provide input to wizards, such as the Active Directory Installation wizard, which is used to add Active Directory to Windows 2000 Server through Setup. The default answer file for Setup is known as Unattend.txt.

API

See *application programming interface*.

APM

See *Advanced Power Management.*

Application media pool

A data repository that determines which media can be accessed by which applications and that sets the policies for that media. There can be any number of application media pools in a Removable Storage system. Applications create application media pools.

Application programming interface (API)

A set of routines that an application uses to request and carry out lower-level services performed by a computer’s operating system. These routines usually carry out maintenance tasks such as managing files and displaying information.

Assistive technology

System extensions, programs, devices, and utilities added to a computer to make it more accessible to users with disabilities.

Asynchronous communication

A form of data transmission in which information is sent and received at irregular intervals, one character at a time. Because data is received at irregular intervals, the receiving modem must be signaled to inform it when the data bits of a character begin and end. This is done by means of start and stop bits.

Asynchronous Transfer Mode (ATM)

A high-speed connection-oriented protocol used to transport many different types of network traffic.

ATM

See *Asynchronous Transfer Mode*.

Attribute (object)

In Active Directory, an attribute describes characteristics of an object and the type of information an object can hold. For each object class, the schema defines what attributes an instance of the class must have and what additional attributes it might have.

Auditing

To track the activities of users by recording selected types of events in the security log of a server or a workstation.

Authentication

A basic security function of cryptography. Authentication verifies the identity of the entities that communicate over the network. For example, the process that verifies the identity of a user who logs on to a computer either locally, at a computer's keyboard, or remotely, through a network connection.

See also *cryptography*; *confidentiality*; *integrity*; *Kerberos authentication protocol*; *nonrepudiation*; *NTLM authentication protocol*.

Authentication Header (AH)

A header that provides integrity, authentication, and anti-replay for the entire packet (both the IP header and the data payload carried in the packet).

Authoritative

In the Domain Name System (DNS), the use of zones by DNS servers to register and resolve a DNS domain name. When a DNS server is configured to host a zone, it is authoritative for names within that zone. DNS servers are granted authority based on information stored in the zone.

See also *zone*.

Automated installation

An unattended setup using one or more of several methods such as Remote Installation Services, bootable CD, and SysPrep.

Automatic caching

A method of automatically storing network files on a user's hard disk drive whenever a file is open so the files can be accessed when the user is not connected to the network.

Automatic Private IP Addressing (APIPA)

A feature of Windows 2000 TCP/IP that automatically configures a unique IP address from the range 169.254.0.1 to 169.254.255.254 and a subnet mask of 255.255.0.0 when the TCP/IP protocol is configured for dynamic addressing and a Dynamic Host Configuration Protocol (DHCP) Server is not available.

Available state

A state in which media can be allocated for use by applications.

Averaging counter

A type of counter that measures a value over time and displays the average of the last two measurements over some other factor (for example, PhysicalDisk\Avg. Disk Bytes/Transfer).

B

Backup

A duplicate copy of a program, a disk, or data, made either for archiving purposes or for safeguarding valuable files from loss should the active copy be damaged or destroyed. Some application programs automatically make backup copies of data files, maintaining both the current version and the preceding version.

Backup operator

A type of local or global group that contains the user rights needed to back up and restore files and folders. Members of the Backup Operators group can back up and restore files and folders regardless of ownership, access permissions, encryption, or auditing settings.

See also *auditing*; *global group*; *local group*; *user rights*.

Backup types

A type that determines which data is backed up and how it is backed up. There are five backup types: copy, daily, differential, incremental, and normal.

See also *copy backup*; *daily backup*; *differential backup*; *incremental backup*; *normal backup*.

Bad block

A disk sector that can no longer be used for data storage, usually due to media damage or imperfections.

Bandwidth

In analog communications, the difference between the highest and lowest frequencies in a given range. For example, a telephone line accommodates a bandwidth of 3,000 Hz, the difference between the lowest (300 Hz) and highest (3,300 Hz) frequencies it can carry. In digital communications, the rate at which information is sent expressed in bits per second (bps).

Barcode

A machine-readable label that identifies an object, such as physical media.

Base file record

The first file record in the master file table (MFT) for a file that has multiple file records. The base file record is the record to which the file's file reference corresponds.

Baseline

A range of measurements derived from performance monitoring that represents acceptable performance under typical operating conditions.

Basic disk

A physical disk that contains primary partitions or extended partitions with logical drives used by Windows 2000 and all versions of Windows NT. Basic disks can also contain volume, striped, mirror, or RAID-5 sets that were created using Windows NT 4.0 or earlier. As long as a compatible file format is used, MS-DOS, Windows 95, Windows 98, and all versions of Windows NT can access basic disks.

Basic input/output system (BIOS)

The set of essential software routines that tests hardware at startup, assists with starting the operating system, and supports the transfer of data among hardware devices. The BIOS is stored in read-only memory (ROM) so that it can be executed when the computer is turned on. Although critical to performance, the BIOS is usually invisible to computer users.

Basic volume

A volume on a basic disk. Basic volumes include primary partitions, logical drives within extended partitions, as well as volume, striped, mirror, or RAID-5 sets that were created using Windows NT 4.0 or earlier. Only basic disks can contain basic volumes. Basic and dynamic volumes cannot exist on the same disk.

Batch program

An ASCII (unformatted text) file containing one or more Windows NT or Windows 2000 commands. A batch program's filename has a .BAT extension. When you type the filename at the command prompt, the commands are processed sequentially. "Script" is often used interchangeably with "batch program" in the Windows NT and Windows 2000 environment.

Bi-directional communication

Communication that occurs in two directions simultaneously. Bi-directional communication is useful in printing where jobs can be sent and printer status can be returned at the same time.

Binding

A process by which software components and layers are linked together. When a network component is installed, the binding relationships and dependencies for the components are established. Binding allows components to communicate with each other.

Binding order

The sequence in which software components, network protocols and network adapters are linked together. When a network component is installed, the binding relationships and dependencies for the components are established.

BIOS

See *basic input/output system.*

BIOS parameter block (BPB)

A series of fields containing data on disk size, geometry variables, and the physical parameters of the volume. The BPB is located within the boot sector.

Boot sector

A critical disk structure for starting your computer, located at sector 1 of each volume or floppy disk. It contains executable code and data that is required by the code, including information used by the file system to access the volume. The boot sector is created when you format the volume.

Bootable CD

An automated installation method that runs Setup from a CD-ROM. This method is useful for computers at remote sites with slow links and no local IT department.

See also *automated installation.*

Bottleneck

A condition, usually involving a hardware resource, which causes the entire system to perform poorly.

BounceKeys

A keyboard filter that assists users whose fingers bounce on the keys when pressing or releasing them.

Bound trap

In programming, a problem in which a set of conditions exceeds a permitted range of values that causes the microprocessor to stop what it is doing and handle the situation in a separate routine.

Browsing

The process of creating and maintaining an up-to-date list of computers and resources on a network or part of a network by one or more designated computers running the Computer Browser service.

See also *Computer Browser service.*

Bulk encryption

A process in which large amounts of data, such as files, e-mail messages, or online communications sessions, are encrypted for confidentiality. It is usually done with a symmetric key algorithm.

See also *encryption*; *symmetric key encryption.*

C

Cable modem

A modem that provides broadband Internet access in the range of 10 to 30 Mbps.

Cache

For DNS and WINS, a local information store of resource records for recently resolved names of remote hosts. Typically, the cache is built dynamically as the computer queries and resolves names; it helps optimize the time required to resolve queried names.

See also *cache file*; *naming service*; *resource record.*

Cache file

A file used by the Domain Name System (DNS) server to preload its names cache when service is started. Also known as the "root hints" file because resource records stored in this file are used by the DNS service to help locate root servers that provide referral to authoritative servers for remote names. For Windows DNS servers, the cache file is named Cache.dns and is located in the %SystemRoot%\System32\Dns folder.

See also *authoritative*; *cache*; *systemroot.*

Caching

The process of storing recently-used data values in a special pool in memory where they are temporarily held for quicker subsequent accesses. For DNS, the ability of DNS servers to store information about the domain namespace learned during the processing and resolution of name queries. In Windows 2000, caching is also available through the DNS client service (resolve) as a way for DNS clients to keep a cache of name information learned during recent queries.

Caching resolve

For Windows 2000, a client-side Domain Name System (DNS) name resolution service that performs caching of recently learned DNS domain name information. The caching resolve service provides system-wide access to DNS-aware programs for resource records obtained from DNS servers during the processing of name queries. Data placed in the cache is used for a limited period of time and aged according to the active Time To Live (TTL) value. You can set the TTL either individually for each resource record (RR) or default to the minimum TTL set in the start of authority RR for the zone.

See also *cache*; *caching*; *expire interval*; *minimum TTL*; *resolve*; *resource record*; *Time To Live (TTL).*

Callback number

The number that a RAS server uses to call back a user. This number can be preset by the administrator or specified by the user at the time of each call, depending on how the administrator configures the user's callback status. The callback number should be the number of the phone line to which the user's modem is connected.

Card Bus

A 32-bit PC Card.

Cartridge

A unit of media of a certain type, such as 8mm tape, magnetic disk, optical disk, or CD-ROM, used by Removable Storage.

Central Processing Unit (CPU)

The part of a computer that has the ability to retrieve, interpret, and execute instructions and to transfer information to and from other resources over the computer's main data-transfer path, the bus. By definition, the CPU is the chip that functions as the "brain" of a computer.

Certificate

A digital document that is commonly used for authentication and secure exchange of information on open networks, such as the Internet, extranets, and intranets. A certificate securely binds a public key to the entity that holds the corresponding private key. Certificates are digitally signed by the issuing certification authority and can be issued for a user, a computer, or a service. The most widely accepted format for certificates is defined by the ITU-T X.509 version 3 international standard.

See also *certification authority*; *private key*; *public key*.

Certificate Services

The Windows 2000 service that issues certificates for a particular CA. It provides customizable services for issuing and managing certificates for the enterprise.

See also *certificate*; *certification authority*.

Certification authority (CA)

An entity responsible for establishing and vouching for the authenticity of public keys belonging to users (end entities) or other certification authorities. Activities of a certification authority can include binding public keys to distinguished names through signed certificates, managing certificate serial numbers, and certificate revocation.

See also *certificate*; *public key*.

Certified-for-Windows Logo

A specification that addresses the requirements of computer users with disabilities to ensure quality and consistency in assertive devices.

Challenge Handshake Authentication Protocol (CHAP)

A challenge-response authentication protocol for PPP connections documented in RFC 1994 that uses the industry-standard Message Digest 5 (MD5) one-way encryption scheme to hash the response to a challenge issued by the remote access server.

Change journal

A feature new to Windows 2000 that tracks changes to NTFS volumes, including additions, deletions, and modifications. The change journal exists on the volume as a sparse file.

Changer

The robotic element of an online library unit.

CHAP

See *Challenge Handshake Authentication Protocol.*

Child object

An object that is the immediate subordinate of another object in a hierarchy. A child object can have only one immediate superior, or parent, object. In Active Directory, the schema determines what classes of objects can be child objects of what other classes of objects. Depending on its class, a child object can also be the parent of other objects.

See also *object*; *parent object.*

CIM (COM Information Model) Object Manager (CIMOM)

A system service that handles interaction between network management applications and providers of local or remote data or system events.

Cipher text

Text that has been encrypted using an encryption key. Cipher text is meaningless to anyone who does not have the decryption key.

See also *decryption*; *encryption*; *encryption key*; *plaintext.*

Client

Any computer or program connecting to, or requesting services of, another computer or program.

See also *server.*

Cluster

A group of independent computer systems known as nodes or hosts, that work together as a single system to ensure that mission-critical applications and resources remain available to clients. A server cluster is the type of cluster that the Cluster service implements. Network Load Balancing provides a software solution for clustering multiple computers running Windows 2000 Server that provides networked services over the Internet and private intranets.

In file systems a cluster is the smallest amount of disk space that can be allocated to hold a file. All file systems used by Windows 2000 organize hard disks based on clusters. The smaller the cluster size, the more efficiently a disk stores information. If no cluster size is specified during formatting, Windows 2000 chooses default sizes based on the size of the volume and the file system used. These defaults are selected to reduce the amount of space lost and the amount of fragmentation on the volume. Also called allocation units.

Cluster recapping

A recovery technique used when Windows 2000 returns a bad sector error to NTFS. NTFS dynamically replaces the cluster containing the bad sector and allocates a new cluster for the data. If the error occurs during a read, NTFS returns a read error to the calling program, and the data is lost. If the error occurs during a write, NTFS writes the data to the new cluster, and no data is lost.

Code page

A page that maps character codes to individual characters. Different code pages include different special characters, typically customized for a language or a group of languages. The system uses code pages to translate keyboard input into character values for non-Unicode based applications, and to translate character values into characters for non-Unicode based output displays.

COM

See *Component Object Model.*

COM port

Short for communications port, the logical address assigned by MS-DOS (versions 3.3 and higher) and Microsoft Windows (including Windows 95, Windows 98, Windows NT and Windows 2000) to each of the four serial ports on an IBM Personal Computer or a PC compatible. COM ports are also known as the actual serial ports on a PC where peripherals, such as printers, scanners, and external modems, are plugged in.

Commit a transaction

To record in the log file the fact that a transaction is complete and has been recorded in the cache.

Common Internet File System (CIFS)

A protocol and a corresponding API used by application programs to request higher level application services. CIFS was formerly known as SMB (Server Message Block).

Compact Disc File System (CDFS)

A 32-bit protected-mode file system that controls access to the contents of CD-ROM drives in Windows 2000.

Compact disc-record able (CD-R)

A type of CD-ROM that can be written once on a CD recorder and read on a CD-ROM drive.

Compact disc-rewritable (CD-RW)

A type of CD-ROM that can be written many times on a CD recorder and read on a CD-ROM drive.

Complementary metal-oxide semiconductor (CMOS)

The battery-packed memory that stores information, such as disk types and amount of memory, used to start the computer.

Component Object Model (COM)

An object-based programming model designed to promote software interoperability; it allows two or more applications or components to easily cooperate with one another, even if they were written by different vendors, at different times, in different programming languages, or if they are running on different computers running different operating systems. COM is the foundation technology upon which broader technologies can be built. Object linking and embedding (OLE) technology and ActiveX are both built on top of COM.

Computer Browser service

A service that maintains an up-to-date list of computers and provides the list to applications when requested. The Computer Browser service provides the computer lists displayed in the My Network Places, Select Computer, and Select Domain dialog boxes and (for Windows 2000 Server only) in the Server Manager window.

Confidentiality

A basic security function of cryptography. Confidentiality provides assurance that only authorized users can read or use confidential or secret information. Without confidentiality, anyone with network access can use readily available tools to eavesdrop on network traffic and intercept valuable proprietary information. For example, an Internet Protocol security service that ensures a message is disclosed only to intended recipients by encrypting the data.

See also *cryptography*; *authentication*; *integrity*; *nonrepudiation*.

Console tree

The tree view pane in a Microsoft Management Console (MMC) that displays the hierarchical namespace. By default it is the left pane of the console window, but it can be hidden. The items in the console tree (for example, Web pages, folders, and controls) and their hierarchical organization determine the management capabilities of a console.

See also *Microsoft Management Console (MMC)*; *namespace*.

Container object

An object that can logically contain other objects. For example, a folder is a container object.

See also *no container object*; *object*.

Copy backup

A backup that copies all selected files but does not mark each file as having been backed up (that is, the archive bit is not set). A copy backup is useful between normal and incremental backups because copying does not affect these other backup operations.

See also *daily backup*; *differential backup*; *incremental backup*; *normal backup*.

CPU

See *Central Processing Unit*.

Cryptography

The art and science of information security. It provides four basic information security functions: confidentiality, integrity, authentication, and nonrepudiation.

See also *confidentiality*; *integrity*; *authentication*; *nonrepudiation*.

D

Daily backup

A backup that copies all selected files that have been modified the day the daily backup is performed. The backed-up files are not marked as having been backed up (that is, the archive bit is not set).

See also *copy backup*; *differential backup*; *incremental backup*; *normal backup*.

Data confidentiality

A service provided by cryptographic technology to assure that data can be read only by authorized users or programs. In a network, data confidentiality ensures that intruders cannot read data. Windows 2000 uses access control mechanisms and encryption, such as DES, 3DES and RSA encryption algorithms, to ensure data confidentiality.

Data Encryption Standard (DES)

An encryption algorithm that uses a 56-bit key, and maps a 64-bit input block to a 64-bit output block. The key appears to be a 64-bit key, but one bit in each of the 8 bytes is used for odd parity, resulting in 56 bits of usable key.

Data integrity

A service provided by cryptographic technology that ensures data has not been modified. In a network environment, data integrity allows the receiver of a message to verify that data has not been modified in transit. Windows 2000 uses access control mechanisms and cryptography, such as RSA public-key signing and shared symmetric key one way hash algorithms, to ensure data integrity.

Data Link Control (DLC)

A protocol used primarily for IBM mainframe computers and printer connectivity.

Data packet

A unit of information transmitted as a whole from one device to another on a network.

Deallocate

To return media to the available state after they have been used by an application.

Decommissioned state

A state that indicates that media have reached their allocation maximum.

Decryption

The process of making encrypted data readable again by converting ciphertext to plaintext.

See also *ciphertext*; *encryption*; *plaintext*.

Default gateway

A configuration item for the TCP/IP protocol that is the IP address of a directly reachable IP router. Configuring a default gateway creates a default route in the IP routing table.

Defragmentation

The process of rewriting parts of a file to contiguous sectors on a hard disk to increase the speed of access and retrieval. When files are updated, the computer tends to save these updates on the largest continuous space on the hard disk, which is often on a different sector than the other parts of the file. When files are thus fragmented, the computer must search the hard disk each time the file is opened to find all of the parts of the file, which slows down response time. In Active Directory, defragmentation rearranges how the data is written in the directory database file to compact it.

See also *fragmentation*.

Desktop

The on-screen work area in which windows, icons, menus, and dialog boxes appear.

Destination directory

The directory (or folder) to which files are copied or moved.

See also *source directory*.

Device driver

A program that allows a specific device, such as a modem, network adapter, or printer, to communicate with Windows 2000. Although a device can be installed on a system, Windows 2000 cannot use the device until the appropriate driver has been installed and configured. If a device is listed in the Hardware Compatibility List (HCL), a driver is usually included with Windows 2000. Device drivers load (for all enabled devices) when a computer is started, and thereafter run invisibly.

See also *Hardware Compatibility List (HCL)*.

Device Manager

An administrative tool that can be used to manage the devices on your computer. Use Device Manager to view and change device properties, update device drivers, configure device settings, and remove devices.

Device Tree

A hierarchical tree that contains the devices configured on the computer.

Differential backup

A backup that copies files created or changed since the last normal or incremental backup. It does not mark files as having been backed up (that is, the archive bit is not set). If you are performing a combination of normal and differential backups, restoring files and folders requires that you have the last normal as well as the last differential backup.

See also *copy backup*; *daily backup*; *incremental backup*; *normal backup*.

Digital audio tape (DAT)

A magnetic medium for recording and storing digital audio data.

Digital certificate

See *certificate*.

Digital linear tape (DLT)

A magnetic medium for backing up data. DLT can transfer data faster than many other types of tape media.

Digital signature

A means for originators of a message, file, or other digitally encoded information to bind their identity to the information. The process of digitally signing information entails transforming the information, as well as some secret information held by the sender, into a tag called a signature. Digital signatures are used in public key environments and they provide nonrepudiation and integrity services.

See also *public key cryptography*.

Digital subscriber line (DSL)

A special communication line that uses modulation technology to maximize the amount of data that can be sent over copper wires. DSL is used for connections from telephone switching stations to a subscriber rather than between switching stations.

Direct hosting

A feature that allows Windows 2000 computers using Microsoft file and print sharing to communicate over a communications protocol, such as TCP or IPX, bypassing the NetBIOS layer.

Direct memory access (DMA)

Memory access that does not involve the microprocessor. DMA is frequently used for data transfer directly between memory and a peripheral device, such as a disk drive.

Directory

An information source that contains information about computer files or other objects. In a file system, a directory stores information about files. In a distributed computing environment (such as a Windows 2000 domain), the directory stores information about objects such as printers, applications, databases, and users.

Directory service

Both the directory information source and the service that make the information available and usable. A directory service enables the user to find an object given any one of its attributes.

See also *Active Directory*; *directory*.

Disable

To make a device nonfunctional. For example, if a device in a hardware profile is disabled, the device cannot be used while using that hardware profile. Disabling a device frees the resources that were allocated to the device.

Discretionary access control list (DACL)

The part of an object's security descriptor that grants or denies specific users and groups permission to access the object. Only the owner of an object can change permissions granted or denied in a DACL; thus access to the object is at the owner's discretion.

See also *access control entry*; *object*; *security descriptor*; *system access control list.*

Disk bottleneck

A condition that occurs when disk performance is reduced to the extent that overall system performance is affected.

Disk quota

The maximum amount of disk space available to a user.

Dismount

To remove a removable tape or disc from a drive.

See also *library*.

Distinguished name

A name that uniquely identifies an object by using the relative distinguished name for the object, plus the names of container objects and domains that contain the object. The distinguished name identifies the object as well as its location in a tree. Every object in Active Directory has a distinguished name. An example of a distinguished name is CN=MyName,CN=Users,DC=Reskit,DC=Com. This distinguished name identifies the "MyName" user object in the reskit.com domain.

Distributed file system (DFS)

A Windows 2000 service consisting of software residing on network servers and clients that transparently links shared folders located on different file servers into a single namespace for improved load sharing and data availability.

Distribution folder

The folder created on the Windows 2000 distribution server to contain the Setup files.

DMA

See *direct memory access*.

DNS

See *Domain Name System*.

DNS server

A computer that runs DNS server programs containing name-to-IP address mappings, IP address-to-name mappings, information about the domain tree structure, and other information. DNS servers also attempt to resolve client queries.

DNS zone

In a DNS database, a zone is a contiguous portion of the DNS tree that is administered as a single separate entity, by a DNS server. The zone contains resource records for all the names within the zone.

Domain

In Windows 2000 and Active Directory, a collection of computers defined by the administrator of a Windows 2000 Server network that share a common directory database. A domain has a unique name and provides access to the centralized user accounts and group accounts maintained by the domain administrator. Each domain has its own security policies and security relationships with other domains and represents a single security boundary of a Windows 2000 computer network. Active Directory is made up of one or more domains, each of which can span more than one physical location. For DNS, a domain is any tree or sub tree within the DNS namespace. Although the names for DNS domains often correspond to Active Directory domains, DNS domains should not be confused with Windows 2000 and Active Directory networking domain.

Domain controller

For a Windows NT Server or Windows 2000 Server domain, the server that authenticates domain logons and maintains the security policy and the security accounts master database for a domain. Domain controllers manage user access to a network, which includes logging on, authentication, and access to the directory and shared resources.

Domain local group

A Windows 2000 group only available in native mode domains that can contain members from anywhere in the forest, in trusted forests, or in a trusted pre-Windows 2000 domain. Domain local groups can only grant permissions to resources within the domain in which they exist. Typically, domain local groups are used to gather security principals from across the forest to control access to resources within the domain.

Domain name

In Windows 2000 and Active Directory, the name given by an administrator to a collection of networked computers that share a common directory. For DNS, domain names are specific node names in the DNS namespace tree. DNS domain names use singular node names, known as "labels," joined together by periods (.) that indicate each node level in the namespace.

See also *Domain Name System (DNS)*; *namespace*.

Domain Name System (DNS)

A hierarchical naming system used for locating domain names on the Internet and on private TCP/IP networks. DNS provides a service for mapping DNS domain names to IP addresses, and vice versa. This allows users, computers, and applications to query the DNS to specify remote systems by fully qualified domain names rather than by IP addresses.

See also *domain*; *Ping*.

Domain tree

In DNS, the inverted hierarchical tree structure that is used to index domain names. Domain trees are similar in purpose and concept to the directory trees used by computer filing systems for disk storage.

See also *domain name*; *namespace*.

DOT4

See *IEEE 1284.4*

Dual boot

A computer configuration that can start two different operating systems.

See also *multiple boot*.

DVD decoder

A hardware or software component that allows a digital video disc (DVD) drive to display movies on your computer screen.

See also *DVD disc*; *DVD drive*.

DVD disc

A type of optical disc storage technology. A digital video disc (DVD) looks like a CD-ROM disc, but it can store greater amounts of data. DVD discs are often used to store full-length movies and other multimedia content that requires large amounts of storage space.

See also *DVD decoder*; *DVD drive*.

DVD drive

A disk storage device that uses digital video disc (DVD) technology. A DVD drive reads both CD-ROM and DVD discs; however, a DVD decoder is necessary to display DVD movies on your computer screen.

See also *DVD decoder*; *DVD disc*.

Dvorak keyboard

An alternative keyboard with a layout that makes the most frequently typed characters more accessible to people who have difficulty typing on the standard QWERTY layout.

Dynamic disk

A physical disk that is managed by Disk Management. Dynamic disks can contain only dynamic volumes (that is, volumes created by using Disk Management). Dynamic disks cannot contain partitions or logical drives, nor can MS-DOS access them.

See also *dynamic volume*; *partition*.

Dynamic Host Configuration Protocol (DHCP)

A networking protocol that provides safe, reliable, and simple TCP/IP network configuration and offers dynamic configuration of Internet Protocol (IP) addresses for computers. DHCP ensures that address conflicts do not occur and helps conserve the use of IP addresses through centralized management of address allocation.

Dynamic priority

The priority value to which a thread's base priority is adjusted to optimize scheduling.

Dynamic volume

A logical volume that is created using Disk Management. Dynamic volumes include simple, spanned, striped, mirrored, and RAID-5 volumes. Dynamic volumes must be created on dynamic disks.

See also *dynamic disk*; *volume*.

Dynamic-link library (DLL)

A feature of the Microsoft Windows family of operating systems and the OS/2 operating system. DLLs allow executable routines, generally serving a specific function or set of functions, to be stored separately as files with .dll extensions, and to be loaded only when needed by the program that calls them.

E

EAP

See *Extensible Authentication Protocol*

EIDE

See *Enhanced Integrated Drive Electronics*

Embedded object

Information created in another application that has been pasted inside a document. When information is embedded, you can edit it in the new document by using toolbars and menus from the original program. When you double-click the embedded icon, the toolbars and menus from the program used to create the information appear. Embedded information is not linked to the original file. If you change information in one place, it is not updated in the other.

See also *linked object.*

Emergency repair disk (ERD)

A disk, created by the Backup utility, that contains copies of three of the files stored in the %SystemRoot%/Repair folder, including Setup. log that contains a list of system files installed on the computer. This disk can be used during the Emergency Repair Process to repair your computer if it will not start or if your system files are damaged or erased.

Encapsulating security payload (ESP)

An IPSec protocol that provides confidentiality, in addition to authentication, integrity, and anti-replay. ESP can be used alone, in combination with AH, or nested with the Layer Two Tunneling Protocol (L2TP). ESP does not normally sign the entire packet unless it is being tunneled. Ordinarily, just the data payload is protected, not the IP header.

Encrypting File System (EFS)

A new feature in Windows 2000 that protects sensitive data in files that is stored on disk using the NTFS file system. It uses symmetric key encryption in conjunction with public key technology to provide confidentiality for files. It runs as an integrated system service, which makes EFS easy to manage, difficult to attack, and transparent to the file owner and to applications.

Encryption

The process of disguising a message or data in such a way as to hide its substance.

Encryption key

A bit string that is used in conjunction with an encryption algorithm to encrypt and decrypt data.

See also *public key*; *private key*; *symmetric key*.

Enhanced Integrated Drive Electronics (EIDE)

An extension of the IDE standard, EIDE is a hardware interface standard for disk drive designs that houses control circuits in the drives themselves. It allows for standardized interfaces to the system bus, while providing for advanced features, such as burst data transfers and direct data access.

Enterprise Resource Planning (ERP)

A software system designed to support and automate the processes of an organization, including manufacturing and distribution, accounting, project management and personnel functions.

Environment variable

A string consisting of environment information, such as a drive, path, or filename, associated with a symbolic name that can be used by Windows NT and Windows 2000. Use the System option in Control Panel or the set command from the command prompt to define environment variables.

ERD

See *emergency repair disk*.

Ethernet

An IEEE 802.3 standard for contention networks. Ethernet uses a bus or star topology and relies on the form of access known as Carrier Sense Multiple Access with Collision Detection (CSMA/DC) to regulate communication line traffic. Network nodes are linked by coaxial cable, fiber-optic cable, or by twisted-pair wiring. Data is transmitted in variable-length frames containing delivery and control information and up to 1,500 bytes of data. The Ethernet standard provides for base band transmission at 10 megabits (10 million bits) per second.

Exabytes

Approximately one quintillion bytes, or one billion billion bytes.

Expire interval

For DNS, the number of seconds that DNS servers operating as secondary masters for a zone use to determine if zone data should be expired when the zone is not refreshed and renewed.

See also *zone*.

Explicit trust relationship

A trust relationship from Windows NT in which an explicit link is made in one direction only. Explicit trusts can also exist between Windows NT domains and Windows 2000 domains, and between forests.

Export

In NFS, to make a file system available by a server to a client for mounting.

Extended Industry Standard Architecture (EISA)

A 32-bit bus standard introduced in 1988 by a consortium of nine computer-industry companies. EISA maintains compatibility with the earlier Industry Standard Architecture (ISA) but provides for additional features.

Extended partition

A portion of a basic disk that can contain logical drives. To have more than four volumes on your basic disk, you need to use an extended partition. Only one of the four partitions allowed per physical disk can be an extended partition, and no primary partition needs to be present to create an extended partition. You can create extended partitions only on basic disks.

See also *basic disk*; *logical drive*; *partition*; *primary partition*; *unallocated space*.

Extensible Authentication Protocol (EAP)

An extension to PPP that allows for arbitrary authentication mechanisms to be employed for the validation of a PPP connection.

Extensible Markup Language (XML)

A meta-markup language that provides a format for describing structured data. This facilitates more precise declarations of content and more meaningful search results across multiple platforms. In addition, XML will enable a new generation of Web-based data viewing and manipulation applications.

F

FAT32

A derivative of the file allocation table file system. FAT32 supports smaller cluster sizes than FAT in the same given disk space, which results in more efficient space allocation on FAT32 drives.

See also *file allocation table*; *NTFS file system*.

Fault tolerance

The assurance of data integrity when hardware failures occur. On the Windows NT and Windows 2000 platforms, fault tolerance is provided by the Ftdisk.sys driver.

Fiber Distributed Data Interface (FDDI)

A type of network media designed to be used with fiber-optic cabling.

See also LocalTalk; Token Ring.

File allocation table (FAT)

A file system based on a file allocation table (FAT) maintained by some operating systems, including Windows NT and Windows 2000, to keep track of the status of various segments of disk space used for file storage.

File record

The row in the master file table (MFT) that corresponds to a particular disk file. The file record is identified by its file reference.

File system

In an operating system, the overall structure in which files are named, stored, and organized. NTFS, FAT, and FAT32 are types of file systems.

File system cache

An area of physical memory that holds frequently used pages. It allows applications and services to locate pages rapidly and reduces disk activity.

File Transfer Protocol (FTP)

A protocol that defines how to transfer files from one computer to another over the Internet. FTP is also a client/server application that moves files using this protocol.

Filter

In IPSec, a rule that provides the ability to trigger security negotiations for a communication based on the source, destination, and type of IP traffic.

See also search filter.

FilterKeys

A Windows 2000 accessibility feature that allows people with physical disabilities to adjust keyboard response time.

See also *BounceKeys*; *RepeatKeys*; *SlowKeys*.

Firewall

A combination of hardware and software that provides a security system, usually to prevent unauthorized access from outside to an internal network or intranet. A firewall prevents direct communication between network and external computers by routing communication through a proxy server outside of the network. The proxy server determines whether it is safe to let a file pass through to the network. A firewall is also called a security-edge gateway.

Folder redirection

A Group Policy option that allows you to redirect designated folders to the network.

Foreground boost

A mechanism that increases the priority of a foreground application.

Forest

A collection of one or more Windows 2000 Active Directory trees, organized as peers and connected by two-way transitive trust relationships between the root domains of each tree. All trees in a forest share a common schema, configuration, and Global Catalog. When a forest contains multiple trees, the trees do not form a contiguous namespace.

Fragmentation

The scattering of parts of the same disk file over different areas of the disk. Fragmentation occurs as files on a disk are deleted and new files are added. It slows disk access and degrades the overall performance of disk operations, although usually not severely.

See also *defragmentation*.

Free media pool

A logical collection of unused data-storage media that can be used by applications or other media pools. When media are no longer needed by an application, they are returned to a free media pool so that they can be used again.

See also *media pool*; *Removable Storage*.

G

Gatekeeper

A server that uses a directory to perform name-to-IP address translation, admission control and call management services in H.323 conferencing.

Gateway

A device connected to multiple physical TCP/IP networks, capable of routing or delivering IP packets between them. A gateway translates between different transport protocols or data formats (for example, IPX and IP) and is generally added to a network primarily for its translation ability.

See also *IP address*; *IP router*.

Global Catalog

A domain controller that contains a partial replica of every domain directory partition in the forest as well as a full replica of its own domain directory partition and the schema and configuration directory partitions. The Global Catalog holds a replica of every object in Active Directory, but each object includes a limited number of its attributes. The attributes in the Global Catalog are those most frequently used in search operations (such as a user's first and last names) and those attributes that are required to locate a full replica of the object. The Global Catalog enables users and applications to find objects in Active Directory given one or more attributes of the target object, without knowing what domain holds the object. The Active Directory replication system builds the Global Catalog automatically. The attributes replicated into the Global Catalog include a base set defined by Microsoft. Administrators can specify additional properties to meet the needs of their installation.

Global group

For Windows 2000 Server, a group that can be used in its own domain, in member servers and in workstations of the domain, and in trusting domains. In all those places a global group can be granted rights and permissions and can become a member of local groups. However, a global group can contain user accounts only from its own domain.

See also *group*; *local group*.

Globally unique identifier (GUID)

A 16-byte value generated from the unique identifier on a device, the current date and time, and a sequence number. A GUID is used to identify a particular device or component.

Graphical Identification and Authentication (GINA)

A DLL loaded during the Windows 2000 Winlogon process, which displays the standard logon dialog box, collects, and processes user logon data for verification.

Graphical user interface (GUI)

A display format, like that of Windows, which represents a program's functions with graphic images such as buttons and icons. GUIs allow a user to perform operations and make choices by pointing and clicking with a mouse.

Group

A collection of users, computers, contacts, and other groups. Groups can be used as security or as e-mail distribution collections. Distribution groups are used only for e-mail. Security groups are used both to grant access to resources and as e-mail distribution lists. In a server cluster, a group is a collection of resources, and the basic unit of failover.

See also *domain local group*; *global group*; *native mode*; *universal group*.

Group Identification (GID)

A group identifier that uniquely identifies a group of users. UNIX uses the GID to identify the group ownership of a file, and to determine access permissions.

Group memberships

The groups to which a user account belongs. Permissions and rights granted to a group are also provided to its members. In most cases, the actions a user can perform in Windows 2000 are determined by the group memberships of the user account to which the user is logged on.

See also *group*.

Group Policy

An administrator's tool for defining and controlling how programs, network resources, and the operating system operate for users and computers in an organization. In an Active Directory environment, Group Policy is applied to users or computers on the basis of their membership in sites, domains, or organizational units.

Group Policy object

A collection of Group Policy settings. Group Policy objects are the documents created by the Group Policy snap-in. Group Policy objects are stored at the domain level, and they affect users and computers contained in sites, domains, and organizational units. Each Windows 2000-based computer has exactly one group of settings stored locally, called the local Group Policy object.

H

H.323

The ITU-T standard for multimedia communications over networks that do not provide a guaranteed quality of service. This standard provides specifications for workstations, devices, and services to carry real-time video, audio, and data or any combination of these elements.

See also *QoS*.

Hardware abstraction layer (HAL)

A thin layer of software provided by the hardware manufacturer that hides, or abstracts, hardware differences from higher layers of the operating system. Through the filter provided by the HAL, different types of hardware all look alike to the rest of the operating system. This allows Windows NT and Windows 2000 to be portable from one hardware platform to another. The HAL also provides routines that allow a single device driver to support the same device on all platforms. The HAL works closely with the kernel.

Hardware Compatibility List (HCL)

A list of the devices supported by Windows 2000, available from the Microsoft Web site.

Hardware malfunction message

A character-based, full-screen error message displayed on a blue background. It indicates the microprocessor detected a hardware error condition from which the system cannot recover.

Hardware profile

A set of changes to the standard configuration of devices and services (including drivers and Win32 services) loaded by Windows 2000 when the system starts. For example, a hardware profile can include an instruction to disable (that is, not load) a driver, or an instruction not to connect an undocked laptop computer to the network. Because of the instructions in this subkey, users can modify the service configuration for a particular use while preserving the standard configuration unchanged for more general uses.

Hardware type

A classification for similar devices. For example, Imaging Device is a hardware type for digital cameras and scanners.

Heartbeat thread

A thread initiated by the Windows NT Virtual DOS Machine (NTVDM) process that interrupts every 55 milliseconds to simulate a timer interrupt.

Hop

In data communications, one segment of the path between routers on a geographically dispersed network. A hop is comparable to one "leg" of a journey that includes intervening stops between the starting point and the destination. The distance between each of those stops (routers) is a communications hop.

Hosts

A local text file in the same format as the 4.3 Berkeley Software Distribution (BSD) UNIX/etc/hosts file. This file maps host names to IP addresses. In Windows 2000, this file is stored in the \%SystemRoot%\System32\Drivers\Etc folder.

Hot keys

A Windows feature that allows quick activation of specified accessibility features through a combination of keys pressed in unison.

HTML+Time

A new feature in Microsoft Internet Explorer 5 that adds timing and media synchronization support to HTML pages. Using a few Extensible Markup Language (XML)-based elements and attributes, you can add images, video, and sounds to an HTML page, and synchronize them with HTML text elements over a specified amount of time. In short, you can use HTML+TIME technology to quickly and easily create multimedia-rich, interactive presentations, with little or no scripting.

Human Interface Device (HID)

A firmware specification that is a new standard for input and output devices such as drawing tablets, keyboards, USB speakers, and other specialized devices designed to improve accessibility.

Hypertext Markup Language (HTML)

A simple markup language used to create hypertext documents that are portable from one platform to another. HTML files are simple ASCII text files with embedded codes (indicated by markup tags) to indicate formatting and hypertext links. HTML is used for formatting documents on the World Wide Web.

Hypertext Transfer Protocol (HTTP)

The protocol used to transfer information on the World Wide Web. An HTTP address (one kind of Uniform Resource Locator [URL]) takes the form: http://www.microsoft.com.

I

I/O request packet (IRP)

Data structures that drivers use to communicate with each other.

ICM

See *Image Color Management.*

IDE

See *integrated device electronics.*

IEEE 1284.4

An IEEE specification, also called DOT4, for supporting multi-function peripherals (MFPs). Windows 2000 has a driver called DOT4 that creates different port settings for each function of an MFP, enabling Windows 2000 print servers to simultaneously send data to multiple parts of an MFP.

IEEE 1394 (Firewire)

A standard for high-speed serial devices such as digital video and digital audio editing equipment.

IIS

See *Internet Information Services.*

ILS

See *Internet locator service.*

Image Color Management (ICM)

The process of image output correction. ICM attempts to make the output more closely match the colors that are input or scanned.

Impersonation

A circumstance that occurs when Windows NT or Windows 2000 allows one process to take on the security attributes of another.

Import media pool

A repository where Removable Storage puts media when it recognizes the on-media identifier (OMID), but does not have the media cataloged in the current Removable Storage database.

Incremental backup

A backup that copies only those files created or changed since the last normal or incremental backup. It marks files as having been backed up (that is, the archive bit is set). If a combination of normal and incremental backups is used to restore your data, you need to have the last normal backup and all subsequent incremental backup sets.

See also *copy backup*; *daily backup*; *differential backup*; *normal backup*.

Independent software vendors (ISVs)

A third-party software developer; an individual or an organization that independently creates computer software.

Industry Standard Architecture (ISA)

A bus design specification that allows components to be added as cards plugged into standard expansion slots in IBM Personal Computers and IBM compatible computers. Originally introduced in the IBM PC/XT with an 8-bit data path, ISA was expanded in 1984, when IBM introduced the PC/AT, to permit a 16-bit data path. A 16-bit ISA slot consists of two separate 8-bit slots mounted end-to-end so that a single 16-bit card plugs into both slots. An 8-bit expansion card can be inserted and used in a 16-bit slot (it occupies only one of the two slots), but a 16-bit expansion card cannot be used in an 8-bit slot.

See also *Extended Industry Standard Architecture*.

Infrared (IR)

Light that is beyond red in the color spectrum. While the light is not visible to the human eye, infrared transmitters and receivers can send and receive infrared signals.

See also *Infrared Data Association*; *infrared device*; *infrared port*.

Infrared Data Association (IrDA)

A networking protocol used to transmit data created by infrared devices. Infrared Data Association is also the name of the industry organization of computer, component, and telecommunications vendors who establish the standards for infrared communication between computers and peripheral devices, such as printers.

See also *infrared*; *infrared device*; *infrared port*.

Infrared device

A computer, or a computer peripheral such as a printer, that can communicate using infrared light.

See also *infrared*.

Infrared port

An optical port on a computer that enables communication with other computers or devices by using infrared light, without cables. Infrared ports can be found on some portable computers, printers, and cameras.

See also *infrared device*.

Input/Output (I/O) port

A channel through which data is transferred between a device and the microprocessor. The port appears to the microprocessor as one or more memory addresses that it can use to send or receive data.

Insert/Eject (IE) port

IE ports, also called "mailslots," offer limited access to the cartridges in a library managed by Removable Storage. When an administrator adds cartridges to a library through an IE port, the cartridges are placed in the IE port and then the library uses the transport to move the cartridges from the IE port to a slot. Some libraries have no IE ports; others have several. Some IE ports handle only one cartridge at a time; others can handle several at one time.

Instantaneous counter

A type of counter that displays the most recent measurement taken by the Performance console.

Institute of Electrical and Electronics Engineers (IEEE)

An organization of engineering and electronics professionals that are notable for developing standards for hardware and software.

Integrated device electronics (IDE)

A type of disk-drive interface in which the controller electronics reside on the drive itself, eliminating the need for a separate adapter card. IDE offers advantages such as look-ahead caching to increase overall performance.

Integrated Services Digital Network (ISDN)

A type of phone line used to enhance WAN speeds. ISDN lines can transmit at speeds of 64 or 128 kilobits per second, as opposed to standard phone lines, which typically transmit at 28.8 kilobits per second. The phone company must install an ISDN line at both the server site and the remote site.

See also *wide area network.*

Integrity

A basic security function of cryptography. Integrity provides verification that the original contents of information have not been altered or corrupted. Without integrity, someone might alter information or the information might become corrupted, but the alteration can go undetected. For example, an Internet Protocol security property that protects data from unauthorized modification in transit, ensuring that the data received is exactly the same as the data sent. Hash functions sign each packet with a cryptographic checksum, which the receiving computer checks before opening the packet. If the packet-and therefore signature-has changed, the packet is discarded.

See also *cryptography*; *authentication*; *confidentiality*; *nonrepudiation.*

IntelliMirror

A set of Windows 2000 features used for desktop change and configuration management. When IntelliMirror is used in both the server and client, the users' data, applications, and settings follow them when they move to another computer.

Interactive logon

A network logon from a computer keyboard, when the user types information in the Logon Information dialog box displayed by the computer's operating system.

Internet

A worldwide public TCP/IP internetwork consisting of thousands of networks, connecting research facilities, universities, libraries, and private companies.

Internet Control Message Protocol (ICMP)

A required maintenance protocol in the TCP/IP suite that reports errors and allows simple connectivity. The Ping tool uses ICMP to perform TCP/IP troubleshooting.

Internet Information Services (IIS)

Software services that support Web site creation, configuration, and management, along with other Internet functions. Internet Information Services include Network News Transfer Protocol (NNTP), File Transfer Protocol (FTP), and Simple Mail Transfer Protocol (SMTP).

See also *File Transfer Protocol*; *Network News Transfer Protocol*; *Simple Mail Transfer Protocol.*

Internet Key Exchange (IKE)

A protocol that establishes the security association and shared keys necessary for two parties to communicate with Internet Protocol security.

Internet locator service (ILS)

An optional component of Microsoft Site Server that creates a dynamic directory of videoconferencing users.

Internet Printing Protocol (IPP)

The protocol that uses the Hypertext Transfer Protocol (HTTP) to send print jobs to printers throughout the world. Windows 2000 supports Internet Printing Protocol (IPP) version 1.0.

Internet Protocol (IP)

A routable protocol in the TCP/IP protocol suite that is responsible for IP addressing, routing, and the fragmentation and reassembly of IP packets.

Internet Protocol security (IPSec)

A set of industry-standard, cryptography-based protection services and protocols. IPSec protects all protocols in the TCP/IP protocol suite and Internet communications using L2TP.

See also *Layer Two Tunneling Protocol.*

Internet service provider (ISP)

A company that provides individuals or companies access to the Internet and the World Wide Web. An ISP provides a telephone number, a user name, a password, and other connection information so users can connect their computers to the ISP's computers. An ISP typically charges a monthly and/or hourly connection fee.

Internetwork Packet Exchange (IPX)

A network protocol native to NetWare that controls addressing and routing of packets within and between LANs. IPX does not guarantee that a message will be complete (no lost packets).

See also *Internetwork Packet Exchange / Sequenced Packet Exchange.*

Internetwork Packet Exchange / Sequenced Packet Exchange (IPX/SPX)

Transport protocols used in Novell NetWare and other networks.

Interrupt

A request for attention from the processor. When the processor receives an interrupt, it suspends its current operations, saves the status of its work, and transfers control to a special routine known as an interrupt handler, which contains the instructions for dealing with the particular situation that caused the interrupt.

Interrupt request (IRQ)

A signal sent by a device to get the attention of the processor when the device is ready to accept or send information. Each device sends its interrupt requests over a specific hardware line, numbered from 0 to 15. Each device must be assigned a unique IRQ number.

Intranet

A network within an organization that uses Internet technologies and protocols but is available only to certain people, such as employees of a company. An intranet is also called a private network.

IP address

A 32-bit address used to identify a node on an IP internetwork. Each node on the IP internetwork must be assigned a unique IP address, which is made up of the network ID, plus a unique host ID. This address is typically represented with the decimal value of each octet separated by a period (for example, 192.168.7.27). In Windows 2000, the IP address can be configured manually or dynamically through DHCP.

See also *Dynamic Host Configuration Protocol*; *node.*

IP router

A system connected to multiple physical TCP/IP networks that can route or deliver IP packets between the networks.

See also *packet*; *router*; *routing*; *Transmission Control Protocol/Internet Protocol.*

IPP

See *Internet Printing Protocol.*

IPSec

See *Internet Protocol security.*

IPSec driver

A driver that uses the IP Filter List from the active IPSec policy to watch for outbound IP packets that must be secured and inbound IP packets that need to be verified and decrypted.

IPSec filter

A part of IPSec security rules that make up an IPSec security policy. IPSec filters determine whether a data packet needs an IPSec action and what the IPSec action is, such as permit, block, or secure. Filters can classify traffic by criteria including source IP address, source subnet mask, destination IP address, IP protocol type, source port, and destination port. Filters are not specific to a network interface.

See also *IPSec security rules.*

IPSec security rules

Rules contained in the IPSec policy that govern how and when an IPSec is invoked. A rule triggers and controls secure communication when a particular source, destination, or traffic type is found. Each IPSec policy may contain one or many rules; any of which may apply to a particular packet. Default rules are provided which encompass a variety of clients and server-based communications or rules can be modified to meet custom requirements.

Irtran-p

A protocol that transfers images from cameras to Windows 2000 computers using infrared transmissions, making a physical cable connection unnecessary.

IrDA

See *Infrared Data Association.*

IRP

See *I/O request packet.*

Isochronous

Time dependent. Refers to processes where data must be delivered within certain time constraints. Multimedia streams require an isochronous transport mechanism to ensure that data is delivered as fast as it is displayed, and to ensure that the audio is synchronized with the video.

J

Job object

A feature in the Win32 API set that makes it possible for groups of processes to be managed with respect to their processor usage and other factors.

K

Kerberos authentication protocol

An authentication mechanism used to verify user or host identity. The Kerberos v5 authentication protocol is the default authentication service for Windows 2000. Internet Protocol security and the QoS Admission Control Service use the Kerberos protocol for authentication.

See also *Internet Protocol security*; *NTLM authentication protocol*; *QoS Admission Control Service*.

Kernel

The core of layered architecture that manages the most basic operations of the operating system and the computer's processor for Windows NT and Windows 2000. The kernel schedules different blocks of executing code, called threads, for the processor to keep it as busy as possible and coordinates multiple processors to optimize performance. The kernel also synchronizes activities among Executive-level subcomponents, such as I/O Manager and Process Manager, and handles hardware exceptions and other hardware-dependent functions. The kernel works closely with the hardware abstraction layer.

Key

A secret code or number required to read, modify, or verify secured data. Keys are used in conjunction with algorithms to secure data. Windows 2000 automatically handles key generation. For the registry, a key is an entry in the registry that can contain both subkeys and entries. In the registry structure, keys are analogous to folders, and entries are analogous to files. In the Registry Editor window, a key appears as a file folder in the left pane. In an answer file, keys are character strings that specify parameters from which Setup obtains the needed data for unattended installation of the operating system.

Keyboard filters

Special timing and other devices that compensate for erratic motion tremors, slow response time, and other mobility impairments.

L

L2TP

See *Layer Two Tunneling Protocol.*

LAN

See *local area network.*

Last Known Good Configuration

A hardware configuration available by pressing F8 during startup. If the current hardware settings prevent the computer from starting, the Last Known Good Configuration can allow the computer to be started and the configuration to be examined. When the Last Known Good Configuration is used, later configuration changes are lost.

Layer 2 forwarding (L2F)

Permits the tunneling of the link layer of higher-level protocols. Using these tunnels, it is possible to separate the location of the initial dial-up server from the physical location at which the dial-up protocol connection is terminated and access to the network is provided.

See also *Layer Two Tunneling Protocol*; *tunnel.*

Layer two Tunneling Protocol (L2TP)

A tunneling protocol that encapsulates PPP frames to be sent over IP, X.25, Frame Relay, or ATM networks. L2TP is a combination of the Point-to-Point Tunneling Protocol (PPTP) and Layer 2 Forwarding (L2F), a technology proposed by Cisco Systems, Inc.

Legend

The area of the System Monitor graph or histogram display that shows computer name, object name, counter name, instances, and other information as a reference to the lines in the graph or the bars in the histogram.

Library

A data-storage system, usually managed by Removable Storage. A library consists of removable media (such as tapes or discs) and a hardware device that can read from or write to the media. There are two major types of libraries: robotic libraries (automated multiple-media, mutative devices) and stand-alone drive libraries (manually operated, single-drive devices). A robotic library is also called a jukebox or changer.

See also *Removable Storage.*

Library request

A request for an online library or stand-alone drive to perform a task. This request can be issued by an application or by Removable Storage.

Lightweight Directory Access Protocol (LDAP)

A directory service protocol that runs directly over TCP/IP and the primary access protocol for Active Directory. LDAP version 3 is defined by a set of Proposed Standard documents in Internet Engineering Task Force (IETF) RFC 2251.

See also *Lightweight Directory Access Protocol application programming interface.*

Lightweight Directory Access Protocol application programming interface (LDAP API)

An API for experienced programmers who want to enable new or existing applications to connect to, search, and update LDAP servers. You can use the LDAP API to write directory-enabled applications that allow LDAP client applications to search for and retrieve information from an LDAP server. LDAP API enables the modification of directory objects, where such modifications are permitted. There are also functions that provide access control for servers, by allowing clients to authenticate themselves.

Line Printer

A connectivity tool that runs on client systems and is used to print files to a computer running an LPD server.

See also *Line Printer Daemon.*

Line Printer Daemon (LPD)

A service on the print server that receives documents (print jobs) from line printer remote (LPR) tools running on client systems.

See also *Line Printer.*

Line Printer Port Monitor

A port monitor that is used to send jobs over TCP/IP from the client running Lprmon.dll to a print server running an LPD (Line Printer Daemon) service. Line Printer Port Monitor can be used to enable Internet printing, UNIX print servers, or Windows 2000 print servers over a TCP/IP network.

Line Printer Remote (LPR)

See *Line Printer.*

Linked object

An object that is inserted into a document but still exists in the source file. When information is linked, the new document is updated automatically if the information in the original document changes.

See also *embedded object*.

Local area network (LAN)

A communications network connecting a group of computers, printers, and other devices located within a relatively limited area (for example, a building). A LAN allows any connected device to interact with any other on the network.

See also *wide area network*.

Local computer

A computer that can be accessed directly without using a communications line or a communications device, such as a network adapter or a modem. Similarly, running a local program means running the program on your computer, as opposed to running it from a server.

Local group

For computers running Windows 2000 Professional and member servers, a group that is granted permissions and rights from its own computer to only those resources on its own computer on which the group resides.

See also *global group*.

Local Security Authority (LSA)

A protected subsystem that authenticates and logs users onto the local system. In addition, the LSA maintains information about all aspects of local security on a system (collectively known as the local security policy), and provides various services for translation between names and identifiers.

Local user profile

A computer-based record maintained about an authorized user that is created automatically on the computer the first time a user logs on to a computer running Windows 2000.

Localmon.dll

The standard print monitor for use with printers connected directly to your computer. If you add a printer to your computer using a serial or parallel port (such as COM1 or LPT1), this is the monitor that is used.

LocalTalk

The Apple networking hardware built into every Macintosh computer. LocalTalk includes the cables and connector boxes to connect components and network devices that are part of the AppleTalk network system. LocalTalk was formerly known as the AppleTalk Personal Network.

Locator service

In a distributed system, a feature that allows a client to find a shared resource or server without providing an address or full name. Generally associated with Active Directory, which provides a locator service.

Logical drive

A volume created within an extended partition on a basic disk. You can format and assign a drive letter to a logical drive. Only basic disks can contain logical drives. A logical drive cannot span multiple disks.

See also *basic disk*; *basic volume*; *extended partition.*

Logical volume

A volume created within an extended partition on a basic disk. You can format and assign a drive letter to a logical drive. Only basic disks can contain logical drives. A logical drive cannot span multiple disks.

See also *basic disk*; *basic volume*; *extended partition.*

Logon script

Files that can be assigned to user accounts. Typically a batch file, a logon script runs automatically every time the user logs on. It can be used to configure a user's working environment at every logon, and it allows an administrator to influence a user's environment without managing all aspects of it. A logon script can be assigned to one or more user accounts.

See also *batch program.*

Long file name (LFN)

A folder name or file name on the FAT file system that is longer than the 8.3 file name standard (up to eight characters followed by a period and an extension of up to three characters). Windows 2000 supports long file names up to the file-name limit of 255 characters. Macintosh users can assign long names to files and folders on the server and, using Services for Macintosh, long names to Macintosh-accessible volumes can be assigned when created. Windows 2000 automatically translates long names of files and folders to 8.3 names for MS-DOS and Windows 3.*x* users.

See also *name mapping*.

Loopback address

The address of the local computer used for routing outgoing packets back to the source computer. This address is used primarily for testing.

M

MAC

See *media access control.*

Magazine

A collection of storage locations, also called "slots," for cartridges in a library managed by Removable Storage. Magazines are usually removable.

Magneto-optic (MO) disk

A high-capacity, erasable storage medium which uses laser beams to heat the disk and magnetically arrange the data.

Magnifier

A screen enlarger that magnifies a portion of the screen in a separate window for users with low vision and for those who require occasional screen magnification for such tasks as editing art.

Manual caching

A method of manually designating network files and folders so they are stored on a user's hard disk and accessible when the user is not connected to the network.

Master Boot Record (MBR)

The first sector on a hard disk, this data structure starts the process of booting the computer. It is the most important area on a hard disk. The MBR contains the partition table for the disk and a small amount of executable code called the master boot code.

Master file table (MFT)

The database that tracks the contents of an NTFS volume. The MFT is a table whose rows correspond to files on the volume and whose columns correspond to the attributes of each file.

Maximum password age

The period of time a password can be used before the system requires the user to change it.

Media

The physical material on which information is recorded and stored.

Media access control

A sublayer of the IEEE 802 specifications that defines network access methods and framing.

Media label library

A dynamic-link library (DLL) that can interpret the format of a media label written by a Removable Storage application.

Media pool

Logical collections of removable media that have the same management policies. Media pools are used by applications to control access to specific tapes or discs within libraries managed by Removable Storage. There are four media pools: Unrecognized, Import, Free, and application-specific. Each media pool can only hold either media or other media pools.

See also *Removable Storage*.

Media states

Descriptions of conditions in which Removable Storage has placed a cartridge that it is managing. The states include Idle, In Use, Mounted, Loaded, and Unloaded.

Memory leak

A condition that occurs when applications allocate memory for use but do not free allocated memory when finished.

Metric

A number used to indicate the cost of a route in the IP routing table to enable the selection of the best route among possible multiple routes to the same destination.

MFP

See *multi-function peripherals*.

Microsoft Challenge Handshake Authentication Protocol version 1 (MS-CHAP v1)

An encrypted authentication mechanism for PPP connections similar to CHAP. The remote access server sends a challenge to the remote access client that consists of a session ID and an arbitrary challenge string. The remote access client must return the user name and a Message Digest 4 (MD4) hash of the challenge string, the session ID, and the MD4-hashed password.

Microsoft Challenge Handshake Authentication Protocol version 2 (MS-CHAP v2)

An encrypted authentication mechanism for PPP connections that provides stronger security than CHAP and MS-CHAP v1. MS-CHAP v2 provides mutual authentication and asymmetric encryption keys.

Microsoft Indexing Service

Software that provides search functions for documents stored on disk, allowing users to search for specific document text or properties.

Microsoft Internet Directory

A Web site provided and maintained by Microsoft used by applications such as NetMeeting to locate people to call on the Internet. The Microsoft Internet Directory is operated through an ILS server.

Microsoft Management Console (MMC)

A framework for hosting administrative consoles. A console is defined by the items on its console tree, which might include folders or other containers, World Wide Web pages, and other administrative items. A console has one or more windows that can provide views of the console tree and the administrative properties, services, and events that are acted on by the items in the console tree. The main MMC window provides commands and tools for authoring consoles. The authoring features of MMC and the console tree might be hidden when a console is in User Mode.

See also *console tree*.

Microsoft Point-to-Point Encryption (MPPE)

A 128/40-bit encryption algorithm using RSA RC4. MPPE provides for packet security between the client and the tunnel server and is useful where IPSec is not available. The 40-bit version addresses localization issues based on current export restrictions. MPPE is compatible with Network Address Translation.

See also *IPSec*.

Microsoft Tape Format (MTF)

The data format used for tapes supported by the Backup application in Windows 2000. There are three major components to MTF: a Tape Data Block (Tape DBLK), otherwise known as the tape header; one or more Data Sets; and On Tape Catalog Information (On Tape Catalog Inf).

Minidrivers

Relatively small, simple drivers or files that contain additional instructions needed by a specific hardware device, to interface with the universal driver for a class of devices.

Minimum TTL

A default Time To Live (TTL) value set in seconds for use with all resource records in a zone. This value is set in the start of authority (SOA) resource record for each zone. By default, the DNS server includes this value in query answers to inform recipients how long it can store and use resource records provided in the query answer before they must expire the stored records data. When TTL values are set for individual resource records, those values will override the minimum TTL.

See also *Time To Live*.

Mirrored volume

A fault-tolerant volume that duplicates data on two physical disks. The mirror is always located on a different disk. If one of the physical disks fails, the data on the failed disk becomes unavailable, but the system continues to operate by using the unaffected disk. A mirrored volume is slower than a RAID-5 volume in read operations but faster in write operations. Mirrored volumes can only be created on dynamic disks. In Windows NT 4.0, a mirrored volume was known as a mirror set.

See also *dynamic disk*; *dynamic volume*; *fault tolerance*; *redundant array of independent disks*; *volume*.

Mixed mode

The default mode setting for domains on Windows 2000 domain controllers. Mixed mode allows Windows 2000 domain controllers and Windows NT backup domain controllers to co-exist in a domain. Mixed mode does not support the universal and nested group enhancements of Windows 2000. You can change the domain mode setting to Windows 2000 native mode after all Windows NT domain controllers are either removed from the domain or upgraded to Windows 2000.

See also *native mode*.

Mode Pruning

A Windows 2000 feature that can be used to remove display modes that the monitor cannot support.

Mount

To place a removable tape or disc into a drive.

See also *library*.

MouseKeys

A feature in Microsoft Windows that allows use of the numeric keyboard to move the mouse pointer.

MP3

Audio compressed in the MPEG1 Layer 3 format

MPEG-2

A standard of video compression and file format developed by the Moving Pictures Experts Group. MPEG-2 offers video resolutions of 720 x 480 and 128 x 720 at 60 frames per second, with full CD-quality audio.

MS-CHAPv2

See *Microsoft Challenge Handshake Authentication Protocol version 2*.

Multicast IP

IP packets sent from a single destination IP address but received and processed by multiple IP hosts, regardless of their location on an IP internetwork.

Multicasting

The process of sending a message simultaneously to more than one destination on a network.

Multihomed computer

A computer that has multiple network adapters or that has been configured with multiple IP addresses for a single network adapter.

Multiple boot

A computer configuration that runs two or more operating systems. For example, Windows 98, MS-DOS, and Windows 2000 operating systems can be installed on the same computer. When the computer is started, any one of the operating systems can be selected.

See also *dual boot*.

N

Name devolution

A process by which a DNS resolver appends one or more domain names to an unqualified domain name, making it a fully qualified domain name, and then submits the fully qualified domain name to a DNS server.

Namespace

A set of unique names for resources or items used in a shared computing environment. The names in a namespace can be resolved to the objects they represent. For Microsoft Management Console (MMC), the namespace is represented by the console tree, which displays all of the snap-ins and resources that are accessible to a console. For Domain Name System (DNS), namespace is the vertical or hierarchical structure of the domain name tree. For example, each domain label, such as "host1" or "example," used in a fully qualified domain name, such as "host1.example.microsoft.com," indicates a branch in the domain namespace tree. For Active Directory, namespace corresponds to the DNS namespace in structure, but resolves Active Directory object names.

Naming service

A service, such as that provided by WINS or DNS, that allows friendly names to be resolved to an address or other specially defined resource data that is used to locate network resources of various types and purposes.

Narrator

A synthesized text-to-speech utility for users who have low vision. Narrator reads aloud most of what the screen displays.

Native mode

The condition in which all domain controllers within a domain are Windows 2000 domain controllers and an administrator has enabled native mode operation (through Active Directory Users and Computers).

See also *mixed mode*.

NDIS miniport drivers

A type of minidriver that interfaces network class devices to NDIS.

Nested groups

A Windows 2000 capability available only in native mode that allows the creation of groups within groups. See also domain local group; forest; global group; trusted forest; universal group.

NetBEUI

See *NetBIOS Extended User Interface.*

NetBIOS Extended User Interface (NetBEUI)

A network protocol native to Microsoft Networking that is usually used in local area networks of one to 200 clients. NetBEUI uses Token Ring source routing as its only method of routing. It is the Microsoft implementation of the NetBIOS standard.

NetBIOS over TCP/IP (NetBT)

A feature that provides the NetBIOS programming interface over the TCP/IP protocol. It is used for monitoring routed servers that use NetBIOS name resolution.

NetWare

Novell's network operating system.

Network adapter

Software or a hardware plug-in board that connects a node or host to a local area network.

Network basic input/output system (NetBIOS)

An application programming interface (API) that can be used by applications on a local area network or computers running MS-DOS, OS/2, or some version of UNIX. NetBIOS provides a uniform set of commands for requesting lower level network services.

Network Control Protocol (NCP)

A protocol within the PPP protocol suite that negotiates the parameters of an individual LAN protocol such as TCP/IP or IPX.

Network Driver Interface Specification (NDIS)

A software component that provides Windows 2000 network protocols a common interface for communications with network adapters. NDIS allows more than one transport protocol to be bound and operate simultaneously over a single network adapter card.

Network file system (NFS)

A service for distributed computing systems that provides a distributed file system, eliminating the need for keeping multiple copies of files on separate computers.

Network Information Service (NIS)

Formerly known as Yellow Pages, NIS is a distributed database service that allows for a shared set of system configuration files on UNIX-based systems, including password, hosts, and group files.

Network News Transfer Protocol (NNTP)

A member of the TCP/IP suite of protocols, used to distribute network news messages to NNTP servers and clients, or newsreaders, on the Internet. NNTP is designed so that news articles are stored on a server in a central database, and the user selects specific items to read.

See also *Transmission Control Protocol/Internet Protocol.*

Network security administrators

Users who manage network and information security. Network security administrators should implement a security plan that addresses network security threats.

Node

In tree structures, a location on the tree that can have links to one or more items below it. In local area networks (LANs), a device that is connected to the network and is capable of communicating with other network devices. In a server cluster, a server that has Cluster service software installed and is a member of the cluster.

See also *local area network.*

Noncontainer object

An object that cannot logically contain other objects. A file is a noncontainer object.

See also *container object*; *object.*

Nonrepudiation

A basic security function of cryptography. Nonrepudiation provides assurance that a party in a communication cannot falsely deny that a part of the communication occurred. Without nonrepudiation, someone can communicate and then later deny the communication or claim that the communication occurred at a different time.

See also *cryptography*; *authentication*; *confidentiality*; *integrity.*

Nonresident attribute

A file attribute whose value is contained in one or more runs, or extents, outside the master file table (MFT) record and separate from the MFT.

Nontransitive trust relationship

A type of trust relationship that is bounded by the two domains in the relationship. For example, if domain A trusts domain B and domain B trusts domain C, there is no trust relationship between domain A and domain C. A nontransitive trust relationship can be a one-way or two-way relationship. It is the only type of trust relationship that can exist between a Windows 2000 domain and a Windows NT domain or between Windows 2000 domains in different forests.

See also *trust relationship*; *transitive trust relationship*.

Normal backup

A backup that copies all selected files and marks each file as backed up (that is, the archive bit is set). With normal backups, only the most recent copy of the backup file or tape is needed to restore all of the files. A normal backup is usually performed the first time a backup set is created.

See also *copy backup*; *daily backup*; *differential backup*; *incremental backup*.

Novell Directory Services (NDS)

On networks running Novell NetWare 4.*x* and NetWare 5.*x*, a distributed database that maintains information about every resource on the network and provides access to these resources.

NT-1 (Network Terminator 1)

A device that terminates an ISDN line at the connection location, commonly through a connection port.

NTFS file system

A recoverable file system designed for use specifically with Windows NT and Windows 2000. NTFS uses database, transaction-processing, and object paradigms to provide data security, file system reliability, and other advanced features. It supports file system recovery, large storage media, and various features for the POSIX subsystem. It also supports object-oriented applications by treating all files as objects with user-defined and system-defined attributes.

NTLM

A security package that provides authentication between clients and servers.

See also *NTLM authentication protocol.*

NTLM authentication protocol

A challenge/response authentication protocol. The NTLM authentication protocol was the default for network authentication in Windows NT version 4.0 and earlier. The protocol continues to be supported in Windows 2000 but no longer is the default.

See also *authentication.*

NWLink

An implementation of the Internetwork Packet Exchange (IPX), Sequenced Packet Exchange (SPX), and NetBIOS protocols used in Novell networks. NWLink is a standard network protocol that supports routing and can support NetWare client/server applications, where NetWare-aware Sockets-based applications communicate with IPX/SPX Sockets-based applications.

See also *Internetwork Packet Exchange*; *network basic input/output system.*

O

Object

An entity, such as a file, folder, shared folder, printer, or Active Directory object, described by a distinct, named set of attributes. For example, the attributes of a File object include its name, location, and size; the attributes of an Active Directory User object might include the user's first name, last name, and e-mail address. For OLE and ActiveX objects, an object can also be any piece of information that can be linked to, or embedded into, another object.

See also *attribute*; *child object*; *container object*; *noncontainer object*; *parent object*.

Object linking and embedding (OLE)

A method for sharing information among applications. Linking an object, such as a graphic, from one document to another inserts a reference to the object into the second document. Any changes you make in the object in the first document will also be made in the second document. Embedding an object inserts a copy of an object from one document into another document. Changes you make in the object in the first document will not be updated in the second unless the embedded object is explicitly updated.

See also *ActiveX*.

Offline media

Media that are not connected to the computer and require external assistance to be accessed.

On-media identifier (OMID)

A label that is electronically recorded on each medium in a Removable Storage system. Removable Storage uses on-media identifiers to track media in the Removable Storage database. An application on-media identifier is a subset of the media label.

On-screen keyboard

A utility that displays a virtual keyboard on a computer screen and allows users with mobility impairments to type using a pointing device or joystick.

OnNow

See *Advanced Configuration and Power Interface*.

Open database connectivity (ODBC)

An application programming interface (API) that enables database applications to access data from a variety of existing data sources.

Open Host Controller Interface (OHCI)

Part of the IEEE 1394 standard. In Windows 2000 Professional, only OHCI-compliant host adapters are supported.

OpenType fonts

Outline fonts that are rendered from line and curve commands, and can be scaled and rotated. OpenType fonts are clear and readable in all sizes and on all output devices supported by Windows 2000. OpenType is an extension of TrueType font technology.

See also *font*; *TrueType fonts*.

Operator request

A request for the operator to perform a task. This request can be issued by an application or by Removable Storage.

Original equipment manufacturer (OEM)

The maker of a piece of equipment. In making computers and computer-related equipment, manufacturers of original equipment typically purchase components from other manufacturers of original equipment and then integrate them into their own products.

Overclocking

Setting a microprocessor to run at speeds above the rated specification.

P

Package

An icon that represents embedded or linked information. That information can consist of a complete file, such as a Paint bitmap, or part of a file, such as a spreadsheet cell. When a package is chosen, the application used to create the object either plays the object (if it is a sound file, for example) or opens and displays the object. If the original information is changed, linked information is then updated. However, embedded information needs to be manually updated. In Systems Management Server, an object that contains the files and instructions for distributing software to a distribution point.

See also *embedded object*; *linked object*; *object linking and embedding*.

Packet

A transmission unit of fixed maximum size that consists of binary information. This information represents both data and a header containing an ID number, source and destination addresses, and error-control data.

Packet assembler/disassembler (PAD)

A connection used in X.25 networks. X.25 PAD boards can be used in place of modems when provided with a compatible COM driver.

PAD

See *packet assembler/disassembler*.

Page fault

An error that occurs when the requested code or data cannot be located in the physical memory that is available to the requesting process.

Page-description language (PDL)

A computer language that describes the arrangement of text and graphics on a printed page.

See also *printer control language*; *PostScript*.

Paging

The process of moving virtual memory back and forth between physical memory and the disk. Paging occurs when physical memory limitations are reached and only occurs for data that is not already "backed" by disk space. For example, file data is not paged out because it already has allocated disk space within a file system.

See also *virtual memory.*

paging file

A hidden file on the hard disk that Windows 2000 uses to hold parts of programs and data files that do not fit in memory. The paging file and physical memory, or RAM, comprise virtual memory. Windows 2000 moves data from the paging file to memory as needed and moves data from memory to the paging file to make room for new data. Also called a swap file.

See also *random access memory*; *virtual memory.*

PAP

See *Password Authentication Protocol.*

Parallel connection

A connection that simultaneously transmits both data and control bits over wires connected in parallel. In general, a parallel connection can move data between devices faster than a serial connection.

Parallel device

A device that uses a parallel connection.

Parallel ports

The input/output connector for a parallel interface device. Printers are generally plugged into a parallel port.

Parent object

The object that is the immediate superior of another object in a hierarchy. A parent object can have multiple subordinate, or child, objects. In Active Directory, the schema determines what objects can be parent objects of what other objects. Depending on its class, a parent object can be the child of another object.

See also *child object*; *object.*

Partition

A logical division of a hard disk. Partitions make it easier to organize information. Each partition can be formatted for a different file system. A partition must be completely contained on one physical disk, and the partition table in the Master Boot Record for a physical disk can contain up to four entries for partitions.

Password authentication protocol (PAP)

A simple, plaintext authentication scheme for authenticating PPP connections. The user name and password are requested by the remote access server and returned by the remote access client in plaintext.

Path

A sequence of directory (or folder) names that specifies the location of a directory, file, or folder within the Windows directory tree. Each directory name and file name within the path must be preceded by a backslash (\). For example, to specify the path of a file named Readme.doc located in the Windows directory on drive C, type C:\Windows\Readme.doc.

PC Card

A removable device, approximately the size of a credit card, that can be plugged into a PCMCIA (Personal Computer Memory Card International Association) slot in a portable computer. PCMCIA devices can include modems, network adapters, and hard disk drives.

PCI

See *Peripheral Component Interconnect.*

PCNFS Daemon (PCNFSD)

A program that receives requests from PC-NFS clients for authentication on remote machines.

Peer-to-peer network

See *workgroup.*

Performance counter

In System Monitor, a data item associated with a performance object. For each counter selected, System Monitor presents a value corresponding to a particular aspect of the performance that is defined for the performance object.

See also *performance object.*

Performance object

In System Monitor, a logical collection of counters that is associated with a resource or service that can be monitored. See also performance counter.

Peripheral

A device, such as a disk drive, printer, modem, or joystick, that is connected to a computer and is controlled by the computer's microprocessor.

Peripheral component interconnect (PCI)

A specification introduced by Intel Corporation that defines a local bus system that allows up to 10 PCI-compliant expansion cards to be installed in the computer.

Permission

A rule associated with an object to regulate which users can gain access to the object and in what manner. Permissions are granted or denied by the object's owner.

See also *access control list*; *object*; *privilege*; *user rights*.

Physical location

The location designation assigned to media managed by Removable Storage. The two classes of physical locations include libraries and offline media physical locations. The offline media physical location is where Removable Storage lists the cartridges that are not in a library. The physical location of cartridges in an online library is the library in which it resides.

Physical media

A storage object that data can be written to, such as a disk or magnetic tape. A physical medium is referenced by its physical media ID (PMID).

Physical object

An object, such as an ATM card or smart card used in conjunction with a piece of information, such as a PIN number, to authenticate users. In two-factor authentication, physical objects are used in conjunction with another secret piece of identification, such as a password, to authenticate users. In two-factor authentication, the physical object might be an ATM card that is used in combination with a PIN to authenticate the user.

Ping

A tool that verifies connections to one or more remote hosts. The ping command uses the ICMP Echo Request and Echo Reply packets to determine whether a particular IP system on a network is functional. Ping is useful for diagnosing IP network or router failures.

See also *Internet Control Message Protocol.*

Pinning

To make a network file or folder available for offline use.

Plaintext

Data that is not encrypted. Sometimes also called clear text.

See also *ciphertext*; *encryption*; *decryption.*

Plug and Play

A set of specifications developed by Intel that allows a computer to automatically detect and configure a device and install the appropriate device drivers.

Point and Print

A way of installing network printers on a user's local computer. Point and Print allows users to initiate a connection to a network printer and loads any required drivers onto the client's computer. When users know which network printer they want to use, Point and Print greatly simplifies the installation process.

Point of presence (POP)

The local access point for a network provider. Each POP provides a telephone number that allows users to make a local call for access to online services.

Point-to-Point Protocol (PPP)

An industry standard suite of protocols for the use of point-to-point links to transport multiprotocol datagrams. PPP is documented in RFC 1661.

Point-to-Point Tunneling Protocol (PPTP)

A tunneling protocol that encapsulates Point-to-Point Protocol (PPP) frames into IP datagrams for transmission over an IP-based internetwork, such as the Internet or a private intranet.

Portable Operating System Interface for UNIX (POSIX)

An IEEE (Institute of Electrical and Electronics Engineers) standard that defines a set of operating-system services. Programs that adhere to the POSIX standard can be easily ported from one system to another. POSIX was based on UNIX system services, but it was created in a way that allows it to be implemented by other operating systems.

POST

See *power-on self test.*

PostScript

A page-description language (PDL) developed by Adobe Systems for printing with laser printers. PostScript offers flexible font capability and high-quality graphics. It is the standard for desktop publishing because it is supported by image setters, the high-resolution printers used by printing services for commercial typesetting.

See also *printer control language*; *page-description language.*

Power-on self test (POST)

A set of routines stored in read-only memory (ROM) that tests various system components such as RAM, the disk drives, and the keyboard, to see if they are properly connected and operating. If problems are found, these routines alert the user with a series of beeps or a message, often accompanied by a diagnostic numeric value. If the POST is successful, it passes control to the bootstrap loader.

PPTP

See *Point-to-Point Tunneling Protocol.*

Primary partition

A volume created using unallocated space on a basic disk. Windows 2000 and other operating systems can start from a primary partition. As many as four primary partitions can be created on a basic disk, or three primary partitions and an extended partition. Primary partitions can be created only on basic disks and cannot be subpartitioned.

See also *basic disk*; *dynamic volume*; *extended partition*; *partition.*

Printer control language (PCL)

The page-description language (PDL) developed by Hewlett Packard for their laser and inkjet printers. Because of the widespread use of laser printers, this command language has become a standard in many printers.

See also *page-description language*; *PostScript.*

Priority

A precedence ranking that determines the order in which the threads of a process are scheduled for the processor.

Priority inversion

The mechanism that allows low-priority threads to run and complete execution rather than being preempted and locking up a resource such as an I/O device.

Private branch exchange (PBX)

An automatic telephone switching system that enables users within an organization to place calls to each other without going through the public telephone network. Users can also place calls to outside numbers.

Private key

The secret half of a cryptographic key pair that is used with a public key algorithm. Private keys are typically used to digitally sign data and to decrypt data that has been encrypted with the corresponding public key.

See also *public key*.

Privilege

A user's right to perform a specific task, usually one that affects an entire computer system rather than a particular object. Administrators assign privileges to individual users or groups of users as part of the security settings for the computer.

See also *access token*; *permission*; *user rights*.

Privileged mode

Also known as kernel mode, the processing mode that allows code to have direct access to all hardware and memory in the system.

Process throttling

A method of restricting the amount of processor time a process consumes, for example, using job object functions.

Processor queue

An instantaneous count of the threads that are ready to run on the system but are waiting because the processor is running other threads.

Protocol

A set of rules and conventions by which two computers pass messages across a network. Networking software usually implements multiple levels of protocols layered one on top of another. Windows NT and Windows 2000 include NetBEUI, TCP/IP, and IPX/SPX-compatible protocols.

Proxy server

A firewall component that manages Internet traffic to and from a local area network and can provide other features, such as document caching and access control. A proxy server can improve performance by supplying frequently requested data, such as a popular Web page, and can filter and discard requests that the owner does not consider appropriate, such as requests for unauthorized access to proprietary files.

See also *firewall*.

Public key

The non-secret half of a cryptographic key pair that is used with a public key algorithm. Public keys are typically used to verify digital signatures or decrypt data that has been encrypted with the corresponding private key.

See also *private key*.

Public key cryptography

A method of cryptography in which two different but complimentary keys are used: a public key and a private key for providing security functions. Public key cryptography is also called asymmetric key cryptography.

See also *cryptography*; *public key*; *private key*.

Public switched telephone network (PSTN)

Standard analog telephone lines, available worldwide.

Q

QoS

See *Quality of Service.*

QoS Admission Control Service

A software service that controls bandwidth and network resources on the subnet to which it is assigned. Important applications can be given more bandwidth, less important applications less bandwidth. The QoS Admission Control Service can be installed on any network-enabled computer running Windows 2000.

Quality of Service (QoS)

A set of quality assurance standards and mechanisms for data transmission, implemented in Windows 2000.

Quantum

Also known as a time slice, the maximum amount of time a thread can run before the system checks for another ready thread of the same priority to run.

Quarter-inch cartridge (QIC)

An older storage technology used with tape backup drives and cartridges. A means of backing up data on computer systems, QIC represents a set of standards devised to enable tapes to be used with drives from different manufacturers. The QIC standards specify the length of tape, the number of recording tracks, and the magnetic strength of the tape coating, all of which determine the amount of information that can be written to the tape. Older QIC-80 drives can hold up to 340 MB of compressed data. Newer versions can hold more than 1 GB of information.

R

RAID-5 volume

A fault-tolerant volume with data and parity striped intermittently across three or more physical disks. Parity is a calculated value that is used to reconstruct data after a failure. If a portion of a physical disk fails, you can recreate the data that was on the failed portion from the remaining data and parity. Also known as a striped volume with parity.

Raster fonts

Fonts that are stored as bitmaps; also called bit-mapped fonts. Raster fonts are designed with a specific size and resolution for a specific printer and cannot be scaled or rotated. If a printer does not support raster fonts, it will not print them.

Rate counter

Similar to an averaging counter, a counter type that samples an increasing count of events over time; the change in the count is divided by the change in time to display a rate of activity.

Read-only memory (ROM)

A semiconductor circuit that contains information that cannot be modified.

Recoverable file system

A file system that ensures that if a power outage or other catastrophic system failure occurs, the file system will not be corrupted and disk modifications will not be left incomplete. The structure of the disk volume is restored to a consistent state when the system restarts.

Recovery Console

A startable, text-mode command interpreter environment separate from the Windows 2000 command prompt that allows the system administrator access to the hard disk of a computer running Windows 2000, regardless of the file format used, for basic troubleshooting and system maintenance tasks.

Redundant array of independent disks (RAID)

A method used to standardize and categorize fault-tolerant disk systems. Six levels gauge various mixes of performance, reliability, and cost. Windows 2000 provides three of the RAID levels: Level 0 (striping) which is not fault-tolerant, Level 1 (mirroring), and Level 5 (striped volume with parity).

See also *fault tolerance*; *mirrored volume*; *RAID-5 volume*; *striped volume.*

Registry

In Windows 2000, Windows NT, Windows 98, and Windows 95, a database of information about a computer's configuration. The registry is organized in a hierarchical structure and consists of subtrees and their keys, hives, and entries.

Relative ID (RID)

The part of a security ID (SID) that uniquely identifies an account or group within a domain.

See also *security ID*.

Remote access server

A Windows 2000 Server-based computer running the Routing and Remote Access service and configured to provide remote access.

Remote procedure call (RPC)

A message-passing facility that allows a distributed application to call services that are available on various computers in a network. Used during remote administration of computers.

Removable Storage

A service used for managing removable media (such as tapes and discs) and storage devices (libraries). Removable Storage allows applications to access and share the same media resources.

See also *library*.

Reparse points

New NTFS file system objects that have a definable attribute containing user-controlled data and are used to extend functionality in the input/output (I/O) subsystem.

Repeat Keys

A feature that allows users with mobility impairments to adjust the repeat rate or to disable the key-repeat function on the keyboard.

See also *FilterKeys*.

Request for Comments (RFC)

A document that defines a standard. RFCs are published by the Internet Engineering Task Force (IETF) and other working groups.

Resident attribute

A file attribute whose value is wholly contained in the file's file record in the master file table (MFT).

Resolver

DNS client programs used to look up DNS name information. Resolvers can be either a small "stub" (a limited set of programming routines that provide basic query functionality) or larger programs that provide additional lookup DNS client functions, such as caching.

See also *caching*; *caching resolver*.

Resource publishing

The process of making an object visible and accessible to users in a Windows 2000 domain. For example, a shared printer resource is published by creating a reference to the printer object in Active Directory.

Resource record (RR)

Information in the DNS database that can be used to process client queries. Each DNS server contains the resource records it needs to answer queries for the portion of the DNS namespace for which it is authoritative.

Response time

The amount of time required to do work from start to finish. In a client/server environment, this is typically measured on the client side.

RGB

The initials of red, green, blue. Used to describe a color monitor or color value.

Roaming user profile

A server-based user profile that is downloaded to the local computer when a user logs on and is updated both locally and on the server when the user logs off. A roaming user profile is available from the server when logging on to any computer that is running Windows 2000 Professional or Windows 2000 Server.

ROM

See *read-only memory.*

Route table

See *routing table.*

Router

A network device that helps LANs and WANs achieve interoperability and connectivity and that can link LANs that have different network topologies, such as Ethernet and Token Ring.

Routing

The process of forwarding a packet through an internetwork from a source host to a destination host.

Routing Information Protocol (RIP)

An industry standard distance vector routing protocol used in small to medium sized IP and IPX internetworks.

Routing table

A database of routes containing information on network IDs, forwarding addresses, and metrics for reachable network segments on an internetwork.

RPC

See *Remote Procedure Call.*

Rules

An IPSec policy mechanism that governs how and when an IPSec policy protects communication. A rule provides the ability to trigger and control secure communication based on the source, destination, and type of IP traffic. Each rule contains a list of IP filters and a collection of security actions that take place upon a match with that filter list.

S

Safe Mode

A method of starting Windows 2000 using basic files and drivers only, without networking. Safe Mode is available by pressing the F8 key when prompted during startup. This allows the computer to start when a problem prevents it from starting normally.

Screen-enlargement utility

A utility that allows the user to magnify a portion of the screen for greater visibility. (Also called a screen magnifier or large-print program.)

Script

A type of program consisting of a set of instructions to an application or utility program. A script usually expresses instructions by using the application's or utility's rules and syntax, combined with simple control structures such as loops and if/then expressions. "Batch program" is often used interchangeably with "script" in the Windows environment.

SCSI

See *Small Computer System Interface.*

SCSI connection

A standard high-speed parallel interface defined by the X3T9.2 committee of the American National Standards Institute (ANSI). A SCSI interface is used to connect microcomputers to SCSI peripheral devices, such as many hard disks and printers, and to other computers and local area networks.

Search filter

An argument in an LDAP search that allows certain entries in the subtree and excludes others. Filters allow you to define search criteria and give you better control to achieve more effective and efficient searches.

Secure Sockets Layer (SSL)

A proposed open standard developed by Netscape Communications for establishing a secure communications channel to prevent the interception of critical information, such as credit card numbers. Primarily, it enables secure electronic financial transactions on the World Wide Web, although it is designed to work on other Internet services as well.

Security Accounts Manager (SAM)

A protected subsystem that manages user and group account information. In Windows NT 4.0, both local and domain security principals are stored by SAM in the registry. In Windows 2000, workstation security accounts are stored by SAM in the local computer registry, and domain controller security accounts are stored in Active Directory.

Security association (SA)

A set of parameters that define the services and mechanisms necessary to protect Internet Protocol security communications.

See also *Internet Protocol security.*

Security descriptor

A data structure that contains security information associated with a protected object. Security descriptors include information about who owns the object, who may access it and in what way, and what types of access will be audited.

See also *access control list*; *object.*

Security event types

Different categories of events about which Windows 2000 can create auditing events. Account logon or object access are examples of security event types.

Security ID (SID)

A data structure of variable length that uniquely identifies user, group, service, and computer accounts within an enterprise. Every account is issued a SID when the account is first created. Access control mechanisms in Windows 2000 identify security principals by SID rather than by name.

See also *relative ID*; *security principal.*

Security method

A process that determines the Internet Protocol security services, key settings, and algorithms that will be used to protect the data during the communication.

Security Parameters Index (SPI)

A unique, identifying value in the SA used to distinguish among multiple security associations existing at the receiving computer.

Security principal

An account-holder, such as a user, computer, or service. Each security principal within a Windows 2000 domain is identified by a unique security ID (SID). When a security principal logs on to a computer running Windows 2000, the Local Security Authority (LSA) authenticates the security principal's account name and password. If the logon is successful, the system creates an access token. Every process executed on behalf of this security principal will have a copy of its access token.

See also *access token*; *security ID*; *security principal name.*

Security principal name

A name that uniquely identifies a user, group, or computer within a single domain. This name is not guaranteed to be unique across domains.

See also *security principal.*

Seek time

The amount of time required for a disk head to position itself at the right disk cylinder to access requested data.

Serial Bus Protocol (SBP-2)

A standard for storage devices, printers, and scanners that is a supplement to the IEEE 1394 specification.

Serial connection

A connection that exchanges information between computers or between computers and peripheral devices one bit at a time over a single channel. Serial communications can be synchronous or asynchronous. Both sender and receiver must use the same baud rate, parity, and control information.

Serial device

A device that uses a serial connection.

SerialKeys

A Windows feature that uses a communications aid interface device to allow keystrokes and mouse controls to be accepted through a computer's serial port.

Server

A computer that provides shared resources to network users.

Server Message Block (SMB)

A file-sharing protocol designed to allow networked computers to transparently access files that reside on remote systems over a variety of networks. The SMB protocol defines a series of commands that pass information between computers. SMB uses four message types: session control, file, printer, and message.

Service access point

A logical address that allows a system to route data between a remote device and the appropriate communications support.

Service Pack

A software upgrade to an existing software distribution that contains updated files consisting of patches and fixes.

Service Profile Identifier (SPID)

A 14-digit number that identifies a specific ISDN line. When establishing ISDN service, your telephone company assigns a SPID to your line.

See also *ISDN*.

Service provider

In TAPI, a dynamic link library (DLL) that provides an interface between an application requesting services and the controlling hardware device. TAPI supports two classes of service providers, media service providers and telephony service providers.

Session key

A key used primarily for encryption and decryption. Session keys are typically used with symmetric encryption algorithms where the same key is used for both encryption and decryption. For this reason, session and symmetric keys usually refer to the same type of key.

See also *symmetric key encryption*.

Sfmmon

A port monitor that is used to send jobs over the AppleTalk protocol to printers such as LaserWriters or those configured with AppleTalk or any AppleTalk spoolers.

Shared folder permissions

Permissions that restrict a shared resource's availability over the network to certain users.

See also *permission*.

Shiva Password Authentication Protocol (SPAP)

A two-way, reversible encryption mechanism for authenticating PPP connections employed by Shiva remote access servers.

Shortcut key navigation indicators

Underlined letters on a menu or control. (Also called access keys or quick-access letters.)

ShowSounds

A global flag that instructs programs to display captions for speech and system sounds to alert users with hearing impairments or people who work in a noisy location such as a factory floor.

Simple Mail Transfer Protocol (SMTP)

A protocol used on the Internet to transfer mail. SMTP is independent of the particular transmission subsystem and requires only a reliable, ordered, data stream channel.

Simple Network Management Protocol (SNMP)

A network management protocol installed with TCP/IP and widely used on TCP/IP and Internet Package Exchange (IPX) networks. SNMP transports management information and commands between a management program run by an administrator and the network management agent running on a host. The SNMP agent sends status information to one or more hosts when the host requests it or when a significant event occurs.

Single-switch device

An alternative input device, such as a voice activation program, that allows a user to scan or select using a single switch.

Slot

Storage locations for cartridges in a library managed by Removable Storage.

SlowKeys

A Windows feature that instructs the computer to disregard keystrokes that are not held down for a minimum period of time, which allows the user to brush against keys without any effect.

See also *FilterKeys*.

Small Computer System Interface (SCSI)

A standard high-speed parallel interface defined by the X3T9.2 committee of the American National Standards Institute (ANSI). A SCSI interface is used for connecting microcomputers to peripheral devices, such as hard disks and printers, and to other computers and local area networks.

Small Office/Home Office (SOHO)

An office with a few computers that can be considered a small business or part of a larger network.

Smart card

A credit card-sized device that is used with a PIN number to enable certificate-based authentication and single sign-on to the enterprise. Smart cards securely store certificates, public and private keys, passwords, and other types of personal information. A smart card reader attached to the computer reads the smart card.

See also *authentication*; *certificate*; *nonrepudiation*.

SNMP

See *Simple Network Management Protocol*.

Software trap

In programming, an event that occurs when a microprocessor detects a problem with executing an instruction, which causes it to stop.

SoundSentry

A Windows feature that produces a visual cue, such as a screen flash or a blinking title bar instead of system sounds.

Source directory

The folder that contains the file or files to be copied or moved.

See also *destination directory*.

SPAP

See *Shiva Password Authentication Protocol.*

Sparse file

A file that is handled in a way that requires less disk space than would otherwise be needed by allocating only meaningful non-zero data. Sparse support allows an application to create very large files without committing disk space for every byte.

Speech synthesizer

An assistive device that produces spoken words, either by splicing together prerecorded words or by programming the computer to produce the sounds that make up spoken words.

Stand-alone drive

An online drive that is not part of a library unit. Removable Storage treats stand-alone drives as online libraries with one drive and a port.

Status area

The area on the taskbar to the right of the taskbar buttons. The status area displays the time and can also contain icons that provide quick access to programs, such as Volume Control and Power Options. Other icons can appear temporarily, providing information about the status of activities. For example, the printer icon appears after a document has been sent to the printer and disappears when printing is complete.

StickyKeys

An accessibility feature built into Windows that causes modifier keys such as SHIFT, CTRL, WINDOWS LOGO, or ALT to stay on after they are pressed, eliminating the need to press multiple keys simultaneously. This feature facilitates the use of modifier keys for users who are unable to hold down one key while pressing another.

Stop error

A serious error that affects the operating system and that could place data at risk. The operating system generates an obvious message, a screen with the Stop message, rather than continuing on, and possibly corrupting data. Also known as a fatal system error.

See also *Stop message.*

Stop message

A character-based, full-screen error message displayed on a blue background. A Stop message indicates that the Windows 2000 kernel detected a condition from which it cannot recover. Each message is uniquely identified by a Stop error code (a hexadecimal number) and a string indicating the error's symbolic name. Stop messages are usually followed by up to four additional hexadecimal numbers, enclosed in parentheses, which identify developer-defined error parameters. A driver or device may be identified as the cause of the error. A series of troubleshooting tips are also displayed, along with an indication that, if the system was configured to do so, a memory dump file was saved for later use by a kernel debugger.

See also *Stop error*.

Streaming media servers

Software (such as Microsoft Media Technologies) that provides multimedia support, allowing you to deliver content by using Advanced Streaming Format over an intranet or the Internet.

Streams

A sequence of bits, bytes, or other small structurally uniform units.

Striped volume

A volume that stores data in stripes on two or more physical disks. Data in a striped volume is allocated alternately and evenly (in stripes) to these disks. Striped volumes offer the best performance of all volumes available in Windows 2000, but they do not provide fault tolerance. If a disk in a striped volume fails, the data in the entire volume is lost. You can create striped volumes only on dynamic disks. Striped volumes cannot be mirrored or extended. In Windows NT 4.0, a striped volume was known as a stripe set.

See also *dynamic disk*; *dynamic volume*; *fault tolerance*; *volume*.

Subkey

In the registry, a key within a key. Subkeys are analogous to subdirectories in the registry hierarchy. Keys and subkeys are similar to the section header in .ini files; however, subkeys can carry out functions.

See also *key*.

Subnet

A subdivision of an IP network. Each subnet has its own unique subnetted network ID.

Subnet mask

A 32-bit value expressed as four decimal numbers from 0 to 255, separated by periods (for example, 255.255.0.0). This number allows TCP/IP to determine the network ID portion of an IP address.

Subnet prioritization

The ordering of multiple IP address mappings from a DNS server so that the resolver orders local resource records first. This reduces network traffic across subnets by forcing computers to connect to network resources that are closer to them.

Subpicture

A data stream contained within a DVD. The Subpicture stream delivers the subtitles and any other add-on data, such as system help or director's comments, which can be displayed while playing multimedia.

Symmetric key

A single key that is used with symmetric encryption algorithms for both encryption and decryption.

See also *bulk encryption*; *encryption*; *decryption*; *session key*.

Symmetric key encryption

An encryption algorithm that requires the same secret key to be used for both encryption and decryption. This is often called secret key encryption. Because of its speed, symmetric encryption is typically used rather than public key encryption when a message sender needs to encrypt large amounts of data.

Synchronization Manager

In Windows 2000, the tool used to ensure that a file or directory on a client computer contains the same data as a matching file or directory on a server.

Syntax

The order in which a command must be typed and the elements that follow the command.

System access control list (SACL)

The part of an object's security descriptor that specifies which events are to be audited per user or group. Examples of auditing events are file access, logon attempts, and system shutdowns.

See also *access control entry*; *discretionary access control list*; *object*; *security descriptor*.

System administrator

A person that administers a computer system or network, including administering user accounts, security, storage space, and backing up data.

System files

Files that are used by Windows to load, configure, and run the operating system. Generally, system files must never be deleted or moved.

System media pool

A pool used to hold cartridges that are not in use. The free pool holds unused cartridges that are available to applications, and the unrecognized and import pools are temporary holding places for cartridges that have been newly placed in a library.

System policy

In network administration, the part of Group Policy that is concerned with the current user and local computer settings in the registry. In Windows 2000, system policy is sometimes called software policy and is one of several services provided by Group Policy, a Microsoft Management Console (MMC) snap-in. The Windows NT 4.0 System Policy Editor, Poledit.exe, is included with Windows 2000 for backward compatibility. That is, administrators need it to set system policy on Windows NT 4.0 and Windows 95 computers.

See also *Microsoft Management Console*; *registry*.

System Policy Editor

The utility Poledit.exe, used by administrators to set system policy on Windows NT 4.0 and Windows 95 computers.

System state data

A collection of system-specific data that can be backed up and restored. For all Windows 2000 operating systems, the System State data includes the registry, the class registration database, and the system boot files.

System volume

The volume that contains the hardware-specific files needed to load Windows 2000. The system volume can be (but does not have to be) the same volume as the boot volume.

See also *volume*.

Systemroot

The path and folder name where the Windows 2000 system files are located. Typically, this is C:\Winnt, although a different drive or folder can be designated when Windows 2000 is installed. The value %systemroot% can be used to replace the actual location of the folder that contains the Windows 2000 system files. To identify your systemroot folder, click Start, click Run, and then type %systemroot%.

T

Taskbar

The bar that contains the Start button and appears by default at the bottom of the desktop. You can use the taskbar buttons to switch between the programs you are running. The taskbar can be hidden, moved to the sides or top of the desktop, or customized in other ways.

See also *desktop*; *taskbar button*; *status area*.

Taskbar button

A button that appears on the taskbar when an application is running.

Tcpmon.ini

The file that specifies whether a device supports multiple ports. If the Tcpmon.ini file indicates that a device can support multiple ports, users a prompted to pick which port should be used during device installation.

Telephony API (TAPI)

An application programming interface (API) used by communications programs to communicate with telephony and network services.

See also *Internet Protocol*.

Terabyte

Approximately one trillion bytes, or one million million bytes.

Terminal Services

Software services that allow client applications to be run on a server so that client computers can function as terminals rather than independent systems. The server provides a multisession environment and runs the Windows-based programs being used on the clients.

See also *client*.

Thread

A type of object within a process that runs program instructions. Using multiple threads allows concurrent operations within a process and enables one process to run different parts of its program on different processors simultaneously. A thread has its own set of registers, its own kernel stack, a thread environment block, and a user stack in the address space of its process.

Thread state

A numeric value indicating the execution state of the thread. Numbered 0 through 5, the states seen most often are 1 for ready, 2 for running, and 5 for waiting.

Throughput

For disks, the transfer capacity of the disk system.

Time To Live (TTL)

A timer value included in packets sent over TCP/IP-based networks that tells the recipients how long to hold or use the packet or any of its included data before expiring and discarding the packet or data.

For DNS, TTL values are used in resource records within a zone to determine how long requesting clients should cache and use this information when it appears in a query response answered by a DNS server for the zone.

Timer bar

The colored bar that moves across the screen according to the frequency of the data-collection update interval.

ToggleKeys

A Windows feature that beeps when one of the locking keys (CAPS LOCK, NUM LOCK, or SCROLL LOCK) is turned on or off.

Token Ring

A type of network media that connects clients in a closed ring and uses token passing to allow clients to use the network.

See also *Fiber Distributed Data Interface.*

Total instance

A unique instance that contains the performance counters that represent the sum of all active instances of an object.

Transitive trust relationship

The trust relationship that inherently exists between Windows 2000 domains in a domain tree or forest, or between trees in a forest, or between forests. When a domain joins an existing forest or domain tree, a transitive trust is automatically established. In Windows 2000 transitive trusts are always two-way relationships.

See also *domain tree*; *forest*; *nontransitive trust relationship.*

Transmission Control Protocol / Internet Protocol (TCP/IP)

A set of software networking protocols widely used on the Internet that provide communications across interconnected networks of computers with diverse hardware architectures and operating systems. TCP/IP includes standards for how computers communicate and conventions for connecting networks and routing traffic.

Transmitting Station ID string (TSID)

A string that specifies the Transmitter Subscriber ID sent by the fax machine when sending a fax to a receiving machine. This string is usually a combination of the fax or telephone number and the name of the business. It is often the same as the Called Subscriber ID.

Transport Layer Security (TLS)

A standard protocol that is used to provide secure Web communications on the Internet or intranets. It enables clients to authenticate servers or, optionally, servers to authenticate clients. It also provides a secure channel by encrypting communications.

Transport protocol

A protocol that defines how data should be presented to the next receiving layer in the Windows NT and Windows 2000 networking model and packages the data accordingly. The transport protocol passes data to the network adapter driver through the network driver interface specification (NDIS) interface and to the redirector through the Transport Driver Interface (TDI).

TrueType fonts

Fonts that are scalable and sometimes generated as bitmaps or soft fonts, depending on the capabilities of your printer. TrueType fonts are device-independent fonts that are stored as outlines. They can be sized to any height, and they can be printed exactly as they appear on the screen.

See also *font*.

Trust relationship

A logical relationship established between domains that allows pass-through authentication in which a trusting domain honors the logon authentications of a trusted domain. User accounts and global groups defined in a trusted domain can be granted rights and permissions in a trusting domain, even though the user accounts or groups do not exist in the trusting domain's directory.

See also *authentication*; *domain*; *two-way trust relationship.*

Trusted forest

A forest that is connected to another forest by explicit or transitive trust.

See also *explicit trust relationship*; *forest*; *transitive trust relationship.*

TSID

See *Transmitting Station ID string.*

Tunnel

The logical path by which the encapsulated packets travel through the transit internetwork.

TWAIN

An acronym for Technology Without An Interesting Name. An industry-standard software protocol and API that provides easy integration of image data between input devices, such as scanners and still image digital cameras, and software applications.

Two-way trust relationship

A link between domains in which each domain trusts user accounts in the other domain to use its resources. Users can log on from computers in either domain to the domain that contains their account.

See also *trust relationship.*

Type 1 fonts

Scalable fonts designed to work with PostScript devices.

See also *font*; *PostScript.*

U

UART

See *Universal Asynchronous Receiver/Transmitter.*

Unallocated space

Available disk space that is not allocated to any partition, logical drive, or volume. The type of object created on unallocated space depends on the disk type (basic or dynamic). For basic disks, unallocated space outside partitions can be used to create primary or extended partitions. Free space inside an extended partition can be used to create a logical drive. For dynamic disks, unallocated space can be used to create dynamic volumes. Unlike basic disks, the exact disk region used is not selected to create the volume.

See also *basic disk*; *dynamic disk*; *extended partition*; *logical drive*; *partition*; *primary partition*; *volume.*

Unicode

A fixed-width, 16-bit character-encoding standard capable of representing the letters and characters of the majority of the world's languages. A consortium of U.S. computer companies developed Unicode.

UniDriver

The UniDriver (or Universal Print Driver) carries out requests (such as printing text, rendering bitmaps, or advancing a page) on most types of printers. The UniDriver accepts information from a printer specific minidriver and uses this information to complete tasks.

Uniform Resource Locator (URL)

An address that uniquely identifies a location on the Internet. A URL for a World Wide Web site is preceded with http://, as in the fictitious URL http://www.example.microsoft.com/. A URL can contain more detail, such as the name of a page of hypertext, usually identified by the file name extension .html or .htm.

See also *HTML*; *HTTP*; *IP address.*

Universal Asynchronous Receiver/Transmitter (UART)

An integrated circuit (silicon chip) that is commonly used in microcomputers to provide asynchronous communications. The UART does parallel-to-serial conversion of data to be transmitted and serial-to-parallel conversion of data received.

See also *asynchronous communication.*

Universal Disk Format (UDF)

A file system defined by the Optical Storage Technology Association (OSTA) that is the successor to the CD-ROM file system (CDFS). UDF is targeted for removable disk media like DVD, CD, and Magneto-Optical (MO) discs.

Universal group

A Windows 2000 group only available in native mode that is valid anywhere in the forest. A universal group appears in the Global Catalog but contains primarily global groups from domains in the forest. This is the simplest form of group and can contain other universal groups, global groups, and users from anywhere in the forest.

See also *domain local group*; *forest*; *Global Catalog.*

Universal Naming Convention (UNC)

A convention for naming files and other resources beginning with two backslashes (\), indicating that the resource exists on a network computer. UNC names conform to the \\SERVERNAME\SHARENAME syntax, where SERVERNAME is the server's name and SHARENAME is the name of the shared resource. The UNC name of a directory or file can also include the directory path after the share name, with the following syntax:
\\SERVERNAME\SHARENAME\DIRECTORY\FILENAME.

Universal Serial Bus (USB)

A serial bus with a bandwidth of 1.5 megabits per second (Mbps) for connecting peripherals to a microcomputer. USB can connect up to 127 peripherals, such as external CD-ROM drives, printers, modems, mice, and keyboards, to the system through a single, general-purpose port. This is accomplished by daisy chaining peripherals together. USB supports hot plugging and multiple data streams.

UNIX

A powerful, multi-user, multitasking operating system initially developed at AT&T Bell Laboratories in 1969 for use on minicomputers. UNIX is considered more portable—that is, less computer-specific—than other operating systems because it is written in C language. Newer versions of UNIX have been developed at the University of California at Berkeley and by AT&T.

Unrecognized pool

A repository for blank media and media that are not recognized by Removable Storage.

Upgrade

When referring to software, to update existing program files, folders, and registry entries to a more recent version. Upgrading, unlike performing a new installation, leaves existing settings and files in place.

URL

See *Uniform Resource Locator.*

USB

See *Universal Serial Bus.*

User account

A record that consists of all the information that defines a user to Windows 2000. This includes the user name and password required for the user to log on, the groups in which the user account has membership, and the rights and permissions the user has for using the computer and network and accessing their resources. For Windows 2000 Professional and member servers, user accounts are managed by using Local Users and Groups. For Windows 2000 Server domain controllers, user accounts are managed by using Microsoft Active Directory Users and Computers.

See also *domain controller*; *group*; *user name.*

User Identification (UID)

A user identifier that uniquely identifies a user. UNIX-bases systems use the UID to identify the owner of files and processes, and to determine access permissions.

User mode

The processing mode in which applications run.

User name

A unique name identifying a user account to Windows 2000. An account's user name must be unique among the other group names and user names within its own domain or workgroup.

User principal name (UPN)

A friendly name assigned to security principals (users and groups) that is shorter than the distinguished name and easier to remember. The default user principal name is composed of the security principal name for the user and the DNS name of the root domain where the user object resides. The user principal name is the preferred logon name for Windows 2000 users and is independent of the distinguished name, so a User object can be moved or renamed without affecting the user's logon name.

See also *distinguished name.*

User profile

A file that contains configuration information for a specific user, such as desktop settings, persistent network connections, and application settings. Each user's preferences are saved to a user profile that Windows NT and Windows 2000 use to configure the desktop each time a user logs on.

User rights

Tasks a user is permitted to perform on a computer system or domain. There are two types of user rights: privileges and logon rights. An example of a privilege is the right to shut down the system. An example of a logon right is the right to log on to a computer locally (at the keyboard). Administrators assign both types to individual users or groups as part of the security settings for the computer.

See also *permission*; *privilege.*

User rights policy

Security settings that manage the assignment of rights to groups and user accounts.

Utility Manager

A function of Windows 2000 that allows administrators to review the status of applications and tools and to customize features and add tools more easily.

V

Value bar

The area of the System Monitor graph or histogram display that shows last, average, minimum and maximum statistics for the selected counter.

Vector fonts

Fonts rendered from a mathematical model, in which each character is defined as a set of lines drawn between points. Vector fonts can be cleanly scaled to any size or aspect ratio.

Video for Windows (VfW)

A format developed by Microsoft for storing video and audio information. Files in this format have an .avi extension. AVI files are limited to 320 x 240 resolution at 30 frames per second, neither of which is adequate for full-screen, full-motion video.

Video Port Extensions (VPE)

A DirectDraw extension to support direct hardware connections from a video decoder and autoflipping in the graphics frame buffer. VPE allows the client to negotiate the connection between the MPEG or NTSC decoder and the video port. VPE also allows the client to control effects in the video stream, such as cropping, scaling, and so on.

Virtual Device Driver (VxD)

Software for Windows that manages a hardware or software system resource. The middle letter in the abbreviation indicates the type of device; x is used where the type of device is not under discussion.

Virtual memory

The space on the hard disk that Windows 2000 uses as memory. Because of virtual memory, the amount of memory taken from the perspective of a process can be much greater than the actual physical memory in the computer. The operating system does this in a way that is transparent to the application, by paging data that does not fit in physical memory to and from the disk at any given instant.

Virtual private network (VPN)

The extension of a private network that encompasses links across shared or public networks, such as the Internet.

Virus scanner

Software used to scan for and eradicate computer viruses, worms, and Trojan horses.

Volume

A portion of a physical disk that functions as though it were a physically separate disk. In My Computer and Windows Explorer, volumes appear as local disks, such as drive C or drive D.

Volume mount points

New system objects in the version of NTFS included with Windows 2000 that represent storage volumes in a persistent, robust manner. Volume mount points allow the operating system to graft the root of a volume onto a directory.

W

WDM Streaming class

The means by which Windows 2000 Professional supports digital video and audio. Enables support for such components as DVD decoders, MPEG decoders, video decoders, tuners, and audio codecs.

Wide area network (WAN)

A communications network connecting geographically separated computers, printers, and other devices. A WAN allows any connected device to interact with any other on the network.

See also *local area network.*

Windows 2000 Multilanguage Version

A version of Windows 2000 that extends the native language support in Windows 2000 by allowing user interface languages to be changed on a per user basis. This version also minimizes the number of language versions you need to deploy across the network.

Windows File Protection (WFP)

A Windows 2000 feature that runs in the background and protects your system files from being overwritten. When a file in a protected folder is modified, WFP determines if the new file is the correct Microsoft version or if the file is digitally signed. If not, the modified file is replaced with a valid version.

Windows Internet Name Service (WINS)

A software service that dynamically maps IP addresses to computer names (NetBIOS names). This allows users to access resources by name instead of requiring them to use IP addresses that are difficult to recognize and remember. WINS servers support clients running Windows NT 4.0 and earlier versions of Windows operating systems.

See also *Domain Name System.*

Windows Update

A Microsoft-owned Web site from which Windows 98 and Windows 2000 users can install or update device drivers. By using an ActiveX control, Windows Update compares the available drivers with those on the user's system and offers to install new or updated versions.

WINS

See *Windows Internet Name Service.*

Winsock

An application programming interface standard for software that provides TCP/IP interface under Windows. Short for Windows Sockets.

See also *TCP/IP.*

Work queue item

A job request of an existing library, made by an application that supports Removable Storage, which is placed in a queue and processed when the library resource becomes available.

Workgroup

A simple grouping of computers intended only to help users find such things as printers and shared folders within that group. Workgroups in Windows 2000 do not offer the centralized user accounts and authentication offered by domains.

Working set

For a process, the amount of physical memory assigned to a process by the operating system.

X

X.25

X.25 is a standard that defines the communications protocol for access to packet-switched networks.

X.400

What is an ISO and ITU standard for addressing and transporting e-mail messages. It conforms to layer 7 of the OSI model and supports several types of transport mechanisms, including Ethernet, X.25, TCP/IP, and dial-up lines.

X.500

The X.500 is the standard for defining a distributed directory service standard and was developed by the International Standards Organization (ISO). This ISO and ITU standard defines how global directories should be structured. X.500 directories are hierarchical, which means that they have different levels for each category of information, such as country, state, and city. X.500 supports X.400 systems.

X Window System

X Windows is a standard set of display-handling routines developed at MIT for UNIX workstations. These routines are used to create hardware-independent graphical user interfaces for UNIX systems.

Y

Ymodem

Ymodem is a variation of the Xmodem file transfer protocol that includes the following enhancements:

1. The ability to transfer information in 1-kilobyte (1,024-byte) blocks

2. The ability to send multiple files (batch file transmission)

3. Cyclical redundancy checking (CRC)

4. The ability to abort transfer by transmitting two CAN (cancel) characters in a row.

Z

ZIPI

A MIDI-like serial data format for musical instruments. ZIPI provides a hierarchical method for addressing instruments and uses an extensible command set.

Zero Wait State

The condition of random access memory (RAM) that is fast enough to respond to the processor without requiring a wait states.

Z axis (X axis)

Used in defining specific graphical display locations. The optical axis that is perpendicular to X and Y axes

Index

TotalRecall Gives You *Four* Levels of Computer Certification Practice Exams, Books, and eBooks

⑩Study formats and prices vary so you can choose one that best fits your level of knowledge and skills.

⑩Each format offers you either free or discounted access to our popular BeachFront Quizzer test engine. See description below.

⑩ALL come with our exclusive Money-Back Guarantee—pass the exam your first time or get money back!

- **1. InsideScoop Certification Success Series**

Paperback books in the InsideScoop series offer a package of comprehensive study manual and CD-ROM of the BeachFront Quizzer test engine with answers/ explanations linked to relevant chapters in an integrated eBook. The study manual includes detailed information about each core exam topic with pre/post assessment quizzes; an abundance of figures, diagrams and photos; chapter summaries; helpful tips and time management techniques for test taking; lists of useful websites, articles and other learning resources; and an extensive glossary of 600 computer, IT, and telecommunications terms.

Books are $89.99

- **2. InsidersChoice Certification Success Series**

Paperback books in the InsidersChoice series offer a package of comprehensive study manual and FREE download of the BeachFront Quizzer test engine with answers/ explanations linked to relevant chapters in an integrated eBook. The study manual includes detailed information about each core exam topic with pre/post assessment quizzes; an abundance of figures, diagrams and photos; chapter summaries; helpful tips and time management techniques for test taking; lists of useful websites, articles and other learning resources; and an extensive glossary of 600 computer, IT, and telecommunications terms.

Paperbacks are $59.99 and eBooks are $44.99

- **3. ExamInsight IT Certification System Series**

Paperback books and eBooks in the ExamInsight series offer a package of compact study guide and 50% discount to purchase a download of the BeachFront Quizzer test engine with answers/ explanations linked to relevant chapters in an integrated eBook. The study guide includes compact information about each core exam topic with pre/post assessment quizzes; an abundance of figures, diagrams and photos; chapter summaries; helpful tips and time management techniques for test taking; and lists of useful websites, articles and other learning resources

Paperbacks are $39.99 and eBooks are $29.99

- **4. ExamWise IT Question Book Series**

Paperback books and eBooks in the ExamWise series offer a package of Q&A workbook and 30-Day FREE access to a BeachFront Quizzer online practice exam. Each ExamWise Q&A workbook offers you approximately 300 practice questions organized by core exam topic. Questions are arranged in a unique format of two questions per right and page, with answers and brief explanations on the reverse page.

Paperbacks are $39.99 and eBooks are $29.99

The BeachFront Quizzer Test Engine Makes Passing Certification Exams as Easy as a Day at the Beach...

The BeachFront Quizzer test engine was pioneered in 1995 by Bruce Moran, an ex-NASA IT professional turned vocational computer instructor and certification trainer before launching his own book publishing operation in 2002. This popular test engine introduced interactive and adaptive features that other publishers have since tried to imitate, but never duplicate. It offers you four helpful study formats:

1) Adaptive technology generates 15-25 questions in 30-minute sessions to help you identify your strengths and weaknesses for each exam topic.

2) Study sessions help strengthen your weakest exam topics by generating up to 250 questions per topic until you can answer each correctly. Explanations for each question are linked to relevant chapters in an eBook study manual and often to web sites to help you develop a complete understanding of why an answer is correct. By focusing on your rough spots, we'll get you certified fast—guaranteed or get money back!

3) Simulated exams generate randomized questions about core exam topics in 60-90 minute sessions and then provide a score summary by topic. Taking multiple practice exams will build your confidence and ability to concentrate during the real deal!

4) Flash card drills present questions to answer mentally and then allow you to click F4 to display the correct answer.

Visit our web sites for more information:

www.TotalRecallPress.com / www.bfq.com

TotalRecall Certification Publications Microsoft

InsideScoop: TotalRecall's Complete Certification System Series:

InsideScoop to MCP / MCSE Certification: **Exam 70-210**
Managing Microsoft Windows 2000 Professional

InsideScoop to MCP / MCSE Certification: **Exam 70-216**
Implementing and Administering a Microsoft Windows 2000 Network Infrastructure

InsideScoop to MCP / MCSE Certification: **Exam 70-217**
Managing a Microsoft Directory Services Infrastructure

InsideScoop to MCP / MCSE Certification: **Exam 70-219**
Designing a Windows 2000 Directory Services Infrastructure

InsideScoop to MCP / MCSE Certification: **Exam 70-220**
Designing Security for a Microsoft Windows 2000 Network

InsideScoop to MCP / MCSE Certification: **Exam 70-221**
Designing a Microsoft Windows 2000 Network Infrastructure

InsideScoop to MCP / MCSE Certification: **Exam 70-227**
Installing, Configuring, and Administering Microsoft Internet Security and Acceleration (ISA) Server 2000, Enterprise Edition

InsideScoop to MCP / MCSE Certification: **Exam 70-270**
Installing, Configuring, and Administering Microsoft Windows XP Professional

InsideScoop to MCP / MCSE Certification: **Exam 70-290**
Managing and Maintaining a Microsoft Windows Server 2003 Environment

InsideScoop to MCP / MCSE Certification: **Exam 70-291**
Managing, and Maintaining a Microsoft Windows Server 2003 Network Infrastructure

InsideScoop to MCP / MCSE Certification: **Exam 70-292**
Managing and Maintaining a Microsoft Windows Server 2003 Environment for an MCSA Certified on Windows 2000

InsideScoop to MCP / MCSE Certification: **Exam 70-293**
Planning and Maintaining a Microsoft Windows Server 2003 Network Infrastructure

InsideScoop to MCP / MCSE Certification: **Exam 70-294**
Plan and Maintain a Microsoft Windows Server 2003 Active Directory Infrastructure

InsideScoop to MCP / MCSE Certification: **Exam 70-296**
Planning, Implementing, and Maintaining a Microsoft Windows Server 2003 Environment for an MCSE Certified on Windows

InsideScoop to MCP / MCSE Certification: **Exam 70-297**
Designing Microsoft Windows Server 2003 Active Directory and Network Infrastructure

InsideScoop to MCP / MCSE Certification: **Exam 70-298**
Designing Security for a Microsoft Server 2003 Network

InsideScoop to MCP / MCSE Certification: **Exam 70-299**
Implementing and Administering Security in a Microsoft Windows Server 2003 Network

ExamInsight: TotalRecall IT Insight Certification Book Series:

ExamInsight For MCP / MCSE Certification: **Exam 70-210**
Managing Microsoft Windows 2000 Professional
ExamInsight For MCP / MCSE Certification: **Exam 70-216**
Implementing and Administering a Microsoft Windows 2000 Network Infrastructure
ExamInsight For MCP / MCSE Certification: **Exam 70-217**
Managing a Microsoft Directory Services Infrastructure
ExamInsight For MCP / MCSE Certification: **Exam 70-219**
Designing a Windows 2000 Directory Services Infrastructure
ExamInsight For MCP / MCSE Certification: **Exam 70-220**
Designing Security for a Microsoft Windows 2000 Network
ExamInsight For MCP / MCSE Certification: **Exam 70-221**
Designing a Microsoft Windows 2000 Network Infrastructure
ExamInsight For MCP / MCSE Certification: **Exam 70-227**
Installing, Configuring, and Administering Microsoft Internet Security and Acceleration (ISA) Server 2000, Enterprise Edition
ExamInsight For MCP / MCSE Certification: **Exam 70-270**
Installing, Configuring, and Administering Microsoft Windows XP Professional
ExamInsight For MCP / MCSE Certification: **Exam 70-290**
Managing and Maintaining a Microsoft Windows Server 2003 Environment
ExamInsight For MCP / MCSE Certification: **Exam 70-291**
Managing, and Maintaining a Microsoft Windows Server 2003 Network Infrastructure
ExamInsight For MCP / MCSE Certification: **Exam 70-292**
Managing and Maintaining a Microsoft Windows Server 2003 Environment for an MCSA Certified on Windows 2000
ExamInsight For MCP / MCSE Certification: **Exam 70-293**
Planning and Maintaining a Microsoft Windows Server 2003 Network Infrastructure
ExamInsight For MCP / MCSE Certification: **Exam 70-294**
Plan and Maintain a Microsoft Windows Server 2003 Active Directory Infrastructure
ExamInsight For MCP / MCSE Certification: **Exam 70-296**
Planning, Implementing, and Maintaining a Microsoft Windows Server 2003 Environment for an MCSE Certified on Windows
ExamInsight For MCP / MCSE Certification: **Exam 70-297**
Designing Microsoft Windows Server 2003 Active Directory and Network Infrastructure
ExamInsight For MCP / MCSE Certification: **Exam 70-298**
Designing Security for a Microsoft Server 2003 Network:
ExamInsight For MCP / MCSE Certification: **Exam 70-299**
Implementing and Administering Security in a Microsoft Windows Server 2003 Network

InsidersChoice: TotalRecall's Insiders Certification System Series:

InsidersChoice to MCP / MCSE Certification: Exam 70-270
Installing, Configuring, and Administering Microsoft Windows XP Professional

InsidersChoice to MCP / MCSE Certification: Exam 70-290
Managing and Maintaining a Microsoft Windows Server 2003 Environment

InsidersChoice to MCP / MCSE Certification: Exam 70-291
Managing, and Maintaining a Microsoft Windows Server 2003 Network Infrastructure

InsidersChoice to MCP / MCSE Certification: Exam 70-292
Managing and Maintaining a Microsoft Windows Server 2003 Environment for an MCSA Certified on Windows 2000

InsidersChoice to MCP / MCSE Certification: Exam 70-293
Planning and Maintaining a Microsoft Windows Server 2003 Network Infrastructure

InsidersChoice to MCP / MCSE Certification: Exam 70-294
Plan and Maintain a Microsoft Windows Server 2003 Active Directory Infrastructure

InsidersChoice to MCP / MCSE Certification: Exam 70-296
Planning, Implementing, and Maintaining a Microsoft Windows Server 2003 Environment for an MCSE Certified on Windows

InsidersChoice to MCP / MCSE Certification: Exam 70-297
Designing Microsoft Windows Server 2003 Active Directory and Network Infrastructure

InsidersChoice to MCP / MCSE Certification: Exam 70-298
Designing Security for a Microsoft Server 2003 Network

InsidersChoice to MCP / MCSE Certification: Exam 70-299
Implementing and Administering Security in a Microsoft Windows Server 2003 Network

ExamWise: TotalRecall IT Insight Certification Book Series:

ExamWise For MCP / MCSE Certification: Exam 70-210
Managing Microsoft Windows 2000 Professional

ExamWise For MCP / MCSE Certification: Exam 70-216
Implementing and Administering a Microsoft Windows 2000 Network Infrastructure

ExamWise For MCP / MCSE Certification: Exam 70-217
Managing a Microsoft Directory Services Infrastructure

ExamWise For MCP / MCSE Certification: Exam 70-219
Designing a Windows 2000 Directory Services Infrastructure

ExamWise For MCP / MCSE Certification: Exam 70-220
Designing Security for a Microsoft Windows 2000 Network

ExamWise For MCP / MCSE Certification: Exam 70-221
Designing a Microsoft Windows 2000 Network Infrastructure

ExamWise For MCP / MCSE Certification: Exam 70-227
Installing, Configuring, and Administering Microsoft Internet Security and Acceleration (ISA) Server 2000, Enterprise Edition

ExamWise For MCP / MCSE Certification: Exam 70-270
Installing, Configuring, and Administering Microsoft Windows XP Professional

ExamWise For MCP / MCSE Certification: Exam 70-290
Managing and Maintaining a Microsoft Windows Server 2003 Environment

ExamWise For MCP / MCSE Certification: Exam 70-291
Managing, and Maintaining a Microsoft Windows Server 2003 Network Infrastructure

ExamWise For MCP / MCSE Certification: Exam 70-292
Managing and Maintaining a Microsoft Windows Server 2003 Environment for an MCSA Certified on Windows 2000

ExamWise For MCP / MCSE Certification: Exam 70-293
Planning and Maintaining a Microsoft Windows Server 2003 Network Infrastructure

ExamWise For MCP / MCSE Certification: Exam 70-294
Plan and Maintain a Microsoft Windows Server 2003 Active Directory Infrastructure

ExamWise For MCP / MCSE Certification: Exam 70-296
Planning, Implementing, and Maintaining a Microsoft Windows Server 2003 Environment for an MCSE Certified on Windows

ExamWise For MCP / MCSE Certification: Exam 70-297
Designing Microsoft Windows Server 2003 Active Directory and Network Infrastructure

ExamWise For MCP / MCSE Certification: Exam 70-298
Designing Security for a Microsoft Server 2003 Network

ExamWise For MCP / MCSE Certification: Exam 70-299
Implementing and Administering Security in a Microsoft Windows Server 2003 Network

TotalRecall Certification Publications

CompTIA Titles

InsideScoop: TotalRecall's Complete Certification System Series:

InsideScoop to **CompTIA A+ Hardware:**	**Exam 220-301**
InsideScoop to **CompTIA A+ OS:**	**Exam 220-302**
InsideScoop to **CompTIA Network+:**	**Exam N10-001**
InsideScoop to **CompTIA Security+ (Second Edition):**	**Exam SY0-101**

InsidersChoice: TotalRecall IT Insight Certification Book Series:

InsidersChoice to **CompTIA A+ Hardware:**	**Exam 220-301**
InsidersChoice to **CompTIA A+ OS:**	**Exam 220-302**
InsidersChoice to **CompTIA Network+:**	**Exam N10-001**
InsidersChoice to **CompTIA Security+: (Second Edition):**	**Exam SY0-001**

ExamInsight: TotalRecall IT Insight Certification Book Series:

ExamInsight For **CompTIA A+ Hardware:**	**Exam 220-301**
ExamInsight For **CompTIA A+ OS:**	**Exam 220-302**
ExamInsight For **CompTIA Network+:**	**Exam N10-001**
ExamInsight For **CompTIA Security+: (Second Edition):**	**Exam SY0-001**

ExamWise: The TotalRecall Question Book Series:

ExamWise For **CompTIA A+ Hardware:**	**Exam 220-301**
ExamWise For **CompTIA A+ OS:**	**Exam 220-302**
ExamWise For **CompTIA Network+:**	**Exam N10-001**
ExamWise For **CompTIA Security+ (Second Edition):**	**Exam SY0-101**
ExamWise For **CompTIA I-Net+ Certification:**	**Exam IK0-002**
ExamWise For CompTIA Server+ Certification:	**Exam SK0-001**

Money Back Book Guarantee

This guarantee applies only to books published by TotalRecall Publications, Inc.! We are so confident in our products, we are prepared to offer the following guarantee to YOU our valued customer: If you do not pass your certification exam after two attempts, we will give money back!

Visit **http://www.totalrecallpress.com**

Select "Money Back Book Guarantee" for details.

Registered book purchasers who qualify will receive

1. Receive a 50% cash refund of purchase price
2. Receive a free TotalRecall book of equal value.

Note: you must pay for shipping and handling.

To qualify for this TotalRecall Guarantee you must meet these requirements and perform the following tasks:

1. Register your purchase at the TotalRecall Web site **http://www.totalrecallpress.com.**
2. Fail the corresponding exam twice (no time limit).
3. Contact TotalRecall for the RMA # and to claim this guarantee
4. Send e-mail to **mailto:Guarantee@totalrecallpress.com.** Subject must contain your Membership # or Registration #.

Ship the following to claim your refund.

1. RMA # from returned e-mail
2. Documents of exam scores for both failed attempts
3. Return the Book to the following address

TotalRecall Publications, Inc.

Attn: Corby Tate

1103 Middlecreek

Friendswood, TX 77546

Contact Information:

bfquiz@swbell.net, **http://www.bfq.com**

888-992-3131, 281-992-3131

281-482-5390 Fax

It's a Passing day here at the BeachFront.

Thank you for using the TotalRecall Success Program.

Bruce Moran, President

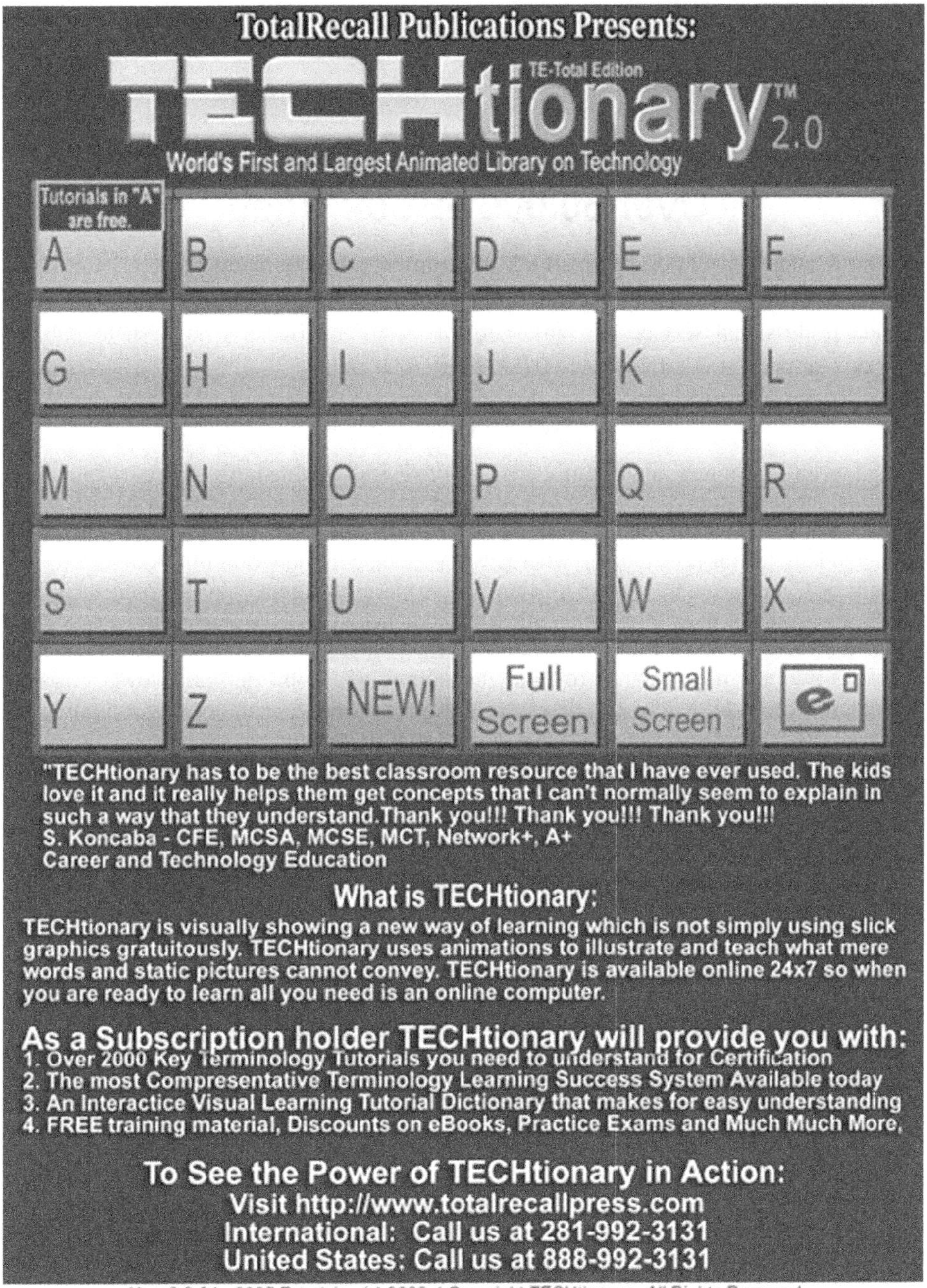
TotalRecall Publications Presents:
TECHtionary™ 2.0
TE-Total Edition
World's First and Largest Animated Library on Technology
Tutorials in "A" are free.
A B C D E F
G H I J K L
M N O P Q R
S T U V W X
Y Z NEW! Full Screen Small Screen e
"TECHtionary has to be the best classroom resource that I have ever used. The kids love it and it really helps them get concepts that I can't normally seem to explain in such a way that they understand.Thank you!!! Thank you!!! Thank you!!!
S. Koncaba - CFE, MCSA, MCSE, MCT, Network+, A+
Career and Technology Education
What is TECHtionary:
TECHtionary is visually showing a new way of learning which is not simply using slick graphics gratuitously. TECHtionary uses animations to illustrate and teach what mere words and static pictures cannot convey. TECHtionary is available online 24x7 so when you are ready to learn all you need is an online computer.
As a Subscription holder TECHtionary will provide you with:
1. Over 2000 Key Terminology Tutorials you need to understand for Certification
2. The most Compresentative Terminology Learning Success System Available today
3. An Interactice Visual Learning Tutorial Dictionary that makes for easy understanding
4. FREE training material, Discounts on eBooks, Practice Exams and Much Much More,
To See the Power of TECHtionary in Action:
Visit http://www.totalrecallpress.com
International: Call us at 281-992-3131
United States: Call us at 888-992-3131

70-291 Download Instructions

BeachFront Quizzer (BFQ) version 4.0 Special Edition

System Requirements: Windows 95 & 98, Windows NT, XP Windows 2000 and Server 2003 with a minimum of 6 MB hard disk space and 16 MB RAM

The Center For Technology Certification, Inc. will help you accomplish your Microsoft Certifications. This state of art software program is designed to cut your study time in half, and get you to a passing level in the easiest and shortest amount of time possible. The program will adapt to you personally, and then lay out a prioritized study plan that will visually show you your progress on a day to day basis. When the software has recognized that you are at a passing level in each objective category, you're ready to sit for the exam! It's really that easy!

Installation Instructions: 70-291 Practice Exam with eBook Visit http://tinyurl.com/5dh7y Download and Install the latest version of the BFQ Engine: File Name Quiz32.exe.

1. Go to http://snipurl.com/MS70291 and download the practice exam ZIP file to a folder on your hard drive.

2. Open the WinZip file and Execute Quiz32.exe OR Execute SetupBFQ.bat to install the practice exam

This will install all software files:

4. Open the LicenseKey.txt file Copy and Insert the 12 digit number **License Key** when requested or type in the following License Key Numbers when requested.

TRP 70-291 Server 2003 MCP/MCSE = 428155697373

The software is very user friendly.

After you get the program installed Open Click on the Help button menu

Select contents for the on-screen manual. (You may want to print the Help File)

You will follow a six step process that will lead you through the program efficiently.

We are here to support you all the way. If you have any technical questions on the content, make sure you contact us. We are very proud of our pass rate, and we want you to contribute.

If you need additional assistance, visit our website www.totalrecallpress.com

Please let me know that the download and installation worked properly.

Thank you for purchasing our product and

Good Luck with your exam!

Sales:

866-992-3398

281-992-3398

Technical Support: info@bfq.com

888-992-3131 or 281-992-3131

Fax 281-482-5390

70-291 Download Instructions

BeachFront Quizzer (BFQ) version 4.0 Special Edition

System Requirements: Windows 95 & 98, NT, XP, 2000 and Server 2003 with a minimum of 6 MB hard disk space and 16 MB RAM.

The Center For Technology Certification, Inc. will help you accomplish your Microsoft Certifications. This state of art software program is designed to cut your study time in half, and get you to a passing level in the easiest and shortest amount of time possible. The program will adapt to you personally, and then lay out a prioritized study plan that will visually show you your progress on a day to day basis. When the software has recognized that you are at a passing level in each objective category, you're ready to sit for the exam. It's really that easy!

Installation Instructions: 70-291 Practice Exam with eBook
Visit http://tinyurl.com/5dh7y Download and Install the latest version of the BFQ Engine: File Name Quiz32.exe.

Visit http://snipurl.com/EI70291 and download the ExamInsight For 70-291 eBook Zip file to a folder on your hard drive.

This will install all software files:
Open the WinZip file and execute the 70-290SE.exe to install the testing software. Open the LicenseKey.txt file Copy and Insert the 12 digit number **License Key** when requested or type in the following License Key Numbers when requested.

TRP 70-291 SE Windows Server 2003 Network Infrastructure = 480345596363
The software is very user friendly.
After you get the program installed Open Click on the Help button menu Select contents for the on-screen manual. (You may want to print the Help File) You will follow a six step process that will lead you through the program efficiently. We are here to support you all the way. If you have any technical questions on the content, make sure you contact us. We are very proud of our pass rate, and we want you to contribute.
If you need additional assistance, visit our website http://www.totalrecallpress.com/ Please let me know that the download and installation worked properly.
Thank you for purchasing our product and Good Luck with your exam!

Sales:
866-992-3398
281-992-3398
Technical Support: info@bfq.com
888-992-3131 or 281-992-3131
Fax 281-482-5390

70-291 Download Instructions

BeachFront Quizzer (BFQ) version 4.0 Special Edition

System Requirements: Windows 95 & 98, Windows NT, XP Windows 2000 and Server 2003 with a minimum of 6 MB hard disk space and 16 MB RAM

The Center For Technology Certification, Inc. will help you accomplish your Microsoft Certifications. This state of art software program is designed to cut your study time in half, and get you to a passing level in the easiest and shortest amount of time possible. The program will adapt to you personally, and then lay out a prioritized study plan that will visually show you your progress on a day to day basis. When the software has recognized that you are at a passing level in each objective category, you're ready to sit for the exam! It's really that easy!!

Installation Instructions: 70-291 Practice Exam with eBook Visit http://tinyurl.com/5dh7y Download and Install the latest version of the BFQ Engine: File Name Quiz32.exe.

1. Go to http://snipurl.com/SE70291 and download the practice exam ZIP file to a folder on your hard drive.
2. Open the WinZip file and Execute Quiz32.exe OR Execute SetupBFQ.bat to install the practice exam

This will install all software files:

4. Open the LicenseKey.txt file Copy and Insert the 12 digit number **License Key** when requested or type in the following License Key Numbers when requested.

TRP 70-291 Windows Server 2003 Environment = 480345596363

The software is very user friendly.

After you get the program installed Open Click on the Help button menu

Select contents for the on-screen manual. (You may want to print the Help File)

You will follow a six step process that will lead you through the program efficiently.

We are here to support you all the way. If you have any technical questions on the content, make sure you contact us. We are very proud of our pass rate, and we want you to contribute.

If you need additional assistance, visit our website www.totalrecallpress.com

Please let me know that the download and installation worked properly.

Thank you for purchasing our product and

Good Luck with your exam!

Sales:

866-992-3398

281-992-3398

Technical Support: info@bfq.com

888-992-3131 or 281-992-3131

Fax 281-482-5390

70-291 CD-ROM Instructions

BeachFront Quizzer (BFQ) version 4.0

System Requirements: Windows 95 & 98, Windows NT, XP Windows 2000 and Server 2003, with a minimum of 6 MB hard disk space and 16 MB RAM.

Installation: The BFQ 70-291 exam will Auto Install. Simply place the CD-ROM in your CD-ROM drive and follow the instructions that appear on your screen, selecting the Windows Server 2003 Network Infrastructure exam.

12-digit Database License Key

TRP 70-291 Windows Server 2003 Network Infrastructure = 428155697373

If you have problems with the automatic installation, use the following procedure:

1) To install the program Run: \Instexe\Quiz32.exe

2) To install Adobe Acrobat Reader Run: Software\Acrobat\ ar505enu.exe

Starting BFQ: To start the program the next time (if it doesn't start automatically), select BeachFront Quizzer 4.0 from the Program's menu. Assistance with running and using BFQ is available under the Help menu.

Good Luck with your certification!

NOTE: THIS BOOK IS GUARANTEED

See details at www.totalrecallpress.com

70-291 Download Instructions

BeachFront Quizzer (BFQ) version 4.0 Special Edition

System Requirements: Windows 95 & 98, NT, XP, 2000 and Server 2003 with a minimum of 6 MB hard disk space and 16 MB RAM.

The Center For Technology Certification, Inc. will help you accomplish your Microsoft Certifications. This state of art software program is designed to cut your study time in half, and get you to a passing level in the easiest and shortest amount of time possible. The program will adapt to you personally, and then lay out a prioritized study plan that will visually show you your progress on a day to day basis. When the software has recognized that you are at a passing level in each objective category, you're ready to sit for the exam. It's really that easy!

Installation Instructions: 70-291 Practice Exam with eBook Visit http://tinyurl.com/5dh7y Download and Install the latest version of the BFQ Engine: File Name Quiz32.exe.

Visit http://snipurl.com/MS70291 and download the InsidersChoice to 70-291 eBook Zip file to a folder on your hard drive.

This will install all software files:

Open the WinZip file and execute the 70-291.exe to install the testing software. Open the LicenseKey.txt file Copy and Insert the 12 digit number **License Key** when requested or type in the following License Key Numbers when requested.

TRP 70-291 Windows Server 2003 Network Infrastructure = 428155697373

The software is very user friendly.

After you get the program installed Open Click on the Help button menu Select contents for the on-screen manual. (You may want to print the Help File) You will follow a six step process that will lead you through the program efficiently. We are here to support you all the way. If you have any technical questions on the content, make sure you contact us. We are very proud of our pass rate, and we want you To Whom It May Concern: contribute.

If you need additional assistance, visit our website http://www.totalrecallpress.com/ Please let me know that the download and installation worked properly.

Thank you for purchasing our product and Good Luck with your exam!

Sales:

866-992-3398

281-992-3398

Technical Support: info@bfq.com

888-992-3131 or 281-992-3131

Fax 281-482-5390

Made in United States
Orlando, FL
19 August 2025

64087517R00431